AF652680

Secularism and Pluralistic Democracy in India

About the Editors

Dr. V. Ragupathy is Professor of Political Science and Development Administration in Gandhigram Rural University, Tamil Nadu. He is in various committees of State Planning Commission, Tamil Nadu, NIRD, Hyderabad, RGNIYD, Chennai and UGC. He had delivered lectures in Institute of Development Studies, University of Susex, UK and Schumacher College, U.K. He had many academic visits to USA, UK, France, Germany, China, Malaysia and Sri Lanka. He published books, edited volumes and research articles on Decentralization, Common Property Resource Management and Empowerment of Women. In collaboration with CSSS, Mumbai, he is currently engaged in a major programme of inclusive society. He has close association with Gandhian Institutions in India and Gandhi Foundation of United States of America.

Dr. (Mrs.) Vasundhara Mohan is Executive Director at the Centre for Study of Society and Secularism in Mumbai. She obtained her Ph.D. (Political Science) from the Rajasthan University, Jaipur. Before joining the Centre, she worked in the Mumbai University (Centre for Central Eurasian Studies) for over 23 years. For her research on Soviet/Russian Nationalities Policy and Gender issues, she worked in a number of academic institutions in Russia, England and the U.S.A. on prestigious scholarships. Twice Salzburg Alumnus, she has published six books and a number of research articles in Indian and Foreign journals. As Executive Director at the CSSS, she is involved in planning and implementation of the Centre's programmes on Peace, Communal Harmony and Women's Empowerment since 2007, besides publishing papers on matters relating to the upliftment of Muslim girls and empowerment of Muslim women.

Secularism and Pluralistic Democracy in India

Edited by

V. Ragupathy
Vasundara Mohan

CONCEPT PUBLISHING COMPANY PVT. LTD.
NEW DELHI-110059

© Editors

All rights reserved. No part of this work may be reproduced, stored, adapted, or transmitted in any form or by any means, electronic, mechanical, photocopying, micro-filming recording or otherwise, or translated in any language, without the prior written permission of the copyright owner and the publisher. The book is sold subject to the condition that it shall not, by way of trade or otherwise, be lent, resold, hired out, or otherwise circulated without the prior publisher's written consent in any form of binding or cover other than that in which it is published.

The views and opinions expressed in this book are author(s) own and the facts reported by him/her have been verified to the extent possible, and the publishers are not in any way liable for the same.

ISBN-13 : 978-81-8069-865-1

First Published 2013

Published and Printed by

Concept Since 1974

Concept Publishing Company Pvt. Ltd.
A/15-16, Commercial Block, Mohan Garden
New Delhi-110059 (India)
T: 25351460, 25351794, *F*: 091-11-25357109
E: publishing@conceptpub.com, W: www.conceptpub.com
Editorial Office: H-13, Bali Nagar, New Delhi-110 015, India.

Cataloging in Publication Data--Courtesy: D.K. Agencies (P) Ltd. <docinfo@dkagencies.com>

Secularism and pluralistic democracy in India / edited by V. Ragupathy, Vasundara Mohan.

p. cm.

Includes bibliographical references (p.) and index.

ISBN 9788180698651

1. Secularism—India—Congresses. 2. Democracy—India—Congresses. 3. Religion and politics—India—Congresses. 4. Religious pluralism—India—Congresses. I. Ragupathy, Varadarajan, 1958- II. Vasundhara Mohan.

DDC 322.10954 23

Foreword

For quite some time, both in the intellectual world of the academia as well as in the practical domain of activists, the concept and practice of secularism in India have been a subject of critical enquiry and debate. The emergence of Hindu communalism as a powerful and influential ideology, and the political support it gained as a result, undermined much of the certainties the secular state had entertained since independence. In actual political and administrative practice, despite the foundation laid by Nehruvian policies, the state has deviated from secular principles and its secular commitment has steadily declined. Simultaneously occurred the religionisation of society, which tended to divide the people on the basis of their religious faith. The success of Hindu communalism to gain control over the government at the Centre was a result of these political and social processes. Martha Nussbaum, an American scholar, has observed that India during the last few years witnessed the near collapse of democracy into religious terror and its rather miraculous survival. It is arguable that the survival was primarily due to the inherent strength of secularism, historically evolved in a multi-religious and multi-cultural society. However, it is equally important to recognize that the near collapse of democracy was a result of the weakness of secular practice. The essays collected together in this volume throw light on these two complex processes. In the bargain they also reflect upon the theoretical approaches which have enriched the discussion on secularism.

The major threat to secularism emanated from the resurgence of Hindu communalism for which the social support mainly came from the fast growing middle class. The neo-liberal policies of the state and the impact of globalization have been the forces which shaped the cultural world of the middle class, which experienced an unprecedented growth during this period. The crisis of identity inherent in this condition was the root of communalism. That by the end of the century the influence of communal forces grew so much to enable them to capture power at the Centre was a result of this development.

Several factors contributed to this political advance. The most decisive among them was religionisation of society which created an unbridgeable gulf between religious communities. The Hindu communal forces led by the Rashtriya Swayam Sevak Sangh (RSS) had unleashed a hate campaign against other communities for a long time. The communal interpretation of history was the pivot of this campaign which was employed to advance the argument that non-Hindus are outsiders and have no right to live in the country. They used the infamous 'two nation theory' to drive home this point. The movement for the demolition of Babri Masjid and the construction of Ram Mandir was the most effective effort of this agenda. The minorities, seized with a complex of insecurity, also sought refuge in religious consolidation and eventually in communalism. The unfortunate consequence of seeking religious solidarity has been ghettoisation which has intensified the sense of insecurity.

Violence is integral to communalism. During the course of the twentieth century the nature of violence that communal forces have indulged in has become unimaginably brutal. In Gujarat and Orissa the nature of violence was unprecedented, both in scale and intensity. All human values, it appears, have been lost. Secularism, therefore, has to launch a struggle, not only for communal harmony and respect for others faith, but also for the restoration of human values.

The record of success of secular forces on both these counts is rather limited. Generally, secularists become active after the event and have no agenda for effective intervention for preventing communal violence or for resisting the spread of communal ideology. The rapid advance of communalism created confusion and uncertainty among the secular camp. Their belief in secularism, at least of some sections, was shaken. Their skepticism embraced not only the secular practice, but also the very concept of secularism. This was primarily because they looked upon Indian secularism as a weaker version of European experience. They failed to recognize that secularization is a universal phenomenon, expressed in manifold ways and what happened in India was a qualitatively different phenomenon with its own characteristics. The skepticism and criticism, even rejection, of secularism emanating from this 'secular'camp have weakened secularism and have indirectly helped communalism. For, their critique is not rooted in creative introspection, but highly coloured by alien experience.

Since independence, particularly during the last couple of decades, secularism in India has been under siege, but it has neither lost its social relevance nor its political importance. In fact, the destiny of the multi-religious Indian society is dependent upon the success or failure of secularism. The contributors to this volume have rightly drawn our attention to the centrality of secular practice both by the state and civil society for the continued welfare of India as a nation.

K.N. Panikkar
Former Chairperson
Centre for Historical Studies (J.N.U.)
&
Former Vice-Chancellor
Sri Sankaracharryar University of
Sanskrit, Kerala

Preface

The six decades of Indian Polity is one of the grand Secular and Pluralistic constitutional experiments of the world. More than one billion people of the sub-continent with ethnic, linguistic, cultural and religious diversities could collectively give themselves a democratic constitution. The strong pluralistic and secular foundations of the nation evolved during the Indian freedom movement have helped Indian democracy to function in spite of many challenges and difficulties. India is not a melting pot of cultures like the United States of America but an enriching mosaic of diversity. The rich diversity cannot be replaced by a monolithic arrangement and diversity is the strength of Indian democracy. But in recent years this diversity of India is threatened. The strong trends of majority and minority syndromes and the communalism of different strands are able to gradually erode India's national unity and pluralistic democracy. Indian democracy is much affected by communalism, casteism and electoral politics tends to divide the country on communal caste and regional lines. Democracy has no meaning without inclusiveness and during the freedom struggle Gandhiji gave more importance to inclusiveness than freedom.

The deficiencies in bringing about inclusive development and inclusive democracy based on justice and equality have given ample opportunity for the rapid growth of communalism, regionalism and terrorism. In the absence of inclusive development marginalized groups move away from main stream politics and seek identity polities. They tend to isolate themselves and fight against the non-responding mainstream polity. Particularly in the context of globalization and unjust economic development, tribals, fishermen and farmers are threatened. Militant groups are able to destabilize democracy. The communal forces are able to create minority phobia to win elections and capture political power. Communalism is used as an easy route to power and at the grassroot level communalism is used by vested interests and criminal forces for selfish ends. In this climate terrorism is able to grow apace.

In this context, the strengthening of secular and plural values of India becomes very important. Against this background the Centre for Study of Society and Secularism, headed by Dr. Asghar Ali Engineer, an eminent peace activist, and the Department of Political Science and Development Administration of Gandhigram Rural Institute–Deemed University—jointly organized a national workshop on "60 Years of Secularism and Pluralistic Democracy in India" April 2010 at Chennai.

The contributions of the participants have been compiled into a volume here. This volume consists of thirteen articles on different themes related to secularism, inclusiveness and democracy.

The articles in the volume give the reader a Kaleidoscopic picture of Indian democracy. The sixty years of Indian republic is still not able to bring a culture of inclusive democracy in India. In recent years different forms of communalism and parochialism are emerging as key players in the electoral politics of India and this is a dark side of Indian democracy. But at the same time electoral democracy has also strengthened the plural nature of Indian political system and Indian democracy has demonstrated that hegemony of any particular group in India is not possible.

We sincerely thank the authors for their contributions for this volume. We want to acknowledge the support and guidance given by Dr. Asghar Ali Engineer in organizing the seminar and bringing out this publication.

V. Ragupathy
Vasundara Mohan

Contents

List of Contributors

Giri, Ananta Kumar, Professor, Madras Institute of Development Studies, 79, Second Main Road, Gandhinagar, Adyar, Chennai.

Engineer, Asghar Ali, Director, Centre for Study of Society and Secularism, Mumbai.

George, M.K., Director, Indian Social Institute, 24 Benson Road, Bangalore.

Engineer, Irfan Ali, Director, Institute of Islamic Studies, Mumbai.

Satish, Kalapana, Child Rights Consultant, 103/62, Karuneegar Street, Thomas Mount Railway Station, Adambakkam, Chennai.

Michael, Vetha Siromony P., Director, Rajiv Gandhi National Institute of Youth Development, Sriperumbudur.

Rajan, Nalini, Professor, Asian School of Journalism, Chennai.

Palanithurai, G., Professor, Rajiv Gandhi Chair for Panchayati Raj Studies, Gandhigram Rural University, Gandhigram.

Palekar, S.A., Professor and Chairman, Department of Political Science, Gulbarga University, Gulbarga, Karnataka.

Patrick, G., Professor, Department of Christian Studies, University of Madras, Chepauk Campus, Chennai.

Ragupathy, V., Professor and Head, Department of Political Science and Development Administration, Gandhigram Rural University, Gandhigram.

Ram, Puniyani, Professor (Retd.), Indian Institute of Technology, Mumbai.

Vasundara, Mohan, Executive Director, Centre for Study of Society and Secularism, Silver Star, 602/603, 6th Floor, Near Santacruz Station, Prabhat Colony, Santacruz (E), Mumbai.

1

Secularism: Indian Dimensions

Asghar Ali Engineer

India became a secular state in the post-colonial era, i.e., after becoming independent in 1947. However, the Constitution that came into force with effect from 26th January, 1950 did not use the word secularism. In other words, India became a secular state more in spirit than in terms of political ideology. The word 'secular' was added during emergency through an amendment. Thus, today our Constitution is a secular Constitution.

What is Secularism ?

Secularism in Indian context was never clearly defined by either our constitutional experts or political ideologues. There are several problems in defining secularism in the Indian context. Both during colonial and post-colonial period, the Indian society has been a traditional society dominated by various customs and traditions with deep religious orientation. For the liberal and progressive intellectuals, on the other hand, secularism meant total exclusion of religion from political arena.

Jawaharlal Nehru, who propounded secular political doctrine since the colonial days, had to come to terms with the traditional Indian society on the one hand, and his western-oriented doctrine of secularism, on the other. Nehru was an agnostic, if not an atheist and was quite critical of religion. He writes in his essay on "Religion, Man and Society": "But it does mean that the religious outlook does not help, and even hinders, the moral and spiritual progress of people, if morality and spirituality is to be judged by this world's standards, and not by the hereafter."[1]

Nehru, while being critical of the role of religion, as a statesman, was well aware of its importance for the masses of India and in his conception secularism in India would mean 'equal protection' for all religions by the state. Unfortunately, due to highly complex historical, political and social developments, even this could not be ensured by the state and secularism did not become a vibrant state policy.

Secularism did not have a precise equivalent in Indian languages as Indian society had never structurally developed any such concept. In Hindi, they coined the term *dharmanirpeksh* (i.e., religiously neutral) but many objected to this term and maintained how Indians could become religiously neutral and proposed, particularly those belonging to the Hindu right, *panthnirpeksh*, i.e., sect-neutral (i.e., there are various sects or paths to divinity or religion and that the state will remain neutral to these paths, i.e., *panths*). But the state stuck to *dharmanirpeksh* and this is what secularism is called in India today.

In Urdu, by no means language only of Muslims but perceived as one, secularism was translated as ironically as *ladiniyyat*, i.e., anti-religion and continued to be in use for almost a decade during the fifties. However, it was a gross misrepresentation of the term in the Indian context and hence subsequently this translation was dropped and as Urdu is quite flexible in adopting words from other languages, it adopted the term 'secular' itself and it is no longer translated.

Thus, the conservatives and rightists maintained that secularism is not in keeping with our traditions and cultural ethos and it is purely a western notion and adopting it would endanger religion and our ancient traditions. However, over a period of time the opposition softened and gradually disappeared. People's apprehensions that it would endanger their religion and traditions were proved wrong as the government was careful not to interfere in religious matters.

Nehruvian Brand of Secularism

However, secularism and its implications continued to be contested in the political arena by the Hindu right and its political implications continue to be challenged even today. Though, all political parties, including the ones like the Shiv Sena and Bharatiya Janata Party (BJP) have accepted secularism, these parties contest the Nehruvian brand of secularism. What is Nehruvian brand of secularism?

According to the RSS and Jan Sangh (now BJP) leaders, Nehruvian brand of secularism has two main pillars; that it is western and against Indian cultural ethos and; secondly, it is based on appeasement of minorities, particularly Muslims. Its western connotation is represented by Nehru's agnosticism and western modernism and its appeasement of minorities is reflected in the Congress policies, particularly its capitulation before conservative Muslim religious and political leaders and refusal to enact uniform civil code as provided in the Article 44 of the Constitution. The Hindu rightwing thus described Nehruvian secularism as 'pseudo-secularism'. It (the Hindu right), on the other hand, developed its own notion of secularism and called it 'positive' secularism and defined it as 'justice for all and discrimination against none'. We will discuss it in more details later in the political context prevailing in eighties of the last century.

The Constitutional Implications of Secularism

How is secularism reflected in the Indian Constitution? Firstly, Articles 14 to 21 of the Constitution guarantee equal rights for all citizens under the broad title Equality before law.[2]

- Article 14 stipulates that 'the State shall not deny to any person equality before the law or equal opportunity of the laws within the territory of India.
- Article 15 prohibits any discrimination on the grounds of religion, race, caste, sex or place of birth.
- Article 16 guarantees equality of opportunity in matters of public employment.
- Article 17 abolishes untouchability.
- Article 18 abolishes conferring of titles, except military or academic distinctions, on any person.
- Article 19 guarantees freedom of speech, freedom of peaceful assembly, freedom to form association and union, freedom to move freely throughout the territory of India and to reside and settle in any part of India and to practice any profession or to carry on any occupation, trade or business.
- Article 20 pertains to protection in respect of conviction for offences.
- Article 21 pertains to protection of life and liberty.

These rights have been rightly termed as fundamental rights and no law can be enacted by the Parliament which is contrary to these rights. However, when emergency was imposed in 1975 and many people were arbitrarily arrested, there was great debate whether Article 21 which guarantees life and liberty can be suspended during emergency and the Supreme Court had ruled in favour of suspension which obviously was not in the spirit of the Constitution.

These fundamental rights are available to all citizens of India irrespective of religion, caste or gender and hence are secular in nature. Thus, the main feature of Indian secularism is the availability of these rights irrespective of one's religious persuasion or one's primordial or acquired identity. Also, negatively defined, Indian state has no religion whereas its citizens can or may not have any religion.

Religious and Cultural Rights

But since India is a multicultural, multi-religious and multi-linguistic society, these fundamental rights which are available to all citizens of India may not suffice and hence other set of rights for religious, cultural and linguistic minorities were also needed and were embodied in the Constitution in Articles 25 to 30. These rights are the hallmark Constitution of Indian and its commitment to secularism.

Article 25 relates to freedom of conscience and free profession, practice and propagation of religion, Article 26 pertains to freedom to manage religious affairs which include managing religious institutions, charitable trusts, etc. Article 27 embodies freedom as to payment of taxes for promotion of any particular religion. Article 28 talks of freedom as to attendance at religious instructions or religious worship in certain educational institutions.

Article 29 is about protection of minorities. Under this article "Any section of the citizens residing in the territory of India or any part thereof having a distinct language, script or culture of its own, shall have right to conserve the same. And lastly, Article 30 pertains to the right of minorities to establish and administer educational institutions. This right is available to all minorities, whether based on religion or language, who shall have the right to establish and administer educational institutions of their choice.[3]

Thus, the rights guaranteed from Articles 14 to 21 and those guaranteed under Articles 25 to 30 are indeed the hallmark of Indian secularism. Indian secularism is thus, positive and unambiguous in nature respecting citizens' right to profess or not to profess religion not only as individuals but also as a corporate body of citizens professing same religion or culture while the state shall have no religion whatsoever.

Secularism and Controversies around the Concept

Here while discussing how secularism has fared in the last sixty years in India, we propose to deal with two principal aspects: Firstly, what controversies surged around this concept in the last sixty years and how they impacted on the Indian society and political culture? Secondly, what are the government and institutional failures in implementing the secular ideology of the state as propounded in the Constitution.

First, we would like to deal with the various controversies surrounding the ideology of secularism. We have already hinted above that the Hindu religious right was sceptical, even suspicious, of this concept and treated it as contrary to, if not downright hostile to Indian culture and ethos. Among the Muslims, while the *Jamiat-ul-Ulama* (an organization of Islamic theologians of India) accepted the concept of secularism as they had actively participated in the freedom struggle and had vigorously opposed partition of India on religious grounds, the *Jamat-e-Islami-Hind,* founded by Maulana Maududi opposed secularism as unislamic and advised Muslims not to participate in the secular government and characterized any participation in it as *haraam* (prohibited).

The *Jamat-e-Islami-Hind*, therefore, refused to participate in the secular governance and did not take part in any political activity until the early nineties when *Babri Masjid* was demolished. It was then that the Jamat formed a secular democratic front and requested Justice Tarkunde, a noted human rights activist, to become its chief patron. The Jamat has not seen back ever since. Earlier the Jamat in India had adopted *Qiyam-e-Din* (establishing religion and consolidating it) as its goal and probably it continues to be its goal.

However, these were the ideological parties of the Muslims and they had their own positions. As far as the Muslim masses were concerned they always saw secularism as the only political ideology which could provide them both guarantee of their rights as well as security and for them Nehru and Nehruvian concept of secularism symbolized secular political culture. They thus always voted either for the Congress or other secular parties like the Socialists, Communists or similar other parties. This led to the charge of vote bank politics by the Hindu right.[4] We will deal with it shortly.

The Hindu Right and Secularism

The Hindu right represented by the RSS and its political front (then) Janasangh and (now) the BJP had severe reservations about the concept of secular politics but gradually they too recognized that one has to accept it as the *fait accompli* of Indian politics and also due to their narrow upper caste political base cannot command sizeable majority in Parliament to amend the Constitution.

Also, the Supreme Court held in the Kesavnanda Bharati's case that the "basic structure of the Constitution could not be abrogated even by a constitutional amendment" which meant that secularism and fundamental rights cannot be changed even by a parliamentary amendment. This was a great setback to the Hindu right and its opposition to secularism as a political ideology. It had no other course but to accept it but find ways to weaken it, if not sabotage it, through other means.

Nehru was already the target of the Hindu right from the day one. He was considered hostile to the Hindu interest. Secularism was projected as a means to grab the minority votes by showing undue favours to them. They coined the term 'minoritism'. They said true secularism would mean "equality for all and discrimination against none" which appealed to the educated middle classes. But such slogans, as we will see, hid much more than what they revealed.

When Indira Gandhi emerged as the undisputed leader of the Congress and the old Congress veterans like Kamraj, Atulya Ghosh, Morarji Desai and others were defeated, she tried to consolidate her political base by nationalizing banks and wooing minorities by putting emphasis on secularism. Thus, the Indira Congress's secularism became a great political challenge both for the old Congress led by these Congress veterans as well as for the Janasangh which was also marginalized by the Indira wave. Both the parties reacted in different ways to safeguard their political positions.

We need not discuss here the way Old Congress (Cong-O) reacted to Mrs. Gandhi's strategy but it is important to discuss how the Hindu right i.e. the Jan Sangh reacted to it. The Jan Sangh was being headed in those days by a more extremist leader Mr. Balraj Madhok. He tried to promote a more militant line by getting a resolution passed by the party for Indianisation of Muslims.

This clearly implied that Muslims were not true Indians and needed to be Indianized by making them accept Indian mainstream culture. What was shocking was that even *Times of India* supported this editorially saying that as there was demand for Indianizing army during the British period, what was wrong to demand Indianisation of Muslims and making them part of Indian mainstream.

There were two occasions when there was almost total polarization on communal lines in the post-Independence period: one, when Indira Gandhi nationalized banks and tried to woo the minorities and second when Mr. Lalkrishna Advani took out *Rath Yatra* on the question of Ram temple and gave the slogan *Mandir wahin banayenge* (we will construct temple at the same place). The whole atmosphere was vitiated on both occasions with communal ethos.

It was in that atmosphere that major communal riots broke out in Ahmedabad in 1969 and more than 1000 Muslims were massacred. A senior journalist Nandan Kagal of the *Indian Express* wrote an article expressing doubts about the loyalty of Muslims to India. Thus, the strategy of the Jan Sangh to weaken secularism seemed to be succeeding by initiating a debate in the public arena about Indianness of Indian Muslims.

Also, it was during this period that the Shiv Sena was formed in Mumbai and Mr. Balasaheb Thackeray took a very militant line, even more militant than the Jan Sangh. He raised a number of local controversies to communalize the situation and riots broke out in Bhivandi and Jalgaon in 1970 in which unofficially 400 persons were killed. Thus, by all means it was highly critical period for Indian secularism.

Indian Muslims and Indianness

Two questions were repeatedly asked about Indian Muslims in those days: one, are Indian Muslims loyal to India or were they Pakistanis at heart? Second, are they part of Indian mainstream? Even academics and scholars often raised these questions. However, no one was clear what they meant by loyalty to Pakistan and what was the definition of Indian mainstream. These words were loosely used.

The only example cited frequently of Muslim loyalty to Pakistan was celebration by some Muslims when Pakistan was won any cricket match. It could not be denied that there were some Muslim youngsters who did feel happy when Pakistan won. However, even this was rather a complex phenomenon. Firstly, it was sympathy rather than loyalty. Sympathy does not have element of disloyalty to one's own country. And this sympathy was found more among North Indian Muslims because of divided families and there were cricket players from Pakistan from these divided families. To term such incidence as loyalty to Pakistan was not technically correct.

Now coming to Indian Muslims not being part of Indian mainstream, there was even more confusion. What is Indian mainstream and who constitutes it? Basically this allegation came from Hindu right and for them Indian mainstream meant upper caste Hindu culture, of which the Vedic culture was the main constituent. In this sense even all Hindus would not be part of such mainstream culture.

In fact there has never been a mainstream Indian culture at any time in the whole of India. The pre-Aryan culture was Dravidian and there were a host of regionally varying cultures some of which were imbibed by the Aryans. India is not at all a mono-cultural country in any sense of the word. And it will be undemocratic to characterize any one culture as mainstream and marginalize other cultures.

North India has had composite culture and various invaders from Greeks to Turks to Moghuls left traces of their respective cultures. Moghuls had greatest impact on Indian culture and the ruling classes evolved a culture during that period which was called interestingly *Ganga-Jamni tahzib*, i.e., the culture of the area between the rivers Ganga and Jamuna. The Sufi saints and various regional *bhakti* movements greatly contributed to this composite culture.

But as the name *Ganga-Jamni* itself indicates it was again essentially a regional culture of North India and the South had its own variety of composite culture with predominant elements of South Indian culture. Quli Qutub Shah of Golconda, Adilshah of Bijapur, Hyder Ali and Tipu Sultan of Mysore and others developed their own variety of composite cultures, none of which can qualify for all India mainstream culture. Muslims were very much part of all these regional cultures and the culture which was dominant in the Ganga-Jamuna region.

Since India is a multi-religious and multicultural country, to promote mono-religious or mono-cultural culture in the name of mainstream culture would seriously weaken our secularism and secular values. In India secularism means religious and cultural pluralism and harmonious co-existence. However, our political culture is at great variance with our constitutional culture. In the post-independence era when our Constitution came into force, our political culture has been more divisive along communal, caste and linguistic lines than integrative. We will throw more light on this a little later.

Education and Secularism

Education is the most powerful tool for promoting respect for other religions, cultures and languages. But, we should also remember that it can be a double-edged sword. Like any other tool, it can both be used and misused. Jawaharlal Nehru had opined that communalism would disappear from this country as modern education will make people more rational and scientific. However, a critical examination of the functioning of our education system in the last sixty years clearly shows that it has been more misused than used.

The main purpose of education is to produce thinking, creative, critical and questioning mind. Knowledge advances with these mental qualities. Conforming mind results in stagnation of knowledge. Our education system hardly promotes these intellectual faculties. It has become stagnant cesspool incapable of producing thinking and critical mind.

What is worse, our education system is inculcating not only a false pride in our past but uncritical acceptance of whatever happened in the past. The Constitution has abolished caste system but our education system goes on reinforcing it not only through textbooks but also by the behaviour of teachers who perpetrate caste divisions in the class room. There have been several reports in the newspapers that children in a class are made to sit on caste lines for mid-day meals. In Gujarat when a *dalit* teacher made them sit together he was immediately transferred.

Also, our education system promotes communal division, even hatred by communalizing medieval history. Medieval history has been reduced to stories of temple demolitions by Muslim rulers as they were opposed to idol worship. Such oversimplification of history results in creating communal hatred against Muslims. What is worse, apart from history textbooks, teachers add their own prejudices as teachers themselves are never trained in secular values.

Many scholars and academics have analyzed these textbooks to show stark communal biases built into them. When the BJP came to power in 1999 the textbooks became even worse. When UPA Government assumed power in 2004 and Mr. Arjun Singh became the Minister for Human Resource Development, he appointed a Committee headed by Prof. Zoya Hasan, which examined the various textbooks prescribed up to matriculation and showed communal biases in them.

Before we discuss communalization of our education system and some of the contents of the textbooks, we should know that there are government schools and private schools and while government schools have to follow the textbooks prescribed by State governments, private schools are free to choose their own textbooks. While mostly lower middle class and poorer class students go to government schools, students from the middle, upper middle and rich classes go to private ones.

Further, there are schools run by *Vidya Bharati,* an organization of the RSS, called *Saraswati Shishu Mandir*. There are other schools run by other *Hindutva* outfits; and madrasas run by various private Muslim organizations. Also, while government schools teach less damaging stuff, schools run by RSS and some of the madrasas do more damage to our secular and pluralist values and sectarian attitude. It is reported that RSS runs more than 32,000 schools which turn out lakhs of students every year with stark communal mindset.

One of the supplementary reader (but compulsory to study for children) says Islam spread in this country on the point of sword and the objective of Islam was to spread terrorism. About Christianity it says that its main aim was to convert Hindus to Christianity.[5] One can well understand the damage such books used in thousands of schools could cause.

Also, it was after the eighties that many States elected BJP governments. If the textbooks taught in schools were bad enough even under the Congress ruled States, they became worse after the BJP governments came to power in several States and in the Centre in 1999. The Madhya Pradesh Government, for example, introduced *Surya Namaskar* (Sun worship) in schools despite protests by secular organizations and minorities.

The Zoya Hasan Committee examined the textbooks prescribed in the D.A.V. group schools and those used in a government school operated by the *Bharatiya Vidya Samiti* in Rajasthan. As in other *Vidya Bharati* schools, students of class 8 have to appear for a public examinations, *Akhil Bharatiya Gyan Pariksha*, conducted by *Vidya Bharati Sanskriti Shiksha Sansthan.* Students of classes 10 and 12 also appear for the *Sansthan's* examinations.[6]

The Report said: "Value education taught from textbooks titled *Sanskara Saurabh* — Both the *Sanskara Saurabh* and the *Bodh Mala* (required reading for an examination conducted on all-India level) contribute significantly to the internalization ... of the norms and values of *Hindutva*.[7] The textbook of Eleventh Standard in Rajasthan, according to Apoorva Anand, a secular activist, says that the best form of government is fascism and best leader is a fascist as he can take prompt decisions in the interest of the nation. Such assertions are in stark contrast to our Constitutional values and yet are taught in public schools". Of course, at that time the BJP was in power both at the Centre and in the State. But even after the Congress returned to power at the Centre and State, PUCL and other NGOs were struggling to get such objectionable statements deleted from the textbooks. This author met the then Human Resource Minister, Shri Arjun Singh and drew his attention to this. He was completely unaware of the contents of the textbooks !

A recent example of how schools are being used to promote *Hindutva* ideology comes from Mumbai. The Shiv Sena-BJP ruled Mumbai Municipal Corporation has asked the Christian missionary schools to allow their female students to wear *bindi* and bangles and also to give them longer holidays for *Ganesh* and Divali festivals.[8] These demands are obviously against constitutional provisions, as Article 30 of the Constitution allows minorities the right to set up their own cultural and educational institutions to promote their own culture, language and religious values. This again shows how secularism is being weakened and taken for a ride by the *Hindutva* forces. Unfortunately they are having free hand.

Demanding that the female students be allowed to wear *bindi* and bangles has not only communal but also a gender bias. Why should a demand be made for *bindis* and bangles only? Is that how Indian culture can be promoted? Are *bindis* and bangles representative of Indian culture? Why should women be made to wear bangles? That has become symbol of femininity rather than gender empowerment.

The examples cited from the textbooks taught in Government and non-government schools show that they are quite harmful to our secular values and multi-culturalism.[9] No wonder that communalism, instead of weakening with the spread of education, is gaining strength. It is the educated classes who are more communal in attitude than the poor and illiterate. Reason is obvious. The poor and illiterate never attend any school or even if they do, quickly drop out and do not imbibe such prejudices.

Thus, it will be seen that our educational system has become part of the problem rather than a solution. It is highly necessary to bring about drastic change in the education system to strengthen secularism and multi-culturalism in India. Also, there is total absence of value-system and emphasis is on information rather than knowledge. Even in the upper class private schools the emphasis is on career building and competition rather than on cooperation and compassion. Quest for truth, very vital element of search for knowledge, goes by total default.

As the American philosopher, Herbert Marcuse said, "Our educational institutions are no more centres of knowledge but centres of acknowledgment; our universities are no more centres of cognition but centres of recognition and they, no wonder, produce one-dimensional person. There is hardly any quest for holistic knowledge. Caste and communal identities are much more important than truth and acceptance of rich diversity in our society".

Communalisation of Politics

Communalization of the education system is the direct result of communalization of politics in our country. India was quite hopeful of building a harmonious society based on its rich diversity in the wake of independence in 1947 despite the grave tragedy of partition and assassination of Mahatma Gandhi at the hands of Nathuram Godse inspired by *Hindutva* ideology.

However, Nehru, who was very hopeful of secularization of our society with modern scientific education, was greatly shocked when India was rocked by communal riots in Jabalpur in 1961. Mr. Katju, then Chief Minister of Madhya Pradesh, a veteran Congressman himself, was accused of lacking the will to quell the riots. In fact, Jabalpur riots proved to be quite catastrophic for our efforts in building secular nationalism. What was worse communal violence graph sharply rose thereafter.

Our polity has been increasingly communalized since there is no serious challenge from secular forces except from higher judiciary as some of the Supreme Court judgments show. The judiciary at lower levels also has also been affected by communal forces. Most of our institutions which go a long way in building a secular nationhood have been communalized; bureaucracy and police included. Army has been an exception but then army does not play crucial role in the socio-political values of the country.

Here, we are basically discussing communalization of our polity over the years. Since ours is what can be called a bewilderingly diverse country, religious, cultural, linguistic and caste identities are exploited by the politicians for mobilizing votes. In a democracy there are certain dilemmas which must be understood and acceptable solutions must be worked out creatively.

Identities can play contradictory roles in a Parliamentary democracy. Our system perpetuates gross injustices with weaker sections of the society like the tribals, *Dalits,* OBCs and minorities. To fight these injustices, the only democratic tool is identity, through which they can be mobilized to protest. That could be a legitimate function of identity in democracy. But then the dilemma is that politicians are not angels. They make unscrupulous use of identity for votes.

While parties representing OBCs and *Dalits* have sharpened caste identities, the religious-right represented by parties like BJP, Shiv Sena, etc. has sharpened communal identities and polarized Hindus and Muslims, thus weakening our secular structure. As more and more people are being mobilized, not based on issues but on caste and communal identities, both casteism and communalism have registered sharp increase rather than weakening with the spread of education.

Thus, this identity based mobilization will continue to pose serious challenge to our secular nation-building. When communal parties saw their base shrinking, they became shriller in raising communal issues. Even secular parties like the Congress could not resist the temptation and often resorted to promoting, directly or indirectly, communal consciousness or even supporting communal riots.

With regard to identity, we have to remember two things: one, the true essence of identity is an authentic sense of belonging to a group—be it tribal, religious, cultural or linguistic, and it is positive in this sense. My identity is my authentic essence of being my authentic self and need not, in this sense be a threat to others. It would help me to understand myself as being a part of one's authentic. My becoming is also partly determined by my being. And that is what identity is all about.

Secondly, no one individual has a single identity; all of us have multiple identities—religious, linguistic, cultural caste, national, etc. We may speak the same language but may have two different linguistic identities; may have the same nationality but two different cultures or ethnicities and so on. Identity becomes a problem when we assert one single identity. For example, when a section of north Indian Muslims asserted their Muslim identity, the result was not only communal violence but division of the country. All those Muslims who demanded Pakistan on the basis of their Muslimness shared same linguistic, cultural and ethnic identities with non-Muslims like Punjabis, Sindhis and Pathans. Thus, the role of identity in secular nation building is quite complex.

When Mrs. Gandhi tried to take support of minorities and tried to project herself as protector of minorities, it became a challenge for the Cong (O) and Jan Sangh and they threw a challenge to Mrs. Gandhi by enhancing their Hindu communal appeal. The Shiv Sena added and abetted the process. Thus, the decade of sixties of the last century ended with more communal polarisation.

However, due to Bangladesh war in the early seventies followed subsequently by emergency, there was relative peace on the communal front. This was further followed by post-emergency situation when the Jan Sangh merged with the Janata Party and took pledge to shun communal politics on the *Samadhi* of Mahatma Gandhi and the Janata Party Government was formed in 1977. Ironically, Mr. Vajpayee who became Foreign Minister under Morarji Desai campaigned along with the Shahi Imam Abdullah Bukhari and north Indian Muslims voted massively for the Janata Party and the Congress lost all the seats in the north India.

This also exposes the BJP propaganda that Muslims always vote for the Congress and the Congress always follows the policy of minority appeasement and hence its secularism is pseudo-secularism. Thus, during 1971 to 1977 there was relative peace and even RSS and the *Jamat-e-Islami* came together in jails and claimed to have understood each other better. But this solidarity was quite ephemeral and lasted no more than a few months.

Soon the Socialist members of the Janata Party like Rajnaraian, Madhu Limaye and George Fernandez raised the question of dual membership (i.e. that of Jan Sangh and of RSS) and the Jan Sangh members refused to resign from the RSS membership. It clearly showed that taking pledge to renounce communal politics was no more than a political strategy rather than a change of heart.

And, hence, soon communal situation began to deteriorate and a number of communal riots took place in Aligarh, Jamshedpur, Varanasi and other places. Through these riots the RSS was sending out a message to the Jan Sangh not to renounce communal politics. Thus, the late-seventies, like the sixties became intensely communal. The Janata Government fell on the dual membership controversy followed by temporary government formed by Chaudhary Charan Singh which hardly lasted for six months.

Mrs. Gandhi returned to power following the elections in 1980. Now Mrs. Gandhi's political strategy saw a sea change. She concluded that Muslim votes are no more solidly behind her and she needed to move on to other voters. There was communal riot in Moradabad in 1980 which shook the entire country. But Mrs. Gandhi, unlike 1969 riots of Ahmedabad, gave it a different political twist.

The Ahmedabad riot of 1969 was a threat to her political existence as she was asserting her secular credentials to woo the minorities. But, the Moradabad riots of 1980, was perceived quite differently by her as an opportunity to woo middle class Hindus and OBCs to compensate for the loss of Muslim votes. Thus, it will be seen that for Mrs. Gandhi secularism was not an ideological conviction like it was for her father Jawaharlal Nehru.

Mrs. Gandhi now began to woo Hindus and through some of her ministers floated the theory that the Moradabad riots were organized on the strength of petro-dollars, i.e., money coming from Arab countries and it became a raging controversy in the media. Throughout this controversy, Mrs. Gandhi remained silent and not once did she deny the role of petro-dollars. Mr. Girilal Jain, editor, *Times of India* wrote a signed editorial blaming petro-dollars and published a series of letters from the readers supportings and opposing this theory. It was interesting that most of those supporting were Hindus and most of those opposing were Muslims. Thus, there was communal polarization even on this question.

In the beginning of the 1980s, the incident of a few *dalits* converting to Islam in Meenakshipuran district in Tamil Nadu took place and this became another controversy which Mrs. Gandhi tried to turn into an opportunity for her political survival. The conversions were linked to the inflow of petro-dollars. In cases, viz., Moradabad riots and Meenakshipuram conversions, there was no iota of proof that petro-dollars were used to finance them and yet Mrs. Gandhi's Government maintained a mysterious silence.

The decade of eighties became intensely communal, even more than communalization at the end of sixties. Mrs. Gandhi was subtly promoting communalization in her own interests and I was told by the much respected senior journalist, Mr. Kuldip Nair, that she was even supported by the RSS in this respect. RSS found in her a more capable Hindu leader than in the BJP leadership whose base had declined. She even appealed to the Hindus of Jammu to vote for her in 1983 elections in J&K saying that the Muslims would kill them in

Kashmir and Sikhs from Punjab (Punjab militancy was at its height at that time). The Hindus of Jammu voted for her party and RSS volunteers worked for her victory.

Thus, it will be seen that even the Congress did not shy away from using the communal card when it came to survival in power. Self-interests are supreme in power struggle. The decade of eighties saw communalism at its height for a number of reasons. Sikh militancy also had its impact on the middle class Hindu mind. Then a large number of major communal riots were taking place in this power game. We will throw light on these riots separately.

The Blue Star operation in 1983 to cleanse the Golden Temple Complex of Bhindranwale and his followers was a catastrophic event which resulted in the assassination of Mrs. Gandhi followed by massacre of 4000 Sikhs in Delhi and several other cities of North India. It is alleged that several top Congress leaders were involved in provoking Hindus against Sikhs. Rajiv Gandhi took over the reins of Congress leadership after Mrs. Gandhi and said, in his speech that 'when a big tree falls there is bound to be a big thud' which was supposedly highly provocative against the Sikhs.

Riding the sympathy wave, Rajiv Gandhi won the 1984 elections with a large majority. He launched a campaign against corruption and was nicknamed Mr. Clean but was soon accused by Mr. V.P. Singh, then Finance Minister, of corruption in the purchase of Bofors guns from Switzerland. As Rajiv Gandhi was young and new to national politics, he mishandled many issues, which the BJP and other opposition parties exploited for their own ends.

In 1985, the Supreme Court delivered judgment in the Shah Bano case, upholding the right to maintenance of a Muslim divorcee woman under Section 125 of the Criminal Procedure Code. The Muslim leadership considered the judgment as interference in Muslim Personal law. There was already a great sense of insecurity among Muslim masses due to communal riots which were taking place in North, Central and Western India and so there was overwhelming response by Muslim masses to the Supreme Court judgment.

Though he first resisted changing the law, Rajiv Gandhi ultimately panicked and nullified the Supreme Court judgment by enacting the Muslim Women's Bill whereby Muslim women lost their right to maintenance under Section 125 of Criminal Procedure Code upon divorce. This enactment had very adverse effect on the Hindu mind and the BJP fully exploited it to its benefit communalizing the situation.

The BJP, which had very badly lost the 1984 elections under the leadership of Vajpayee, was waiting for such an opportunity.

The BJP accused that the Congress, with its pseudo-secularism, was trying to appease the minorities (read Muslims) and offered "positive secularism" which meant "justice for all and discrimination against none". But, as we know, in 1977 the Jan Sangh had taken a pledge under the leadership of Jayaprakash Narayan to give up communalism and follow secularism and Gandhian socialism but it proved disastrous for it.

Thus, calling the Congress secularism as 'pseudo' and its own as 'positive' the BJP relegitimized its avowal of 'secularism'. But it was much more deceptive. It was during this period that the BJP resorted to communal politics with a view to revive itself and the decade of eighties became the decade of communalism in the post-independence era. During the late-sixties, when faced with secular challenge from Mrs. Gandhi after the split in the Congress, the Jan Sangh went for communalization overdrive, which it repeated during the eighties. It indeed posed serious challenge to secularism.

The BJP had already raised the issue of *Ramjanamabhoomi* and demanded construction of a grand Ram Temple in place of Babri Masjid and raised the slogan '*mandir wahin banayenge*' (will construct temple there only, i.e., where the Babri Masjid stands). The whole issue was intensely communalized as Rajiv Gandhi, already apprehensive of the loss of Hindu votes with the enactment of the Muslim Women's Act, ordered the opening of lock of Babri Masjid doors to enable Hindus worship the idol of Ram Lalla. It is alleged that Arun Nehru advised him to do so to regain Hindu votes. But ironically he angered both and lost their support.

When the V.P. Singh Government came to power in 1989, BJP was part of the alliance which further complicated the communal situation. The BJP had joined the V.P. Singh Government with a view to serve its own communal agenda. In order to increase his support base and to emerge as the messiah of OBCs, V.P. Singh implemented the Mandal Commission Report giving reservation to OBCs which the Congress Government had avoided.

This alarmed the BJP which thought it would split Hindu votes and OBCs will now rally round V.P. Singh. The BJP, therefore, decided to consolidate the Hindu votes by intensifying the *Ramjanamabhoomi* movement as Ram is held in high esteem by all sections of Hindus from upper castes to OBCs to *dalits*. It is interesting to note that

V.P. Singh announced implementation of Mandal Commission Report on 8th August, 1990 and L.K. Advani announced his *Rath Yatra* (Rath is a religious vehicle of gods in Hindu mythology) to campaign for *Ramjanamabhoomi* temple.

It will be seen that the *Ramjanammabhoomi* movement was purely a political movement launched by the BJP to widen its political base and it was gross misuse of religion for political purposes and it was Mr. Advani's *Rath Yatra* which greatly communalized the Indian polity towards the end of 80s of the last century. The misuse of religion is obvious when we see that the *yatra* was planned from Somnath temple to *Ramjanamabhoomi* site in Ayodhya.

More than 300 small and big riots took place when the *Rath Yatra* was proceeding. The *Times of India* editorially described it as "blood yatra" because of the riots. In fact a Toyota truck was converted into a *Rath* shape making it fully air-conditioned and equipped with stage and audio system. Lakhs of supporters of the BJP joined the *yatra* from place to place and BJP succeeded in making a dent in the OBC vote bank and weaning away a large section of the OBC from V.P. Singh.

The V.P. Singh Government was highly embarrassed by the *Rath Yatra*, which was a betrayal of the ruling alliance agenda but the BJP hardly cared for it and was determined to encash communal passions into Hindu votes. Thus, V.P. Singh decided to arrest L.K. Advani which would certainly have resulted in BJP withdrawing its support and the fall of his government. But for Mr. Singh there was no alternative. The *yatra* was posing a serious communal challenge.

Mr. Singh was trying to emerge not only as the messiah of OBCs but also of minorities. Also others like the Samajwadi Party of Mulayam Singh Yadav and Rashtriya Janata Dal of Lalu Prasad Yadav and the left parties like the CPM, CPI etc. were also part of the alliance and all these parties were highly uncomfortable with the *Rath Yatra* and wanted Advani to be arrested. At last Mr. Singh asked Lalu Prasad Yadav to arrest Advani in Bihar and his Government fell, leading to another General Election in 1990.

It was during this election that Rajiv Gandhi was assassinated in May 1990 by the LTTE and Mr. P.V. Narasimha Rao became the Prime Minister of India. BJP also increased its strength due to *Ramjanamabhoomi* movement sentiments among a large section of Hindus, both upper castes and OBCs. It kept on insisting on constructing

Ram temple in place of Babri Masjid. All attempts to find a solution failed as the BJP was adamant and wanted to come to power by misusing this religious issue.

The BJP announced *Karseva* at Ayodhya on two occasions. *Karseva* (voluntary service) is basically a Sikh tradition and not a Hindu one. But BJP tried to use it for its own political purposes. In October 1990 when Mulayam Singh Yadav was Chief Minister of U.P. BJP announced *Karseva* but Mulayam Singh sealed all routes and claimed that even a bird cannot enter Ayodhya. However, lot of policemen in charge of sealing Ayodhya were sympathetic to the *Ramjanamabhoomi* movement due to its religious appeal and thousands of '*karsevaks*' could enter the city and tried to mob Babri Masjid.

The Police had to resort to firing in which three people were killed but the RSS and BJP spread the rumour that 300 people died and furnished wrong names and addresses of those 'died'. Later the whole thing was exposed. Some Hindi papers, in order to either increase their circulation or out of sympathy with BJP, helped spread these rumours and the Press Council of India strongly reprimanded these Hindi papers for their irresponsible behaviour and ignoring journalistic ethics.

The BJP again announced '*Karseva*' on 6th December, 1992 when all attempts to resolve the issue failed. Now BJP Government was in power in U.P. led by Kalyan Singh, himself an OBC leader. All secular parties including the Congress were worried that the *Karseva* may result in harming the Masjid which the media generally referred to as '*vivadit dhancha* (controversial structure)' though obviously it was a mosque.

But the BJP maintained that *Karseva* would mean only singing *bhajans* (Hindu devotional songs) and no harm will come to the Babri structure. Kalyan Singh even filed an affidavit to this effect in the Supreme Court and Mr. Vajpayee gave an assurance in the National Integration Council that the *Karseva* would mean only singing *bhajans.* However, this affidavit and Mr. Vajpayee's assurances came to a naught on 6th December, 1992 when *karsevaks* demolished Babri Masjid right in the presence of top BJP leaders like L.K. Advani, Murli Manohar Joshi, Vinay Katyar and several others.

According to Mrs. Anju Gupta, an IPS officer in charge of Mr. Advani's security, he allegedly delivered provocative speech. She told the CBI Court that Advani "looked euphoric" and "his provocative speech infused enthusiasm amongst *karsevaks*". She also said the BJP leaders including Advani, celebrated the demolition.[10]

These are, to say the least, serious charges made by a responsible IPS officer.

Demolition of the Babri Masjid was a serious blow to Indian secularism which is primarily based on religious pluralism, tolerance and respect for all faiths. And Babri Masjid was demolished because of intensive campaign for building Ram Temple in its place by a responsible political party which swore by 'secularism'. However, cases are still pending even 17 years after the demolition and no one has been brought to justice so far. This by itself is a sad commentary on the way law and order machinery functions.

It must also be said, and it is equally important in the context of secular governance of this country, that the Congress Government was no less responsible for the demolition. Prime Minister, Narasimha Rao was accused of negligence in protecting the religious structure which was under grave threat. The BSF and other Central security forces detailed for the purpose had already prepared a detailed plan to protect the mosque with minimum loss of life but they never received any instructions to go into action until the mosque was demolished.[11]

Senior Congress leaders like Arjun Singh were also of the opinion that no action was taken by the Central Government at the appropriate time. It is unfortunate that Justice Liberahan Commission thought it fit to give clean chit to Narasimha Rao Government despite evidence to the contrary. Of course, he dismissed the Kalyan Singh Government after the demolition holding him responsible for its protection.

BJP had already communalized Indian society through its high pitched communal campaign for Ram Mandir. Demolition of Babri Masjid further intensified it and communal violence broke out in a number of cities and towns like Mumbai, Surat, Ahmedabad, Kanpur, Bhopal, etc. The Mumbai and Surat riots were indeed of grave proportions and in Mumbai riots alone accounted for more than 1,000 lives lost.

Due to *Ramjanamabhoomi* Mandir campaign, BJP successfully widened its political base and could win over a sizeable vote bank of OBCs and could come to power in several States like U.P., M.P., Gujarat and Maharashtra (along with the Shiv Sena as a senior partner). Wherever, it came to power it did so by using communal card and further intensified communalism after coming to power. The BJP-led NDA Government ultimately came to power at the Centre also in 1999.

The BJP coming to power at the State or Central level, as pointed out above, has had grave implications, as far as consolidation of communal forces are concerned. There are several communal outfits like RSS, Bajrang Dal, Vidya Bharati Ashrams, cultural institutions and so on. The States run by BJP grants them financial as well as land grants thus making them much stronger. These institutions, in turn, indulge in communal propaganda which strengthens BJP politically.

Also, when there is state patronage, government servants are likely to develop links with these institutions. In fact, the M.P. Government even permitted its servants to attend RSS *shakhas* which is otherwise not permissible. The RSS *shakhas* are held on government lands without any restrictions. The BJP Government introduces various Hindu rituals like *Surya Namaskar*, etc., in schools and other educational institutions. It prescribes textbooks with open communal bias as we have already discussed above at length.

While in power at the Centre the BJP has potential for much greater damage. As soon as the BJP-led government came to power, it appointed a commission led by Justice Venkatachaliah with a view to amending the Constitution at the instance of VHP and the main intention was to take away Article 30 of the Constitution which gives religious and linguistic minorities the right to establish their own institutions.

However, it was not easy to restructure the Constitution for a number of reasons. Firstly, the Supreme Court judgment earlier referred to ruled out any change in the basic structure of the Constitution. Secondly, there was widespread opposition from secular forces and also 'secular' allies in the NDA like the Telugu Desam Party, Janata Dal (United) led by Sharad Yadav, etc. Thus, the terms of reference had to be whittled down and it came to nothing.

The NDA Government also reconstituted NCERT (National Council for Educational Research and Training) which is a premier body for preparing textbooks and laying guidelines for them. Prof. Murli Manohar Joshi, who became the Minister for Human Resources Development, had a passion for Indianizing everything including science. Thus, NCERT textbooks were prepared accordingly and tried to undermine religious pluralism of India which is the main pillar of Indian secularism.

The BJP had come to power on the *Hindutva* agenda which had mainly three elements, i.e., (1) To Construct Ram Temple at Ayodhya; (2) to bring Uniform Civil Code as per the Directive Principle of the Constitution, and (3) to delete Article 370 of the Constitution giving special status to Jammu and Kashmir. However, it could not implement any of this during its six-year tenure as other partners of NDA would not permit and also secular forces in the country were strongly opposed to this *Hindutva* agenda.

But, on the other hand, BJP could exploit this to its own advantage by projecting itself as a martyr to the pseudo-secular forces in the country which did not allow *Hindutva* agenda to be implemented. This generated more intensified communalism among its own cadres. Thus, it would be seen that during the eighties of the last century communal forces consolidated themselves to the maximum extent by using *Ramjanamabhoomi*-Babri Masjid controversy on the one hand, and the Mandal Commission controversy, on the other. It came to be popularly known as *Mandal and Kamandal* (A vessel carried by the Hindu mendicants and *sadhus*).

It was during this period that secular India faced maximum communal threat and secular forces stood considerably weakened. Jawaharlal Nehru had thought that with the spread of education scientific temper will spread and communalism will become a history. But, in his optimism, he discounted many other forces which were working and helping communal attitude to spread much faster than scientific temperament.

To cultivate scientific temperament one has to work harder, swimming against the tide, whereas to strengthen communal attitude one has everything, from religion to customs to traditional culture, on one's side. Thus, for the BJP initially it was easier to communalize Indian polity but it ran into problems on other issues. It had projected itself as a party with difference, i.e., more disciplined and clean as compared to the Congress which was corrupt and faction ridden.

This proved to be no more than an illusion. Soon BJP became as corrupt as the Congress and faction ridden too. The real test lies not while being in opposition but only when one comes to power. In fact, it allotted so many petrol pumps to its own people that *the Indian Express* came out with a headline *The Pump Parivar*. Also, during the Kargil war there were serious allegations of corruption in army purchases and *Tehelka* did a sting operation exposing ruling politicians and Army officers accepting bribes. Even the BJP President was shown in a sting operation accepting bribe and seriously embarrassed, RSS called it 'a student gone astray'.

Along with communalization and corruption, communal violence also increased culminating in the 2002 genocide in Gujarat and ultimately the BJP lost power in 2004 elections despite its slogan of

India Shining. India shined but ironically in a different way: by coming out of BJP's darkness of communalism. People of India felt suffocated under communal darkness and were keen to emerge out of this darkness at the first available opportunity.

Communal Violence in Post-Independence India

Like communalism, communal violence also became an integral part of secular India in post-independence India thanks to communalization of various democratic institutions. It is important to note that communal violence may not take place even when communalism is spreading in the society. It takes place on a larger scale only when it is needed by the communal forces. Communalism is a necessary condition for communal violence but communal violence is not so for communalism.

For example, from 1950 to 1961, when the first major riots took place in Jabalpur, there were no major communal riots in India (except some minor ones) but that did not mean India was free of communalism. The Jan Sangh was formed in early fifties by Shymaprasad Mukherjee and the Jan Sangh. Though very weak then, it was busy spreading communal propaganda on political plane and the RSS formed in 1925 was running its *shakhas* (branches) throughout India.

It was only in 1961 that the first major communal riot took place in Jabalpur which shook the whole country and Jawaharlal Nehru was so shocked, it is said, by the Jabalpur riots on the one hand, and the Chinese invasion on the other, that he took ill and could never recover. True or not, it is a fact that the Jabalpur riots took place when the Congress was ruling in M.P. and Mr. Katju, a senior Congress leader was the Chief Minister.

When Mrs. Subhadra Joshi, close to Nehru, was sent as his representative for restoring peace, she was cold-shouldered by the M.P. Government and her booking in the Government rest house was also cancelled on some pretext. It showed how indifferent Mr. Katju was towards communal violence which was taking place. The State Reserved Police was committing atrocities against the minorities. A delegation of senior journalists led by Shri Sitaram Kolpe of *Free Press Journal* visited Jabalpur and prepared a detailed report which was carried by *Blitz* edited by Mr. Karanjia. It gave the gory details of not only the riots but also how the State institutions were communalized.

Since the Jabalpur riots, it has been an unending story of communal violence in post-independence India. Several major and minor riots have been taking place every year which are monitored by the Centre for the Study of Society and Secularism, Mumbai. During the sixties, seventies and eighties some of the most communally sensitive States were West Bengal (Until Left Front which came to power effectively controlled communal riots), U.P., Bihar (until Lalu Prasad Yadav's RJD came to power in early nineties), Maharashtra, Gujarat, Madhya Pradesh, and Orissa.

Gujarat witnessed communal frenzy in 1969 of which we have already spoken and there too the Congress (O) Government led by Hitendra Desai remained a mute spectator and more than 1,000 Muslims were killed. Gujarat riots in 1969 were followed by Bhivandi-Jalgaon riots in 1970 directly provoked by Shiv Sena-RSS combination in which 250 persons were killed. Justice Madon Commission Report is a landmark document in this respect.[12]

After the Jalgaon-Bhivandi riots, there was relative peace on communal front due to developments like the Bangladesh war in 1971, followed by Jayaprakash Narain's movement against Mrs. Gandhi and declaration of emergency from 1975 to 1977 and formation of the Janata Party Government in which the Jan Sangh had also merged.

But the communal scene aggravated in 1977 when the Janata Party was driven with the dual membership controversy and RSS became hyper-active to send a signal to the Jan Sangh members not to yield their RSS membership under pressure from socialist leaders and several major riots took place in places like Aligarh, Benaras, Jamshedpur, etc. All these riots witnessed unprecedented communal frenzy and it appeared as if the secular project was failing. It was indeed a very critical period for India's secular polity.

These riots were followed by the Moradabad riots in 1980 which, though started as Police-Muslim riot, soon were taken over by vested interests, culminating in Hindu-Muslim riots. Moradabad riot was the turning point in the history of communal violence in post-independence India.[13] Thus, as pointed out earlier, the decade of 80s of last century became the most critical decade as far as spread of communalism and communal violence is concerned.

Riots took place one after the other from 1980 onwards. There was a major communal flare up in Biharsharif in 1981, followed by communal riot in Meerut and Baroda in 1982 which in turn followed by communal catastrophe in Nelli, Assam in 1983 in which according to unofficial figures more than 3,000 persons were killed, mainly Assamese Muslims and Muslims of East Bengal origin who had migrated to Assam in 30s and 40s of the twentieth century.

Nelli riot was followed by Bhivandi-Mumbai riots of May 1984 and anti-Sikh riots of November 1984 following the assassination of Rajiv Gandhi. There were communal riots in Ahmedabad again in 1985 after Solanki won Gujarat elections in February 1985 by giving reservations to people belonging to the KHAM categories, i.e., Kshatriya, Harijans, Adivasis and Muslims. The BJP launched a movement against Solanki and riots continued for more than a year until Solanki resigned as Chief Minister in October 1986.

In the 1985 Ahmedabad riots, builders also played a major role in the last phase. They spread rumours in the old city to frighten people so that they run away. Later, in collusion with the police, the hutments were torched and after the plot of land was cleared, the builders bought them for major construction projects. The Amarsinh Chowdhury Government issued an ordinance to deregister such properties to control riots. Thus, economic factors also played a major role in certain riots.

Among the major riots, the 1985 Gujarat riots were followed by Meerut riots of 1987 which too were unprecedented in scale as well as brutalities. What was utterly shocking in the Meerut riots of 1987 was that on 23rd May, Commandant Tripathi of U.P. Armed Police ordered young Muslim boys to be picked up from Hashimpura locality in Meerut and shoot them dead. Some 42 young men were pulled out of their houses, loaded into trucks, taken to nearby Hindon Canal, shot and their bodies thrown into the canal. Fortunately, two of them survived miraculously to tell the tale. This was U.P. Police's method of stopping communal riots by terrorizing young Muslim boys. These police officers have still not been brought to justice and the case lingers on. Probably they will never be.

The Meerut riot was followed by Bhagalpur riots in Bihar in 1989 which, in scale and brutalities, even outdid the Meerut riots. A police sub-inspector killed several Muslims in a village and buried their bodies in a field and grew cauliflower over the graves. More than 800 persons were killed in the Bhagalpur massacre. Thus, the decade of eighties ended with a major communal violence in Bihar.

Then of course, came Advani's *Rath Yatra*, which turned into *blood yatra* and more than 300 small and big riots took place in its wake, as indicated above. The demolition of Babri Masjid witnessed renewed communal frenzy and in Mumbai riots alone more than 1,000 people were killed followed by several other cities like Surat which otherwise was considered a peaceful city and had no history of communal violence. The sustained BJP rule had communalized even such otherwise peaceful cities.

After Mumbai riots of 1992-93, there was a lull in communal violence from 1993 to 1998 as the BJP, which had drawn lot of resentment for demolition of Babri Masjid, decided to play its communal profile down and also there was political turmoil at the Centre. Next riot took place in Coimbatore in Tamil Nadu in which some 40 persons were killed. The riot in Coimbatore was partly the result of extremist activities of a Muslim group and partly due to economic competition between well established *Marwari* traders and newly arrived Kerala Muslims from the Gulf.

After 1998, it was Gujarat in 2002 which, perhaps, was the largest and most intense riot in the post-independence period.[14] It attracted world attention, more so as it was almost State-sponsored violence, something which had never happened before. More than 2,000 people were killed with unprecedented brutalities and scores of women including pregnant women, were raped. Details of these riots need not detain us here.

One thing that is clear in all these riots listed and briefly described above is that there was state complicity, connivance or indifference towards violence, for without such state complicity or indifference no major riot can ever take place. If state does not want, no communal violence can last for more than 24 hours and can be controlled with minimum damage to life and property.

Secondly, communal violence, as in popular perception, does not take place on account of religious teachings, much less due to clash of religions; it takes place, mainly, due to clash of political interests. Thirdly, no major communal riot can take place without planning and careful execution. Fourthly, the real cause of communal violence is not a sparking event as is often thought, like cow slaughter or molestation of a girl or eve teasing, etc. Real causes are of political interests.

Communal violence in India has never been successfully fought as most political parties use it as a political instrument to mobilize votes except perhaps the left parties. West Bengal was a communal tinder box before the left front came to power but during its thirty years rule no major communal riot took place except in Nadia district in 1979 in which 28 persons were killed and 1400 houses in 12 villages were burnt down. The two communities clashed after a spate of robberies for which both communities blamed each other.[15]

Since Gujarat 2002, though no major communal violence has taken place, communal riots on smaller scale keep taking place throughout India. There has been no year which can be cited as free of communal violence. It is indeed a great shame for a secular country like India that it did not have riot-free year since independence. Thankfully no major riot has taken place since Gujarat as the communal issues which BJP raised have lost steam and people no longer respond to the *Hindutva* agenda. Yet, because of constant communal propaganda riots do break out here and there.

It is also interesting to note that since Babri demolition and loss of BJP rule, the communal profile of U.P. and Bihar, which are otherwise highly communally sensitive, has radically changed due to a combination of *dalit* and OBC parties coming to power. In the post-Babri Masjid demolition period, UP has either been ruled by Samajwadi Party of Mulayam Singh or Bahujan Samaj Party of Mayawati, a party of *dalits*. Both badly need Muslim support and hence take extra care to prevent communal violence.

In Bihar too, Lalu Prasad Yadav's RJD came to power and he too needed Muslim support and ruled over Bihar with what was known as MY (Muslim-Yadav) combination and hence took care to prevent communal violence. All this clearly shows that without state complicity no major communal riot can take place.

However, unlike OBC and *dalit* parties, the Congress, which also depended on Muslim votes, did not exert to prevent communal violence as many major communal riots, right up to end of eighties and beginning of nineties, took place during its regime. What could be the reason? Firstly, ideologically Congress was committed to secularism but several of its senior leaders had communal outlook or wanted to exploit communal sentiments for political purposes.

The best examples are those of Chief Minister Sampurnanand of U.P. in 1948 who remained a mute spectator when RSS installed *Ram Lalla* idol in Babri Masjid and did not take action even after Nehru and Sardar Patel wrote to him, and of Shri Katju, the Chief Minister of M.P. when Jabalpur communal violence broke out in 1961 and despite Nehru's emissary Subhadra Joshi being sent, did not take any action against communal elements and there was widespread destruction.

The Congress leaders also had a smug feeling that Muslims have no alternative but to vote for the Congress as the only alternative was Jan Sangh or BJP after 1980. Also, in the faction fight among the Congress leaders, one faction used communal card against the other. Shri S.K. Patil was instrumental in promoting Shiv Sena to defeat Krishna Menon in Mumbai Parliamentary Elections as he leaned towards the left. Shiv Sena subsequently posed a great communal challenge and was instrumental in promoting several communal riots in Maharashtra. Mr. Vasantdada Patil also used Shiv Sena in his factional fight and 1984 Bhivandi-Mumbai riots took place.

But when the power equations changed and caste-based parties came to power in post-Mandal situation, Muslims had an alternative among different secular parties and neither of these parties could take Muslim vote for granted except in States like Gujarat where BJP was in power. Caste-based parties like those of Lalu, Mulayam and Mayawati wanted to wean Muslims away from Congress and hence they saw to it that communal violence is prevented. The Congress in its heydays had no such fear and its communal-minded leaders hardly felt uncomfortable with communal violence, even at times patronizing it for factional politics.

Violence against Christians

So far we have mainly dealt with violence against Muslims. Sikhs faced violence only once in the post-Indira Gandhi assassination period in 1984. However, until recently Christians were spared, though there was continuous RSS propaganda that they convert Hindus to Christianity. It is also important to note that Christians did foresee problems in future and when communal violence was taking place mainly against Muslims in eighties, many Christian NGOs and others had taken the initiative to fight communalism and were organizing workshops, seminars and inter-faith meetings.

It was even argued by some scholars that there is no communal violence against Christians as they render important services to the country, impart education through their institutions and provide health services through hospitals and, therefore, are held in high esteem. Muslims, on the other hand, provide no such services and are not even loyal to the country and hence strong prejudices against them and even some well meaning Hindus become hostile to them.

That this argument was not tenable was proved when the *Sangh Parivar* started communal campaign against Christians too. Since, the early nineties they started targeting both Islam and Christianity as foreign religions and hence part of the problem for Indian nationalism, which is essentially Hindu in origin. In the beginning there were sporadic attacks on Christian churches, schools and priests. Even when priests were preaching to their own people, they were accused of converting and attacked.

The culmination of this communal campaign was large scale communal violence against Christians in Kandhamal district of Orissa where BJP was an ally in the Government led by Biju Janata Dal. It was a mass scale violence against Christians for the first time in Indian history. More than 40 persons were killed, many women raped including a nun and more than 40,000 Christians ran to jungles and lived in relief camps.

The violence in Orissa was triggered by the murder of a VHP leader Laxamananda who was campaigning against conversion of *dalits*. Even though the Naxalites claimed responsibility for the murder and gave televised interview in this respect, the violence did not abate. As the BJP was an ally, Navin Patnaik, the Chief Minister did not act. The BJP and VHP were mainly involved in provoking and sustaining violence. The police, as usual, either did not act or sided with the rioters. Christians were mainly targeted by the *Sangh Parivar* when violence against Muslims was becoming counter-productive and they needed another enemy to target.

Also, after demolition of the Babri Masjid and fizzling out of *Ramjanamabhoomi* movement, the VHP and Bajrang Dal, the two most militant Hindu organizations, needed some issue in their political kitty and Christians came handy for this purpose.

Conclusion

It will be seen from the above discussion that India faced difficult challenges right from the beginning. The real question is how did it fare in facing these challenges and what are the problems that need to be addressed? India, as pointed out earlier, is a country of bewildering diversity and to carve out a homogeneous nation out of such diversity and that too within a democratic framework is a challenging task not without political hazards.

In fact, Europe and America began to face such a challenge in what has come to be known as post-industrial and post-modern society when people from former colonies began to migrate to their metropolitan countries and western societies began to become culturally diverse societies. In view of the developing diversity, the western social scientists coined the term 'multiculturalism' and also began to talk about inter-cultural and inter-faith dialogue.

Post 9/11, the situation got further aggravated and the Muslim minority in western countries started facing multiple challenges, including religious prejudices and security threats besides being marginalized. Most of the European countries are thinking of banning the face veil. While Belgium has already done so, France is in the process of legislating a ban on *niqab* and Switzerland, a country with a measure of linguistic diversity, has even banned minarets.

Thus, secularism in the west was alright as long as it was confined to western culture which was considered basically a Christian culture but it failed and intolerance came to the surface the moment it was faced with non-western, non-Christian cultures, particularly Islamic culture. And we also know how Prof. Huntington came out with a theory of clash of civilizations and his book got rave reviews in the western press as if it was some great discovery. In fact, it was a manifestation of intolerance in as much as Western culture, (read Christian culture) cannot co-exist with non-Christian cultures.

Thus, it will be seen that promoting harmonious living between diverse cultures is always a challenging task and India too had to face this challenge in the process of nation-building. Here, we have to take into account two factors: first, that even before we began to live in a secular democratic nation after our Constitution came into force, we already had behind us more than a thousand-year tradition of religious and cultural diversity and rich tradition of composite culture.

Secondly, due to global developments and increasing awareness of religious and ethnic identities, a new religious and ethnic resurgence had began which has been described by western social scientist and western media as 'religious fundamentalism' and religion became an increasingly important factor in politics. This factor was further aggravated by the collapse of communism on the one hand, and, Islamic revolution in Iran, on the other.

It also impacted Indian political development. Along with the resurgence of caste identity, there was also a resurgence of religious identities during the eighties in India. In fact, the decade of eighties was the most challenging for Indian diversity too, particularly religious and caste diversity. It led to caste and religious confrontation. Caste confrontation was easier to manage as it was fragmentation within one religious tradition but religious confrontation was more difficult to manage as it pertained to different faiths and traditions.

However, it must be admitted that despite such difficult challenges, India has not fared badly on the whole. Communalism and religious fundamentalism could not acquire serious proportions in the long run and India is not experiencing as severe a problem of religious fundamentalism as Pakistan is experiencing. What is worse, Pakistan is experiencing religious fundamentalism even though there is only one religious community in that country. It also fell apart in 1971 when Bengali-speaking Muslims refused to share nationhood with Punjabi-speaking Muslims and Urdu speaking Muslims do face problems of their own.

However, India has remained united despite religious diversity within the framework of secular democracy and today BJP is feeling more and more isolated and has to scale down its Hindu militancy as it is not paying political dividends; at least for the time being. In fact, there were fierce debates within the BJP whether it lost 2009 elections because of overemphasizing Hindu fundamentalism by its leaders like Varun Gandhi and others.

Having said this, I must also say that communalism continues to be a challenge before us and all our democratic institutions have been affected and contaminated. The real antidote for it is our secular values and secular polity. Though identity politics cannot be completely ruled out in a democratic polity, it should not be overemphasized as it is being done by our politicians and certainly should not be at the cost of our socio-economic problems and problems of modernity.

Thus, our political culture should be reoriented towards core-values of our Constitution. It will not only strengthen our unity in diversity but would also enable us to concentrate on the real challenges that we face in the twenty-first century. Parties like BJP or Muslim fundamentalism by SIMI can only play disruptive and destructive role in the society. It is for secular minded individuals and organizations to effectively intervene and restore our constitutional values in our political life.

NOTES

1. *Jawaharlal Nehru on Communalism*, Nandlal Gupta (Ed.), Delhi (2006), Hope India.

2. See, The Constitution of India.
3. *Ibid.*
4. Basic Structure, Constitution of India. Available at http/ en.wikipedia.org/wiki/basic_structure.
5. A study of these supplementary readings has been carried out by senior journalist and activist Shri L.S. Hardinia of Bhopal, M.P. He has with him the entire set of these books.
6. *Government of India,* Ministry of Human Resource Development, Committee of Central Advisory Board for Education, Regulatory Mechanism for Textbooks and Parallel Textbooks Taught in Schools Outside The Government System: A Report, New Delhi (2005), p. 62.
7. *Ibid.*, p. 62.
8. *Times of India (Mumbai edition)*, 21st May, 2010.
9. *Indian History Congress (Executive Committee), History in the New NCERT Textbooks: A Report and an Index of Errors,* Irfan Habib, Suvira Jaiswal and Aditya Mukherjee, Kolkata (2003).
10. *The Indian Express* (Mumbai edition), 1st April, 2010.
11. In a seminar held at the VRPF Academy, Mount Abu, the Director, Border Security Force, explained with the help of a map where the forces were stationed and how they were waiting for instructions but received none. This author, who was one of the resource persons at the seminar, heard the whole story.
12. *Government Press*, Justice Madon Commission Report on Jalgaon-Bhivandi Riots, Mumbai (1972).
13. For an account of all these riots, see Asghar Ali Engineer, *Communal Riots After Independence—A Comprehensive Account,* Delhi (2204), (Shipra Publications.
14. See Asghar Ali Engineer (Ed.), The *Gujarat Carnage, Hyderabad (2003),* Orient Blackswan Private Limited.
15. See *Communal Riots After Independence, Ibid.*, p. 50.

2

Spiritual Cultivation for a Secular Society

Ananta Kumar Giri

> Exiting from the palaces and mansions of the powerful, faith—joined by philosophical wisdom—is beginning to take shelter in inconspicuous smallness, in those recesses of ordinary life unavailable to co-optation.
>
> —Fred Dallmayr (2005), *Small Wonder: Global Power and Its Discontents*, p. 4.

> [. . . . .] being able to laugh at oneself would entail not less but more transcendence. It is a piece of folk wisdom that Kierkegaard knew well.
>
> —Walter Lowe (2002), *Second Thoughts about Transcendence*, p. 246.

> To undertake contemplative cultural critique is to engage in transcoding. For, notwithstanding the theological roots of Western rationality, the language and concepts of socio-cultural analysis are, for the most part, thoroughly secular. To bring the insights of spiritual and secular knowledge to bear on current phenomena thus requires one to translate between and across epistemes or ways of knowing. Many tend to see these two forms of knowledge as autonomous and incompatible, and choose to privilege one or the other. However, there is much that is common to the emancipatory streams within both knowledge traditions.
>
> —Lata Mani (2009), *Sacred Secular: Contemplative Cultural Critique*, p. 2.

> The arts are contributing to a deeper, may be even spiritual, examination of life, and so what it means to be human is expressed in a variety of cultural and literary revivals in different regions of the world. Thus, the post-modern world is turning out to be a post-secular world as well. It is giving rise to what is increasingly called post-modern theology and spirituality, which recognizes that identity is linked to relationships with the family, society, and the natural world, which can be seen as part of a larger divine reality.
>
> —Scott M. Thomas (2005), *The Global Resurgence of Religion and the Transformation of International Relations: The Struggle for the Soul of the Twenty-First Century*, p. 45.

The Problem

Much water has flown down Jordan, Jhelum, Ganges, Cauvery, Mahanadi, Thames, Rhines and Mississippi since the dawn of humanity and the Independence of India and in recent years much discussion has taken place on the nature of secularism in India, its uses and abuses. Broadly speaking, we can classify various contending positions on secularism in India into three approaches: (a) those who defend the secular character of Indian Republic as enshrined in the Constitution of India; (b) those who oppose it on the ground that the practice of Indian state-led secularism has been a pseudo-secularism; and (c) those who critique that secularism is Western in origin and we must have something in its place which is appropriate to centuries long tradition of India of spontaneous religious harmony and inter-religious co-existence. While I do not want to spend much time on the second argument of pseudo-secularism which has been offered by Hindu fundamentalist forces with an eye on religious minorities, I wish to come directly to the first and the third argument and draw our attention to a dead-end in which both the approaches are locked at present and how both need to rethink secularism and reshape it with a spiritual cultivation of self and society. The defense of secularism in the face of the rising fundamentalism in Indian body polity, especially on the wake of the 1992 demolition of Babri Masjid in Ayodhya which was a watershed in the history of secularism in post-independent India, by many left-wing scholars and constitutional experts has been mechanical and it does not wish to make a dialogue with the transcendental dimension of religion. Religion is a false consciousness to these secularists but even if it is a false consciousness, it is a reality in the lives of millions of people in Indian sub-continent as it is in many parts of the world, including the so-called secularized universe of North America and Western Europe. How do we come to terms with religion if from the beginning we label it as a form of false consciousness? It is probably for this reason that Andre Beteille, himself an ardent defender of secularism in contemporary India, tells us: "If civil society is pluralistic and tolerant in its very nature, then it would be absurd for it to wish to expel religious institutions from its fold or to denigrate its beliefs as a form of false consciousness" (Beteille, 1996: 23). Beteille warns us against what he calls the "adoption of a militantly secular ideology": "Our Constitution is based, I believe wisely, on the separation between religion and politics, and on their mutual toleration. Civil Society must find ways of creating and nurturing secular institutions, but that objective is likely to be hindered by the adoption of a militantly secular ideology" (*ibid*). And here as William Connolly argues from the other side of the Atlantic who is more self-critical about secularism than Beteille: "The historical *modus vivendi* of secularism, while seeking to chastise religious dogmatism, embodies unacknowledged elements of immodesty in itself. The very intensity of the struggle it wages against religious tolerance may widen blind spots with respect to itself" (Connolly, 1999: 4).

It is a fact of living that Hindus, Muslims, Christians, Jains, Buddhists, tribals and people of other religious faiths live in India and the key question for an agenda of secularism is to ensure, facilitate and enhance toleration among people of different religious faiths. But defenders of secularism have not told us much how to have, ensure and facilitate toleration not only as a static equilibrium but as a dynamic movement of life which creates "fusions of horizons" in the people who are part of this process of inter-subjective and inter-religious (also multi-religious) interaction. Similarly, those who oppose secularism on the ground that it has originated in the socio-historical context of Western Europe which has a monoculture of Christianity and is not applicable to our ethos of religious pluralism and present "Anti-Secular Manifestoes" (*cf.* Nandy, 1985) do not say that they want our society and politics to be guided by religious authorities. In other words, their agenda is not one of a return to a theocracy or "establishment of a Hindu state" (Madan, 1992: 408). But they do not spell out clearly their positive agenda and whether their desire to relate to religion authentically and sympathetically supports violence and authoritarianism perpetrated in the name of religion.

A clear example of this ambivalence is the work of Ashis Nandy and T.N. Madan, two of our main proponents of the third approach to secularism mentioned above. Both of them make a cultural critique of the agenda of secularism and in the process rope in Gandhi. For example, in his now-famous address, "Secularism in its Place," fist presented as the Anniversary Distinguished Lecture on the occasion of the 1987 Annual Meetings of the American Association of Asian Studies, Madan (1992: 408) writes: "Perhaps men of religion such as Mahatma Gandhi would be our best teachers on the proper relation between religion and politics—values and interests—underlining not only the possibilities of inter-religious understanding, which is not the same thing as an emaciated version of mutual tolerance or respect, but also opening out avenues of a spiritually justified limitation of the role of religious institutions in certain areas of contemporary life". But Madan does not take further the issue of spiritual critique of religion which he just hints at with his phrase "spiritually justified limitation of the role of religion" (*ibid*). If secularism now has to be redefined as "religious pluralism," as Madan argues (Madan, 1997: 262) then how does it relate to non-religious participation in our public life and what is its ethos of engagement—ethics of self-cultivation, terms of public dialogue and politics of becoming? (*cf.* Connolly, 1999). Furthermore, Madan does not realize that the proposed intermixture of secularism and faith is not simply a given one—as Madan seems to be suggesting—but has to be an object of a spiritual *sadhana*. Madan does not explore the preparation in self and society that is required to make this possible. Gandhian agenda of secularism is a transformative agenda of alternative practice and movement at the level of self, culture and society. In Gandhi, in order to be secular, i.e., to be able to accept each other coming from different backgrounds of religious faith, one has to be spiritual but this spirituality is a matter of conscious striving, *sadhana* and struggle. It is an aspect of continuous self-cultivation in the life of both individuals and societies. Therefore, Gandhi used to have inter-faith prayer meetings everyday. But this aspect of the Gandhian agenda of spiritual cultivation of self and society does not find much place in Madan's critique even in his latest work, *Modern Myth and Locked Minds* (*cf.* Madan, 1997).

In this context of the dead-end in the discourse and practice of secularism, Indian society specifically and the present-day world more generally, this chapter in our engagement in knowledge and human liberation explores the pathways of a spiritual reshaping of secularism from an emergent transdisciplinary perspective involving dialogues with sociology, anthropology, political theory, theology, philosophy and literature. From the perspective of spiritual cultivation, it redefines secularism as genuine cohabitation, acceptance of each and respect for each other (facilitated by appropriate ontological cultivation and intersubjective dialogue), non-violence and self-emptying or *kenosis vis-ā-vis* one's will to power, domination and annihilation. It argues that both the critics and defenders of secularism need a radical spiritual supplement for a fuller realization of their potential, and preparing them against one-sided self-closure of and for simultaneous critique of religious tradition and secular state. Cultivation in spirituality would enable us to reconstitute secularism as genuine pluralism, both ontological and social, and characterized by a striving for realization of non-duality between self and other, self and society, among religious groups, and between the religious spheres and the state. A spiritual cultivation would enable us to realize the plurivocal dimensions of our beings as well as broaden and deepen civil society and public sphere as a space of meditative and multidimensional pluralism. Our contemporary conceptions of civil society and public sphere suffer from a rationalist and secularist blindness where sources from religions and spirituality are automatically excluded and a spiritual cultivation for a secular society contributes to a contemporary renewal of public sphere beyond the rationalist gaze of Kant, Rawls and Habermas. Thus, starting with the specific debate about secularism in contemporary Indian society, this chapter touches some of the broad themes of modernity, discusses the emergent evolutionary calling of practical spirituality, and points to the need for realization of non-duality and transcendence in self, society and polity as a way of spiritualizing secularism and modernity, self and the public sphere. Spiritualization here is not bound to religion, belief in a personal God, theistic beliefs and other familiar orthodoxies but embodies a permanent critique of violation of life and incessant striving for establishment of relationships of dignity.

Critiques of Secularism and the Calling of Spiritual Transformations

In the Indian context, Ashis Nandy and T.N. Madan have been at the forefront of presenting a cultural critique of secularism as a statist, hegemonic and culturally alien ideology. For Nandy (1985), much violence has been perpetrated by the secularist state and it is the ideology of secularism that not only makes us look at religion with suspicion but also does not enable us to build on traditionally existent people's capacity for co-existence. Madan's critique of secularism also begins with such a view. The problem of secularism in India for Madan is the problem of a "modernist minority" which is "beset with deep anxieties about the future of secularism in the country and South Asia generally" who in their attempt to rescue secularism, want to "foster modern scientific temper" as a foundation for secularism (Madan, 1992: 396).

But in Madan's critique of secularism the issue is not only between modernity and tradition but also between different religious traditions in the way they classify the world. For Madan, the modernist ideology of secularism has its most comfortable home in Christian religious tradition, namely in its supposed neat distinction between the sacred and the secular. In other religious traditions such as Hinduism and Islam, for Madan, though there is a distinction between the two the secular is always hierarchically encompassed by the religious. Madan's argument is that since a majority of people of South Asia are vibrant followers of other religions, they have a problem in feeling at home in the dichotomy between the sacred and the secular. In the words of Madan, "...the Hindu tradition does not provide us with a dualistic view of the kind that Christianity does. I find that a Hindu or a Sikh or a Muslim for that matter would find it more difficult to make sense of the notion of 'privatization of religion' than perhaps a Christian does" (Madan in Bhargava, 1998: 319).

Madan's reflections on comparative religious approaches to secularity call for a deeper anthropology of religions, particularly of Christianity which in the Indian context is a neglected domain of inquiry. It remains to be ethnographically validated if Protestant Christians are more secular or feel more at home with the ideology of secularism in a multi-religious society such as India or even in Western Europe and North America. Furthermore, in the last quarter century we have witnessed intense mobilization against privatization of religion globally in which many Christian movements including Protestant ones such as liberation theology and Habitat for Humanity have been key actors (Beyer, 1994; Giri, 2002a). For Madan, secularism is a gift of Christianity but Madan himself says that it is Protestantism which has made a fuller delivery of this gift possible. But even in understanding post-Reformation ideal of secularism there is a problem here as it neglects the trajectory of what Charles Taylor (1996) calls Catholic modernity. It is the Catholic encounter with modernity, as Alexis de Tocqueville (1961) suggests from his encounter with the dialectic of individualism and equality in American democracy, which has struggled more on the side of equality rather than just feel satisfied with possessive individualism.[1]

What should be taken note of here is that Gianni Vattimo, a critical philosopher of our times who comes to his Christian faith taking both Nietzsche and Heidegger seriously, also makes a similar argument about secularism and Christianity. For Vattimo (1999), there is an intimate connection between the secular project and the Christian vocation in the world as Jesus Christ makes a break with violence. In making the connection between secularization and Christianity, Vattimo urges us to realize that secularization here is characterized by the striving for non-violence, kenosis or self-emptying which also means "self-abasing" oneself in love, and charity—namely interpretive charity with regard to supposedly sanctioned divine commands and laws. For Vattimo, secularization means working with a "non-violent and non-absolute God", a God who is "post-metaphysical". In the words of Vattimo: "[. . . .] If the natural sacred is the violent mechanism that Jesus came to unveil and undermine, it is possible that secularization—which also constitutes the Church's loss of temporal authority and human reason's increasing autonomy from its dependence upon an absolute God, a fearful Judge who so transcends our ideas about good and evil as to appear as a capricious or bizarre sovereign—is precisely a positive effect of Jesus' teaching, and not a way of moving away from it" (*ibid.*, 41; also see, Taylor, 1996).

For Vattimo, non-violence inaugurated by Jesus's break with the supposed violence of the natural sacred, is an important part of the secular vocation. As Madan's formulations suffer from a weak anthropology and theology of Christianity, Vattimo's suffer from a messianic zeal of it and lacks a cross-cultural and cross-religious realization that all sacred is not violent. The God of *Taitteriya Upanishad* where God meditates upon himself to bring forth a world is not violent. But this apart, Vattimo's reflections urge us to realize the many other dimensions in the connection between Christian vocation and secularization. Secularization here is not confined to the neat distinction between the sacred and the secular but points to normative ideals of non-violence, *kenosis* or self-emptying, and charity—ideals which call for appropriate self-realization and institutional transformations. These ideals, arguing with Vattimo against Vattimo, are not only the legacy of Christianity, and they can work as a critique of both religion and secularism conventionally understood. If we understand secularism as *kenosis* or self-emptying then one challenge of being secular is to empty oneself from one's will to power. Secularism as self-emptying of power poses enormous challenge to the prevalent conceptions of secularism and models of emancipation as empowerment and urges us to realize that emancipation as politics of empowerment must have within itself an ethics and spirituality of self-cultivation so that one does not become a slave to one's will to power in one's private life and the public sphere. Secularism as *kenosis* or self-emptying *vis-à-vis* one's will to power challenges us not to be obsessed with, as Foucault urges in his *Care of the Self*, "exercising power over others" and to be concerned with discovering and realizing "what one is purely in relation to oneself" (Foucault, 1986: 85). Secularism as *kenosis* can thus be linked to Foucauldian care of the self: "It is then a matter of forming and recognizing oneself as the subject of one's own actions, not through a system of signs denoting power over others, but through a relation that depends as little possible on status, and its external forms" (*ibid*).

Madan concludes his address, "Secularism in its Place," with a passionate urging to take both religion and secularism seriously. But the task of taking both religion and secularism also entails a mutual critique, and a foundational interrogation and broadening of categories. In his critique, Madan presents us a cross-cultural interrogation of what may be called the ideology of secularism. Secular ideology for Madan leads to "the marginalization of religious faith". The more foundational problem for Madan which he expresses in the words of Falzur Rahman is: "Secularism destroys the sanctity and universality (transcendence) of all moral values" (Madan, 1992: 402). But does secularism do this or has to necessarily to do this? Does religion always promote moral values? Does invocation of transcendence necessarily lead to human emancipation? What kind of ultimate values lead to human annihilation and what kind of ultimate values lead to human flourishing including a mutual sharing of each other's ultimate values? If, as Vattimo (1999: 90) suggests, love is the ultimate value and all of us have sinned because we have failed in love, then should we be prepared to reject religions if they fail us in love?

Madan himself says that religious traditions of South Asia are "totalizing in character, claiming all of a follower's life" but in our engagement with religion should we support its totalitarianism. I am sure for Madan, respect for religion does not mean support for a totalitarian determination of life in the name of religion. Taking religion seriously means engaging ourselves with a critique of it, certainly a connected critique to begin with. What we need here is a critique of religion, and not only secularism, and in this realize the significance of secularism as it has loosened the totalitarian hold of religion and has contributed to the quest and realization of human freedom. As Thomas Pantham argues, "The problematic relationship between religion and politics in the West had its analogues in India too. Despite important philosophical or metaphysical differences between them, both European Christianity and Indian religions rationalized in their own ways, a feudal order of social inequalities prevailing during the medieval period" (Pantham, 1999: 182). And in the medieval world a radical interrogation of religion as a partner in social exploitation was articulated by varieties of socio-spiritual movements such as the Anabaptists in Europe (*cf.* Mauss, 1979) and *Bhakti* (devotional) movements in India. *Bhakti* movements were spiritually inspired socio-spiritual movements which fought against caste and gender hierarchy in medieval India. The work of spirituality in *Bhakti* movements involved a critique of religion as a partner in systemic oppression of society and quest for establishment of relationships of dignity. As critic and essayist Chittaranjan Das argues: "To go inside in the life of the spirit is also to expand oneself in terms of consciousness, to break down the separating wall between oneself and the all. Self-realization with the medieval saints of India was not a running away from the world to what is called to save one's soul; it is being reborn ego less, so that you are able to look at the whole world in a different eye. You become a rebel because you want the relationships and arrangements of society to be determined anew" (Das, 1982b: 80). Thus secularism as a fight for human emancipation and striving for realization of human freedom has also an origin in spiritual protests in both India as well as Europe and this helps us to deconstruct religion as we take it seriously. In medieval India *Bhakti* movements characterized by a quest for love and non-violence have been the forbearers of secularism and modernity, what JPS Uberoi (1996) calls Indian modernity which started with Kabir and has found an ally in Gandhi, among others, in the midway. But what is interesting is that this spiritual origin of secularism buttresses the non-violent character of it as pointed to us by Vattimo and is characterized by a religion, spirituality and praxis of love. Spirituality as a movement of transformation in self and society and embodied in the life and work of Antigone, Socrates, Buddha, Jesus, Kabir, Guru Nanak, Meister Eckhart, *Bhakti* movements, Ali Shariati, and innumerable movements of what can be called practical spirituality all over the world—provides not only a critique of secularism but also a radical interrogation of religion. It is my submission that both the critiques as well as defense of secularism would be enriched by bringing the vision and practice of spirituality not only to our discourse but also to our practice.

But opening ourselves to such sources of secularism calls for crossing the borders of conventional academic boundaries. When we look at the discursive field of secularism this seems to be a crucial challenge as it is bounded by a dualistic logic and is one dimensional and mono-disciplinary. In contemporary Indian society and scholarship, it is a field which suffers from the blindness of disciplinary exclusivity which affects both the critics and defenders. The political scientists writing here talk mostly of state, to some extent of civil society, and of course always of Constitution. And anthropologists such as Madan or cultural critics such as Nandy enter the field with an a priori privileging of the religious and faith in its capacity for tolerance in the pre-modern life-world. But if one of the tasks before us is an interpretative task of providing more clarity to the agenda of secularism, as Madan challenges us in the Indian context and Connolly in the Euro-American world, then what is called for is a creative embodiment of transdisciplinarity. This calls for political scientists to go beyond the secured logic of Constitution and state and anthropologists to acknowledge, as Andre Beteille (1992, 2002) would urge, that contemporary Indian society is governed not only by *Dharmasastras* but also by Constitution. But again he called for transdisciplinary participation here must have within it the perspective of spiritual movements and seekers and cross the boundaries between sociology and spiritual seeking. A spiritual process of abandonment and creative exploration is central to the practice of transdisciplinarity and the discursive field of secularism calls for a spiritual interrogation of our disciplinary homes in anthropology, sociology, philosophy, theology and even spirituality (Giri, 2000).[2]

Such a transdisciplinary participation has not only semantic function or scholastic utility: it has important implications for our art of learning and living in a secular society understood as a plural society. Consider here Ashis Nandy's statement: "As far as public morality goes, statecraft in India may have something to learn from Hinduism, Islam or Sikhism; but Hinduism, Islam and Sikhism have very little to learn from the contribution from state secular practices" (quoted in Pantham, 1999: 177). But do not Muslim males who do not give alimony to their divorced wives and caste Hindus who burn *dalits* have something to learn from Constitution of India ? Even do not the well-meaning Hindus, Muslims and Sikhs have something to learn from the secular principles of Indian Constitution?

Thus, in rethinking secularism the challenge is a multidimensional learning—lateral as well as vertical, and a simultaneous critique of both religious tradition and modern state. A transdisciplinary participation in secularism with a radical spiritual supplement can prepare us against one-sided confident self-closure and for simultaneous critique of both religious traditions and the secular state. And here Gandhi can help us in not only discovering the religious resources for living in a secular society but also in initiating a spiritual transformation of the telos and the machinery of modern state. For Gandhi, "the modern state itself needs to be 'civilized' by integrating it with spirituality or morality" (Pantham, 1999: 183). As Thomas Pantham argues: "[. . . .] Gandhi seems to have inaugurated a postliberal, ethical-secular trajectory of relationship between politics and religion in which their relative autonomy from each other is used in moral-political experiments or campaigns for the reconstruction of both the religious traditions and the modern State [. . . .]" (*ibid*: 181). Unfortunately, this aspect of Gandhian critique of a moral transformation of state has not received much attention from either the critics or the defenders of secularism.

Gandhi is dear to many of us but the question is how far, deep and up we wish to walk with him. One important implication of holding the hands of Gandhi is that we strive to learn about each other's religions. Madan finds it difficult and here gives the analogy of difficulty of multilingual learning in India (Madan 1997: 277). But if secularism as a dignified mode of inter-religious and plural existence has to succeed then learning about each other's religion is a must. As Gandhi tells us:

> I hold that it is the duty of every cultured man or woman to read sympathetically the scriptures of the world. If we are to respect others' religions as we would have them to respect our own, a friendly study of the world's religions is a sacred duty. We need not dread, upon our grown up children, the influence of scriptures other than our own. We liberalize their outlook upon life by encouraging them to study freely all that is clean. [. . . .] For myself, I regard my study of and reverence for the *Bible*, the *Quran*, and the other scriptures to be wholly consistent with my claim to be a staunch Sanatani Hindu. He is no Sanatani Hindu who is narrow, bigoted, and considers evil to be good if it has the sanction of antiquity and is to be found supported in any Sanskrit book (quoted in Sharma, 1995: 89-90).

However, the invocation of Gandhi in the reshaping of secularism does not go unchallenged. Political scientist, Paul Brass (1998) finds the invocation of Gandhi in the critique of secularism offered by Nandy and Madan problematic. For Brass, "The peaceful pursuit of interreligious dialogue through the 'recovery of religious tolerance' has no meaning for those groups who have seen themselves as oppressed and discriminated against in Hindu society: Muslims, Backward Castes, Scheduled Castes and Scheduled Tribes (Brass, 1998: 493). But Brass has to help us understand how even for these groups tolerance is possible without cultivation of the capacity of tolerance at the levels of individuals and groups? And here Gandhi is important because Gandhi urges us through the example of his life and death to be ever prepared for the knockings of the other in our house and open our doors. As JPS Uberoi argues: "[. . . .]Gandhi would always look the other in the eye as his second self and offer truthful dialogue and non-violent conversation without the fear of the possible consequences" (Uberoi, 2002: 121). Gandhian agenda is not confined only to the search for "transcendent interreligious truths" as Brass makes it to be. Learning to hold the hands of the other from other religions here on Earth—in Noakhali, in Delhi, in Sevagram, in Lahore and in Amritsar—is an important part of the Gandhian way of life.

Defense of Secularism

Towards a Spiritual Transformation of Justification and Application

Co-existence and toleration are important aspects of the way of life which Gandhi inspires us to lead. Even defenders of secularism in the Indian context are coming to realize that toleration is the single most important task facing us now insofar as the issue of secularism is concerned. For example, in his recent insightful reflection on the predicament of secularism, "Secularism and its Discontents", Amartya Sen (1996) argues that the key question for an agenda of secularism is the question of symmetric treatment of religions, groups, individual and other autonomies. For Sen, a secular state has a moral duty to ensure such a symmetric treatment among religions and does not agree with critics of secularism such as Nandy that such a practice is inevitably accompanied by the increase in the power of the state to perpetrate violence on people in the name of defending secularism.

But how do we cultivate and facilitate the capacity for symmetric and fair treatment to each other on the part of individuals and groups? Here, Sen does not go much farther and deeper. He does not address the ontological preparation that is required for such a mode of life to exist in our society and politics. Similar is the problem with another thinker such as Partha Chatterjee (1994) who titles his contribution on the subject as "Secularism and Toleration." But Chatterjee does not tell us how we can cultivate toleration among members of different religious faiths. And like Sen, Chatterjee finds a panacea only in secular politics. For Chatterjee, by the initiation of a politics of representative democracy among the minorities to run their religious affairs such as the Muslim Wakf Board or the Akal Takht, we can help initiate reform within these and create a more favourable condition for inter-group toleration. But is this enough to ensure toleration? Practice of toleration requires a preparation in the life of individuals for another religion, another world, and this is not a matter of politics alone.

The same challenge of self-cultivation and transformation we find in the defense of secularism offered by other political scientists of India. They defend secularism as part of democratic equality. Manoranjan Mohanty makes a distinction between secularism—hegemonic and democratic. Mohanty would agree with critics of secularism such as Madan and Nandy that there is a danger in making it only an ideology of the state or an elite and would want secularism to be part of ongoing democratic mobilization and transformation of Indian society. Continuing the same engagement with democracy, though a bit more constitutional rather mobilizational as in the case of Mohanty, Neera Chandhoke (1999) defends secularism as defense of minority rights which is part of a broader agenda of democratic equality. For her, "...societies that are deeply polarized on the matter of religion, such as India or Northern Ireland, will need to institute protections for minorities against majoritarianism" (Chandhoke, 1999: 7). But Chandhoke also argues, implicitly suggesting the argument of Uberoi that the problem of humanity cannot be solved "within a framework of majority and minority" (*cf.* Uberoi, 2002: 120): "...the right of a minority community to its own identity and practices has to be balanced with respect for the rights of other communities to their own identity and practices. [. . . .] *the struggle for recognition that is simultaneously a search for dignity, directs our attention to the intersubjective conditions of human realization*" (Chandhoke, 1999: 19; emphasis added).

To this defense of secularism Rajeev Bhargava contributes important clarifications by redefining secularism contextually. He develops a notion of contextual secularism partly out of the recognition of the problem posed by Nandy and Madan that there is very little sensitivity to religious pluralism in the state-centric discourse of secularism. Contextual secularism recognizes that "many forms of separation lie between total exclusion and complete fusion" (Bhargava, 1998: 516). Contextual secularism for Bhargava is political secularism, not ideological secularism, and "political secularism demands only that everyone—believer, non-believer—gives up a bit of what is of exclusive importance in order to sustain that which is generally valuable" (*ibid*: 496).

But is politics enough in realizing political secularism or does it need an appropriate ethics and spirituality? Is realization of democratic equality possible only by institution of group rights in the Constitution or does it require appropriate self-cultivation and ontological preparation in self and society for inviting the other into the hard core of the "political" self. And this requires not only a Rawlsian political liberalism and Habermasian inclusion of the other but also a spiritual praxis of self-opening and self-transformation which is conspicuous by its absence in Rawls and Habermas (*cf.* Cohen, 2001; Giri, 2002b). Bhargava's conception of political secularism uncritically reflects a Rawlsian project of liberalism but the challenge now to realize the limits of Rawls. As Connolly urges us to realize: "*But secularism is the last historical moment in the politics of becoming Rawlsian categories authorize us to acknowledge*. Rawls wants us to freeze the liberal conception of the person and the secular conception of public space today while everything else in and around the culture undergoes change" (Connolly, 1999: 66; emphasis in the original).

Chandhoke herself writes that "we need not value pluralism although we are faced with a plural society" (Chandhoke, 1999: 297). This urges us to realize that even if we institute pluralism constitutionally we may not embody a plural mode of being or what William Connolly calls "the ethos of pluralization" (Connolly, 2001). As Connolly would suggest, for embodying an ethos of pluralization we need to be self-reflective about the modernist privileging of epistemology and open ourselves to ontological journeys. However, this calls for not only a multidimensional conception of pluralism and public sphere as Connolly suggests but also a multi-layered conception of being which is suggested in Connolly's conception of "plurivocity of being." But Connolly's "plurivocity of being" only stops at the foothills of Nietzsche and thus it is no wonder that the only other dimension of plurivocality of being that we are opened to in Connolly is the dimension of the infrarational. But here a cross-cultural and trans-civilizational philosophical and spiritual engagement can help us realize that it is not only Nietzschean and Deleuzean infrarational which constitute the other dimension of plurivocality of being but also Sri Aurobindo's supra-rational and Roy Bhaskar's "transcendentally real self" (Bhaskar, 2002: 139) which is characterized by the striving for realization of non-duality in a world of duality and strife. For Sri Aurobindo, the "supra-rational dimension" of our being enables us to overcome the limitations of our mind, especially our "desire-mind," and enable us to "have the joy of contact in diverse oneness" (Sri Aurobindo, 1950: 484).

A multidimensionally rich conception of self-facilitates the realization of secularism as multidimensional pluralism by facilitating not only public contestations of one's fundamentals but also a sharing of selves, a creative interpenetration between the self and other, or as Uberoi would say, an exchange of self, not only of gifts (Uberoi, 2002). And this sharing in self and society is preeminently a spiritual activity. Thus, in the political reshaping of secularism as democratic equality a spiritual foundation is helpful. But spiritual processes of transformation are not foundational only in a genealogical sense but in a critically constitutive sense of permanent critique and refiguration. Spirituality as a permanent critique of violation of life and the destructive logic of power provides us with a much needed perspective of "limits", i.e., the realization of "limits of politics" to both the confident and self-critical political scientists of our times (see Lalcau, 1992).[3] As Roberto M. Unger, himself a political and legal theorist, tells us: there are two kinds of sacred—a transcendental sacred and a social sacred and whenever a system of power loses touch with the transcendental sacred it can and very often present oppression as manifestation and justification for the social sacred and there may not be any critical ground to critique such an unjust arrangement (Unger, 1987). And here as Alberto Melucci (1996: 171), a sociologist, urges us to realize:

> Instrumental rationality has restored the world to mankind's scope of operation, but it also denies humanity all chances to transcend reality, it devalues everything that resists subsumption under the instrumental action. Society thus becomes a system of apparatuses identical with its own actions and intolerant of any diversity. The sacred thus emerges as an appeal to a possible other, as the voice of what is not but could be. Divested of the ritual trappings of the churches, the sacred thus becomes a purely cultural form of resistance which counters the presumption of power by affirming the right to desire—to hope that the world is more than what actually is.

Melucci's critique of instrumental rationality in modernity is in tune with Gandhi's and even has a resonance in Weber. As Madan helps us understand this: "A Gandhian critique of secularism in terms of ultimate values and individual responsibility is in some respects similar to Max Weber's concern with the problem of value. What Gandhi and Weber are saying is that secularized world is inherently unstable because it elevates to the realm of ultimate values the only value it knows and these are instrumental values" (Madan, 1997: 237-38). These critiques point to a spiritual horizon of secularism not as a way of providing a stable ground to the inherent instability of secularism but as a permanently moving frame of criticism. But understanding this requires not only a transformation in our political reasoning but also sociological reasoning. Sociology has been part of the project of modernity which believes that it can "provide a privileged or authoritative interpretation of social events", making it a hegemonic discourse while "all others, including religious utopias, derivative" (Wuthnow, 1991: 14). But opening ourselves to spiritual critique and transformations calls for us to "interpret the significance of contemporary movements in terms of hopes and aspirations of their participants, including their hopes for salvation and spiritual renewal [. . . .]" (*ibid*).

The Calling of Mutual Learning and Cultivating Non-Dual Pluralism

If toleration is the most important part of the agenda of secularism then we must lay its seed in our minds and hearts and for this it is important for us to learn about each other, know each other in an open-ended spirit of exploration, dialogue and creation of a new ground of life. Such a mode of learning is pre-eminently a spiritual activity. Spirituality is about the quality of relationship between the self and the other (*cf.* Kurien, 1997); in fact, spirituality lies in the heart of relationships or at the mid-point of relationships, to borrow a phrase from Martin Heidegger (*cf.* Dallmayr, 1996). And for a more dignified relationship, we must prepare ourselves for it by being engaged in multifarious practices of education, self-cultivation or Bildung (*cf.* Dumont, 1994) and to understand the spiritual foundations for a secular society.

But now there is a shocking ignorance about each other's religion. In a society like contemporary Indian society not only are we not taught about it in schools because of the secular injunctions against it nor do we have any opportunity for this in civil society. If we do not know anything about each other's religions then how can we accept each other's religions? It is true that knowing is not enough but this is an important part of a more inclusive process of feeling and realization. But how do we learn about each other's religions? If the Hindus learn about Islam only from the *Rastriya Swayam Sevak Sangha* and the *Viswa Hindu Parishad* (sectarian Hindu organizations) and Muslims learn about Hindus from sectarian Islamic organizations, then what is the nature of our knowledge of each other? Is this not a knowledge of hatred only? Is there any knowledge here where we have already formulated our objects of knowledge in an a priori mode?

In this context, it is helpful to listen to my discussion with a follower of a Hindu socio-spiritual movement. This movement is an exciting one and it believes that we should accept all religions. *Sarva dharma samabhava* (Goodwill towards all religions) is not enough; we must have *sarva dharma swikara*—acceptance of all religions. This movement also believes that Hindus should accept Jesus as the eleventh incarnation of God and Prophet Mohammed as the twelfth. But when I asked him does he know anything about Jesus or Mohammed, he told me: " I am sorry that I do not know anything". I told him: "But the city in which you live has so many Muslims. Could not you make a little effort"? Then he told me: "Yes, there is an eagerness within me. But it stays at a subterranean level of my consciousness. It is helpful if we have organizations to activate this dormant eagerness within me". Thus, the challenge of education I am pleading for goes much deeper and here we must have appropriate institutional condition for learning both at the level of state and civil society (also see Sharma, 1996).

If secularism has to be redefined as pluralism and multiculturalism then we must confront the epistemic task of living in such a plural and multi-religious society (*cf.* Mohanty, 1998). As has been suggested, learning about other religions, cultures and communities is an important part of this epistemic engagement. But learning is not simply a question of epistemology but involves ontological preparation and work on self-development on the part of self, culture and society.

To live in a multi-religious, multi-cultural and plural society we need a new ethics, politics and spirituality of self-cultivation. And it is this focus on self-cultivation which is missing in our discourse on both secularism and pluralism. In Indian sociology, T.K. Oommen (2002) is a passionate advocate of pluralism but his pluralism remains at the boundaries of groups and it does not have a project of what can be called ontological pluralism. The Ontological pluralism calls for realization of non-dual plurivocality in our beings. Roy Bhaskar, the philosopher of critical realism, who has taken critical realism into new depths and horizons of spiritual strivings, provides us glimpses of non-dual self-realization as an important part of realization of ontological and sociological pluralism (see Bhaskar, 2000; 2002). For Bhaskar, "the possibility of human emancipation depends upon expanding the zone of non-duality within our lives; and in the first instance upon shedding our own heteronomy so that we become in a way non-dual beings in a world of duality" (Bhaskar, 2002: 11).

There are several implications of realization of non-duality for the project of reshaping secularism. One implication is that there is no point in thinking about the relationship between the religious and the secular in terms of an essential opposition. But the other implication for us in this path of engagement is to open ourselves to emergent evolutionary happening and possibility. As Uberoi suggests, which reminds us of Sri Aurobindo: "[. . . .] the theory of evolution means to us, not chiefly or only development of what is complex out of simple, but also the development of many varieties of existence out of the original few, and without humanity in anyway losing the unity of its universe of discourse" (Uberoi, 2002: 130).

The Calling of an Emergent Evolution

Transcendence and Practical Spirituality

(a) The Calling of a New Transcendence

And I would like to submit that the emergence of transcendence as an existence sphere and value sphere of self and society along with "the standard three some of science, morality and religion" (*cf.* Schrag, 1997: 148) is an important part of the contemporary processes of spiritual evolution. Fred Dallmayr's following comments make this clear: "There are plenty of signs in our time that a narrowly confined immanence cannot satisfy human longings and aspirations. What needs to be recognized is that longing for transcendence, even a transcendental holism, are vibrantly alive today in many societies on the level of the ordinary life-world—far removed from traditional holistic power structures" (Dallmayr, 2001: 17). And as Jean-Luc Nancy argues: "It is precisely the immanence of man to man, or it is man, taken absolutely, considered as the immanent being par excellence, that constitutes the stumbling block to a thinking of community" (quoted in Dallmayr, 1998: 281).

But the process of unification in the emergent sphere of transcendence as it relates to other domains of our lives is different from the familiar process of universalistic unification. It is not the simple formula of unity-in-diversity as Uberoi suggests. It is a process of unification where unity is always a deferred state. As Scharg urges, "[. . . .] it is a dynamics of unification that is always an "ing", a process of unifying, rather than an "ed", a finalized result" (Schrag, 1997: 129). Schrag builds upon Kierkegaard and urges us to overcome the facile dualism between transcendence and immanence. What is helpful is that in contemporary philosophy and theology we have passionate reformulation of not only the relationship between transcendence and immanence but the very categories themselves. Building on the philosophical and theological works of Jacques Derrida and Luce Irigaray, John D. Caputo writes: "The new idea of transcendence turns on a new and positive idea of the finite, not as confining limit, as in Kant's example of the dove that thinks it is confined by the air that sustains it...[Rather] transcendence [is] life in the elements, in the enveloping medium in which soul and body 'marry.' What then is God's transcendence? Who is the God who comes after metaphysics? Not a God of infinite distance from earth and flesh, but the infinite freedom to make Godself immanent in the finite, incarnate" (Caputo, 2002: 14-15). Giving a new interpretation to Derrida's famous dictum "God is Wholly Other," Walter Lowe (2002) writes in his "Second Thoughts About Transcendence": "Surely we have the option of reading "God is other" as "God is different" and "God as Wholly Other" as "God differing-differently." There would then be the conceptual space to conceive that 'divine transcendence' might refer, perhaps, to God's freedom. Then transcendence would cease to be the opposite of immanence; for a God of freedom would not be isolated in some lofty place but would be capable of being immanent precisely because of being transcendent, i.e., free" (Lowe, 2002: 250).

For Derrida, there is no problem and in fact it is a blessing if we do not take the name of God. As Caputo (2002) interprets the Derridean pathway: "Save everything about God save the name of God, lest it become an idol that blocks our way". This Derridean refusal to name God and abandonment is noticed in the *Bhakti* movements of India. Here, Chittaranjan Das's work on *Bhakti* movements and spiritual evolution deserves our careful attention. Das (1982a) tells us in his study of Bhakti literature of India that saint Pundarika Das of Karnataka in his poems has described Rama and Krishna as *Idli* and *Dosha* (items of food in South India). In Orissa, while the Panchasakhas—Achyutananda Das, Balram Das, Ararkhita Das *et al.* have transcended many idols and arrived at Jagannatha as Brahma the blind tribal poet and spiritual prophet Bhima Bhoi in nineteenth century has transcended Jagannatha himself and made him a watchman in the house of *Sunya*—Emptiness (Das, 2001). This refusal to name God and abandonment has affinity with the path of spiritual seeking and enlightenment charted by Buddha.

Luc Irigaray has been another source of inspiration in contemporary rethinking of transcendence as the air we breathe. Irigaray has been an important source of inspiration in rethinking religion as a process of being divine reminding us of Sri Aurobindo's pathway of life divine (*cf.* Jantzen, 2002; Sri Aurobindo, 1951). Irigaray provides us a critique of religion, namely Christian religion from the point of view of feminine spirituality. A woman, a client in psychoanalysis, tells Irigaray, "At the point in the mass when they, the (spiritual) father and son, are reciting together the ritual words of the consecration, saying 'This is my body, this is my blood', I bleed" (*cf.* Jantzen, 2002). Irigaray points to the shifting trajectory of Christian theology and in the Indian context Felix Wilfred (1999) points to its mystical dimensions. Wilfred presents us the agenda of a situated Christian theology taking into consideration the cultural and spiritual aspirations of Asia. For Wilfred Christianity in the new millennium, not only in India but around the world, should not only assert its prophetic truths but open itself to the mysterious dimension of religion, spirituality and the human condition. In the words of Wilfred: "The Christian attempts to cross over to the other, to the different, has been by and large from the pole of being or fullness. This naturally creates problems, which can be overcome by activating the ability also to cross over from the pole of nothingness or emptiness" (Wilfred, 1999: xiii).

(b) The Calling of Practical Spirituality

At this point the work of German theologian Johannes B. Metz (1981) deserves our careful attention. He says that the quest for unity cannot be achieved on the level of faith but has to be a practical quest, the practical quest of addressing the concrete problems of men and women here on Earth. We can utilize this as a turning point for discussing practical spirituality as an emergent mode in many world religions now. Swami Vivekananda had spoken about it more than hundred years ago and the previous chapter has described the emerging vision and practice of practical spirituality.

What is to be noted that practically spirituality can be looked at as an emergent global genre. Consider for instance the shifting contours of spirituality in contemporary American Society. For Robert Wuthnow in contemporary American society there is a shift from a "spirituality of dwelling" to a "spirituality of seeking" (Wuthnow,

1998). "A spirituality of dwelling emphasizes habitation: God occupies a definite place in the universe" (Wuthnow, 1998: 10). It "emphasizes an orderly, systematic understanding of life" (*ibid.*, 8). But a spirituality of habitation and dwelling is inadequate to satisfy our multiple aspirations at present when the secured houses of our lives are in a flux. This creates the context for the emergence of a "spirituality of seeking" which is "closely connected to the fact that people increasingly create a sense of personal identity through an active sequence of searching and selecting" (*ibid.*, 18). But Wuthnow makes it clear that a spirituality of seeking in itself is inadequate to come to terms with challenges of self-development and responsibility to the other and the world as it offers only "fleeting encounters with the sacred" (*ibid.*, 8). Spirituality of seeking suffers from the danger of making seekers of spirituality satisfied with temporary spiritual sensations and needs to be supplemented by what Wuthnow calls "practice-oriented spirituality". Practice-oriented spirituality provides multiple grounds for combining spiritual practice and social service. Practice-oriented spirituality is not confined to moments of spiritual sensations but touches all aspects of our life: "[. . . .] the point of spiritual practice is not to elevate an isolated set of activities over the rest of life but to electrify the spiritual impulse that animates all of life" (Wuthnow, 1998: 198).

The significance of practical spirituality as a global genre is attested by many observers of the contemporary scene such as Peter Beyer (1994) who argues that "pure religion" is at a disadvantage in the global society and the solution to its increasing and inevitable privatization lies in finding "effective religious applications". Thus, in order to be of interest to both believers and non-believers, religions have to undertake activities which ameliorate the conditions of poverty and suffering, build the foundations for what Giddens calls a "generative well-being" (Giddens, 1994) and through this act of building encourage the participants to develop themselves ethically, morally, and spiritually. But the practical activities of religion are not just "applied" where application is dissociated from what Kierkegaard (1962; also Giri and Quarles von Ufford, 2000) calls a transcendental inspiration of love. The applied activities of practical spirituality manifest themselves through various projects—both the life-projects where the actors are committed to a cause and live in accordance with such a commitment and social projects where religious movements are engaged in a concrete activity as building houses as in the case of Habitat for Humanity or building water harvesting structures in case of *swadhyaya*—but these projects are not merely instances of "application"; they are manifestations of an integral mode of engagement where applied activities are nourished by a spiritual relationship with the Transcendent. Thus, the applied projects of such movements of practical spirituality are different from projects of mere application which is the case with many development projects of our times (*cf.* Quarles van Ufford and Giri, 2003). Practice and practical work in such movements differ from the familiar anthropological category of practice outlined by Bourdieu (*cf.* Bourdieu, 1971) and the notion of practical discourse presented by Habermas (1990) as both the categories refer only to rational strategies and rational deliberations of actors and are not linked to spiritual realization and transcendent self-awareness of actors. The applied activities of movements of practical spirituality transcend the familiar dichotomies between Transcendence and Immanence; in fact, their projects of social action for the other which are simultaneously initiatives in self-development transcend the familiar dichotomies between transcendence and immanence and exist at the "mid-point" of the relationship between transcendence and immanence.

This border crossing between transcendence and immanence also involves transformations in the ethico-moral horizons of religions. While in the past, moral considerations meant "sin, ignorance, etc." (*cf.* Beyer, 1990: 360), now the condition of our life and society—the nature of poverty, social justice, quality of our love—is the subject of ethico-moral engagement. As Vattimo challenges us: "We all stand in need of forgiveness; not because we have broken sacred principles that were metaphysically sanctioned, but rather we have because we have 'failed' toward those whom we are supposed to love" (Vattimo, 1990: 90).

On the Way towards Conclusion

Spirituality as a Permanent Critique and Creativity

In this chapter we have explored different pathways of spiritual cultivation for realization of plurivocal beings and a multi-dimensionally rich public sphere. We began this essay with a caution from Jacques Derrida that we should be on our guard so that we do not authorize in the name of religion. In exploring spiritual cultivation for a secular society am I authorizing in the name of spirituality? Here I have not provided a definition of spirituality but spirituality for me lies in the in-between lines and embodies a permanent quest for realization of relationships of dignity. But it would be a mistake to look at spirituality as a stable foundation, as the ultimate truth, and as solution to all our problems. It is also important not to forget that spiritual movements many a time are entrapped in a logic of authoritarianism and individual salvation (*cf.* Krishna, 1996). In this context, as we work on spiritual cultivation for a secular society, the challenge before spirituality now is to continue to fight for radical democracy and universality—a universality which transgresses the boundaries of self and other, creates new intimacies and solidarities across boundaries and participates in the struggle for creation and nurturance of transformative institutions of justice, well-being and dignity.

NOTES

1. Tocqueville writes: "If Catholicism predisposes the faithful to obedience, it certainly does not prepare them for inequality: but the contrary may be said of Protestantism, which generally tends to make men independent, more than to render them equal" (Tocqueville, 1961: 356).
2. Of course, admirable exceptions in this field are J.P.S. Uberoi's (1996) *Religion, Civil Society and State: A Study of Sikhism* and Felix Wilfred's (2000) *Asian Dreams and Christian Hopes* which embody a simultaneous and sometimes transgressive engagement with politics, religion, theology and spirituality.
3. This is as much a challenge for Neera Chandhoke and Rajeev Bhargava as for William Connolly. It is striking that Connolly's inspiring conception of "politics of being" has no engagement with the issue of self-cultivation in terms of, among others, developing kenosis or self-emptying *vis-ā-vis* the will to power. Note here the way Connolly defines "politics of being," and compare this, without judgment, with the vocation of being articulated by Roy Bhaskar described later in the essay: "By the politics of becoming I mean that paradoxical politics by which new cultural identities are formed out of unexpected energies and institutionally congealed injuries. The politics of becoming emerges out of the energies, suffering, and the lines of flight available to culturally defined differences in a particular institutional constellation" (Connolly, 1999: 57).

REFERENCES

A Glimpse into Oriya Literature. Bhubaneswar: Orissa Sahitya Akademi, 1982b.

After Heaven: Spirituality in America since the 1950s. California, 1998.

Alternative Visions: Pathways in the Global Village. Lanham, MD: Rowman & Littlefield, 1998.

Antinomies of Society. Delhi: Oxford University Press, 2002.

Asian Dreams and Christian Hopes. Delhi: ISCPK, 2000.

Basu, Kaushik & Sanjay Subramaniam. (eds). *Unravelling the Nation: Sectarian Conflict and India's Secular Identity*. New Delhi: Penguin Books, 1996.

Beteille, Andre, *Society and Politics in India: Essays in a Comparative Perspective*. Delhi: Oxford University Press, 1992.

Beyer, Peter F. *Religion and Globalization*. London: Sage, 1994.

Bhargava, Rajeev. (eds.) *Secularism and its Critics*. Delhi: Oxford University Press, 1998.

Bhaskar, Roy. *From East to West: The Odyssey of a Soul*. London: Routledge, 2000.

Bhinna Jane Vivekananda [Another Vivekananda]. Cuttack: The Universe, 1996.

Bourdieu, Pierre. 1971. *Outline of a Theory of Practice*. Cambridge: Cambridge University Press.

Brass, Paul R. 1998. "Secularism Out of Its Place." *Contributions to Indian Sociology*, 32 (2): 485-505.

Building in the Margins of Shacks: The Vision and Projects of Habitat for Humanity. New Delhi: Orient Longman, 2002a.

Caputo, John D. 2002. "Introduction: Who Comes After the God of Metaphysics?" In *idem* (ed.), *The Religious*. Oxford: Blackwell.

Chandhoke, Neera. 1999. *Beyond Secularism: The Rights of Religious Minorities*. Delhi: Oxford University Press.

Chatterjee, Partha. 1994. "Secularism and Toleration." *Economic and Political Weekly*. July 9.

Civil Society and its Institutions. Calcutta: The First Fulbright Memorial Lecture, 1996.

Cohen, G.A. 2001. If you're Egalitarian, How come you are so rich? Cambridge, MA: Harvard University Press.

Connolly, William. 1999. Why I am not a Secularist. Minneapolis: University of Minnesota Press.

Conversations and Transformations: Towards a New Ethics of Self and Society. Lanham, MD: Lexington Books & Rowman and Littlefield, 2002.

Dallmayr, Fred. 1996. *The Other Heidegger*. Ithaca: Cornell U. Press.

Das, Chittaranjan. 1982a. Santha Sahitya [Literature of the Saints]. Bhubaneswar: Orissa Sahitya Akademi.

Dekhu Dekhu Keba Sahu [How Can one tolerate all these one sees]. Bhubaneswar: Siksha Sadhana, 2001.

Derrida, Jacques. 1998. "Faith and Knowledge: Two Sources of 'Religion' at the Limits of Reason Alone". In Jacques Derrida and Giani Vattimo, (eds.), *Religion*. Cambridge: Polity Press.

Dumont. L. 1994. *German Ideology*. Chicago: University of Chicago Press.

Foucault, Michel. 1986. *Care of the Self*. New York: Pantheon.

"Freedom of Religion." *Economic and Political Weekly*, 2003.

Giddens, Anthony. 1994. *Beyond Left and Right: The Future of Radical Politics*. Cambridge: Polity Press.

Giri, Ananta & Philip Quarles van Ufford. 2000. Reconstituting Development as a Shared Responsibility: Ethics, Aesthetics and A Creative Shaping of Human Possibilities. Madras Institute of Development Studies: Working Paper.

Giri, Ananta Kumar. 1998. "The Quest for a Universal Morality: Jurgen Habermas and Sri Aurobindo". In *idem*, *Global Transformations: Postmdoernity and Beyond*. Jaipur & Delhi: Rawat Publications.

"Global Modernities." University of Notre Dame: Unpublished Paper, 2001.

Habermas, Jurgen. 1990. *Moral Consciousness and Communicative Action*. Cambridge: Polity Press.

Jantzen, Grace M. 2002. "'Barely By a Breath...': Irigaray on Rethinking Religion". In John Caputo (ed.), *The Religious*. Oxford: Basil Blackwell.

Joas, Hans. 2000. *Genesis of Values*. Cambridge: Polity Press.

Kierkegaard, Soren. 1962. *Works of Love*. New York: Harper and Row.

Krishna, Daya. 1996. *The Problematic and Conceptual Structure of Classical Indian Thought about Man*, Society and Polity. Delhi: Oxford University Press.

Kurien, C.T. 1996. *"The Material and Spiritual in Social Life"*. Text of the Public Lecture on the occasion of the 317th Anniversary of St. Mary's Church, Chennai, October 28.

Laclau, Ernesto. 1992. "Beyond Emancipation". *Development and Change*.

Life Divine. Pondicherry: Sri Aurobindo Ashram, 1951.

Lowe, Walter. 2002. "Second Thoughts About Transcendence". In John Caputo (ed.), *The Religious*. Oxford: Basil Blackwell.

Madan, T.N. 1992. "Secularism in its Place." In *idem*, ed., *Religion in India*. Delhi: Oxford University Press.

Mani, Lata. 2009. *Sacred Secular: Contemplative Cultural Critique*. Delhi: Routledge.

Matustik, Martin J. 1997. *Postnational Identity: Critical Theory and Existential Philosophy in Habermas*, Kierkegaard, and Havel. New York: The Guilford Press.

Mauss. Marcel. 1979. "The Category of the Person". In *idem*, *Sociology and Psychology: Essays*. London: Routledge and Kegan Paul.

Melucci, Alberto. 1996. *Challenging Codes*. Cambridge: Polity Press.

Metz, Johannes B. 1981. "Towards Second Reformation: The Future of Christianity in a Post-Bourgeoisie World." *Cross Currents*, XXXI (1).

Modern Myths, Locked Minds. Delhi: Oxford University. Press, 1997.

Mohanty, Manoranjan. "Secularism: Hegemonic and Democratic." *Economic and Political Weekly*.

Mohanty, Satya P. 1998. *Literary Theory and the Claims of History*. Delhi: Oxford University Press.

Nandy, Ashis. 1985. "An Anti-Secular Manifesto." *Seminar*, 314: 14-24.

Oommen, T.K. 2002. *Pluralism, Identity, Equality*. Delhi: Oxford University Press.

Pande, G.C. 1989. *The Meaning and Process of Culture as Philosophy of History*. Allahabad: Raka Prakashan.

Pantham, Thomas. 1999. "Indian Secularism and its Critics". In *Border Crossings: Toward A Comparative Political Theory*, ed., Fred Dallmayr. Lexington Books.

Quarles van Ufford, Philip & Ananta Kumar Giri. 2003. eds. A Moral Critique of Development: In *Search of Global Responsibilities*. London: Routledge.

Reflections on Meta Reality: Transcendence, Emancipation and Everyday Life. New Delhi: Sage Publications, 2002.

Religion, Civil Society and State: A Study of Sikhism. Delhi: Oxford University Press, 1996.

Sen, Amartya. 1987. "Secularism and its Discontents". In Kaushik Basu *et al.* eds., *Unravelling the Nation*. New Delhi: Penguin.

Sharma, Arvind. 1995. *Hinduism for Our Times*. Delhi: Oxford University Press.

Sri Aurobindo. 1950. *The Synthesis of Yoga*. Pondicherry: Sri Aurobindo Ashram.

Sunderrajan, R. 1998. *Beyond the Crisis of European Sciences: New Beginnings*. Shimla: Indian Institute of Advanced Studies.

Taylor, Charles. 1996. *A Catholic Modernity*? Dayton, Ohio: University of Dayton Press.

"The Calling of a Creative Transdisciplinarity." *Futures* 34: 103-115, 2000.

The Ethos of Pluralization. Minneapolis: University of Minnesota Press, 2001.

The European Modernity: Truth, Science and Method. Delhi: Oxford University Press, 2002.

Thomas, Scott M. 2005. *The Global Resurgence of Religion and the Transformation of International Relations: The Struggle for the Soul of the Twenty-First Century*. NY: Palgrave Macmillan.

Tocqueville, Alexis de. 1961. *Democracy in America*, Vol. 1. New York: Schokcen Books.

Uberoi, J.P.S. 1984. *The Other Mind of Europe: Goethe as a Scientist*. Delhi: Oxford University Press.

Unger, Roberto M. 1987. *False Necessity: Anti-Necessitarian Social Theory in the Service of Radical Democracy*. Cambridge: Cambridge University Press.

Van der veer, Peter. 1996. *Religious Nationalism: Hindus and Muslims of India*. Delhi: Oxford University Press.

Vattimo, Gianni. 1999. Belief. Cambridge: Polity Press.

Vivekananda, Swami. 1991. *The Collected Works of Swami Vivekananda*. Calcutta: Ramakrishna Mission Publications.

Wilfred, Felix. 1999. "Introduction: The Art of Negotiating the Frontiers". The Special Issue of *Concilium* on "Frontier Violations". April.

Wuthnow, Robert. 1991. "Understanding Religion and Politics." *Daedalus*, 120 (3): 1-20.

3

Sixty Years of Secularism and Pluralistic Democracy: An Overview

M.K. George

The Dream

A billion people of diverse ethnic, linguistic, cultural and religious background living as one nation under the protection of a Democratic Constitution, Striving for inclusive development, through inclusive democracy, based on Justice and Equality and building a cultural mosaic of our nation.

This dream is best symbolized and manifested in the Preamble of our Constitution. It says,

> We, The People of India, having solemnly resolved to constitute India into a Sovereign Socialist Secular Democratic Republic and to secure to all its citizens: Justice, social, economic and political; *Liberty* of thought, expression, belief, faith and worship; *Equality* of status and of opportunity; and to promote among them all *Fraternity* assuring the dignity of the individual and the unity and integrity of the Nation.

The Preamble to our Constitution, as we know, serves two purposes:

(i) It indicates the source from which the Constitution derives its authority;
(ii) It also states the objects, which the Constitution seeks to establish and promote.

The Preamble seeks to establish what Mahatma Gandhi described as The India of my Dreams, "...an India in which the poorest shall feel that it is their country in whose making they have an effective voice; ...an India in which all communities shall leave in perfect harmony. There can be no room in such an India for the curse of untouchability or the curse of Intoxicating drinks and drugs. Woman will enjoy as the same rights as man".

Part of the dream is the appreciation for a pluralistic, multicultural society. Multiculturalism is not just a statement of fact, it is also a value. It cherishes cultural diversity and envisions a society in which different communities forge a common identity while retaining their cultural provenance. When modern democratic societies embrace multiculturalism they demonstrate a deeper and more profound egalitarian impulse within them than the mere presence of plural cultures. Multiculturalism acknowledges the existence of diverse communities, but what is more important is that it accords positive value to the collective identities of all ethnic communities. It pictures a society which is characterized not by multiple cultural solitudes or endemic cultural strife, but by communities living together and participating as equal partners in national political life.

Multiculturalism acquires its value primarily because of the historical experience of the dangers of political majoritarianism which are by now widely accepted. 'They have become an assimilated ingredient in the metabolism of modern democracies. Multiculturalism adds to this awareness by sensitizing us to the dangers of cultural majoritarianism. In particular, it points to the way in which cultural majoritarianism disadvantages minorities, alienates of them, enhances conflicts between communities and limits of self-understanding.'

We value, first and foremost, multiculturalism not just as the acceptance of diversity and multiple solitudes without a common public agenda and multiculturalism is neither a gift of liberal democracy nor an optional policy within a democracy. It is not as if a democracy can choose to be multicultural or not. Every democracy must necessarily be multicultural if the democratic and liberal temper in it is to survive. Far from being an option, multiculturalism actually gives democracy its health and vigour. Multiculturalism is not only about inter-group relations but also informs relations within a community. Respect for other cultures is always premised on first respecting the individual citizen.

The Reality

A Volatile Situation

The India we live in today is far from this dream. If one-third of the country is ruled not by the State, but by rebel groups, if one-third to fifty per-cent or more of the population does not have enough to eat, if communal riots happen at regular intervals, if increasing demands for autonomy and even separate states continue, then we know that the reality is far from wholesome. The situation is in many ways very volatile. Analysis of the changing morphology of a typical riot in Bareilly and Hyderabad showed the subtle way in which fear and communal divisions are deepened through what was called "a new level of control over the riot machinery by the *Hindutva* forces" which meant that they modulate the violence, an ominous sign for the future.

Ambedkar's Warnings and the State of the Republic

Ramachandra Guha (2010) in an insightful analysis points out the three warnings Ambedkar had issued and their status now. The first was his urging his compatriots to abandon the bloody methods of revolution. He had written, "There can be no justification for these unconstitutional methods. These methods are nothing but the grammar of anarchy and the sooner they are abandoned, the better for us". But see the situation in which we live now.

The second warning was about "dynastic democracy". The situation beginning with the Congress Party, right down to the Communist parties, remains sadly far distant from the dream of Ambedkar.

The third and most important warning: "Political democracy cannot last unless there lies at the base of it social democracy. On the social plane, we have in India a society based on the principle of graded inequality, which means elevation for some and degradation for others. ....How long shall we continue to live this life of contradictions? How long shall we continue to deny equality in our social and economic life? If we continue to deny it for long, we will do so only by putting our political democracy in peril. We must remove this contradiction at the earliest possible moment or else those who suffer from inequality will blow up the structure of political democracy which this Assembly has so laboriously built up".

Majority-Minority Syndrome

A syndrome, probably most strongly manifested in the 1940s leading to the partition of India, has continued to hold sway on the Indian polity. Every communal riot deepens its roots. As pointed out by Rajeev Bhargava (2002), the syndrome points to the breakdown of basic trust and common understanding between the majority and the minority. It is dreadful in its impact leading to a diseased network of neurotic relations, so completely poisoned and accompanied by a conglomerate of negative emotions. With the syndrome, animosity circulates freely, eventually leading to paranoia, antagonistic games, and an emotional arms race. Unfortunately, with the unique tradition of Indian history, the syndrome is accompanied by and results in persistent and very real discrimination, humiliation, marginalization, exclusion or subordination of minorities. In cases like Gujarat riot, it has threatened the very survival of a minority community.

The recent instance of Tslima Nasrin's alleged article on *purdah* led to a bout of violence which resulted in the death of two people in Shimoga, Karnataka on March 1, 2010. How could an article, apparently, not even authored by her or in another version on the event, Edited version by the newspaper could provoke such violence. Observers remarked that the protests were a sign that the Muslim leadership in the State had failed to control the more extremist members of the community at a time when a sober response discussing the quality of the article was required.

From the analytical point of view, this is what majority-minority syndrome does. It divides the nation, breeds hierarchy, mindlessly detracts from welfare and development and, by inhibiting reforms, restricts freedom, stultifies communities and emboldens a morally obnoxious conservatism. No wonder then that even a small trigger can ignite large fires.

Communal Forces—Communal Politics

"The Indian State has betrayed the principle of secularism by being partial to the religion of the majority—Hinduism—and over and against the religion of the minorities. (Meera Nanda, 2010). It is the sad part of the history of India that every political party has used communal forces for electoral gain. In the heart of hearts everyone seems to be a fundamentalist, the difference being only whether you are a soft or hard core fundamentalist. Though there are optimists like Asghar Ali Engineer who argue that, "it will be seen that no political party can survive on communal flare for long. Like a heady wine it goes up fast but then declines even faster. Such parties do not have any base or even ideals to claim people's support. Hate politics has serious limitation", the power of communal politics is not to be overlooked. *Hindutva* forces particularly do home work and wait for an opportunity to strike. Other political parties hesitate not to use communal forces as and when it suits them.

Regionalism and Separatist Movements

Petty regionalism is killing Indian republic. Existence and continuation of regional inequalities both among States and within states create the feeling of neglect, deprivation and of discrimination. In a country which is multi-ethnic and multi-religious, with groups concentrated in States or regions, these disparities also become cause of social conflicts leading to political and administrative problems. In any case, regional imbalances are a major cause of regionalism in India in many ways. While some of the movements like Telengana movement has a history and justification of its own, many others do not have a justifiable reason other than vested political interests. Regional and separatist movements are allegedly getting linked to outside interests which in turn further weaken the State. The face of the Indian republic is no way glossed by the regional and separatist.

Widespread Social Exclusion and Marginalization

Globalization and Neo-Liberal Policies

Neoliberalism is clearly resuming its stalled march, adopting a Thatcherite strategy for doing so. But the UPA government miscalculates by ignoring the fact that, unlike in Thatcher's Britain, "the affluent middle class wooing is a minuscule segment of our society, while those squeezed by neoliberalism, the workers, pedants, agricultural labourers, and petty producers, constitute its overwhelming majority" (Editorial, *Frontline*, March 26, 2010).

- Identity Politics
- Ghettoisation

- Militancy, Terrorism, Naxalism
- Rising Religiosity and Fundamentalism

Rising religiosity in India is demolishing four of the most cherished myths of secularization theory.

- *The myth of the prosperous non-believer*: In India, the rich and the upper castes and the more educated continued to pray more than other social group. Equally, the subaltern group is also praying more. But the interesting thing is that a growth of religiosity among the rich, rather than a decline even in the face of economic growth.
- *The myth of privatization of faith*: The argument was as societies become modern, religion will recede from the public sphere to private lives. On the contrary, both the upper castes and *dalits* show an increase in public religious events.
- *The myth of deritualization*: Imagine, instead of deritualizing we have entered an era of e-pujas, remote darshans, and computer generated horoscopes and so on.
- *The myth of rationalism and temper*: Language of science is used to justify religious beliefs. For instance, in the name of 'scientific Hinduism', promotion of universities in Vedic sciences, patronage of *gurus*, pilgrim centres, etc., continue at will.

Most observers are confirming the fact popular religiosity is on the rise in societies undergoing rapid economic changes under the current conditions of globalization.

Apathy, Negligence and Aggression

The Challenge

1. Widespread education for multicultural sensitivity;
2. Search for alternatives: TINA-TIAN;
3. Vouching by the Constitution;
4. Preferential treatment to the excluded, marginalized;
5. Critical use of media;
6. Joining hands with Civil Society groups across borders; and
7. Kindle the light of hope.

Conclusion

The Story of the 100th Monkey Phenomenon (by Ken Keyes, jr.)

The Japanese monkey, Macaca fuscata, had been observed in the wild for a period of over 30 years.

In 1952, on the Island of Koshima, scientists were providing monkeys with sweet potatoes dropped in the sand. The monkeys liked the taste of the raw sweet potatoes, but they found the dirt unpleasant.

An 18 month-old female named Imo found she could solve the problem by washing the potatoes in a nearby stream. She taught this trick to her mother. Her playmates also learned this new way and they taught their mothers too.

This cultural innovation was gradually picked up by various monkeys before the eyes of the scientists.

Between 1952 and 1958 all the young monkeys learned to wash the sandy sweet potatoes to make them more palatable.

Only the adults who imitated their children learned this social improvement. Other adults kept eating the dirty sweet potatoes.

Then something startling took place. In the autumn of 1958, a certain number of Koshima monkeys were washing sweet potatoes—the exact number is not known.

Let us suppose that when the sun rose one morning there were 99 monkeys on Koshima Island who had learned to wash their sweet potatoes.

Let us further suppose that later that morning, the hundredth monkey learned to wash potatoes.

Then it Happened !

By that evening almost everyone in the tribe was washing sweet potatoes before eating them.

The added energy of this hundredth monkey somehow created an ideological breakthrough !

But notice

A most surprising thing observed by these scientists was that the habit of washing sweet potatoes then jumped over the sea....

Colonies of monkeys on other islands and the mainland troop of monkeys at Takasakiyama began washing their sweet potatoes.

Thus, when a certain critical number achieves awareness, this new awareness may be communicated from mind to mind.

Although the exact number may vary, this Hundredth Monkey Phenomenon means that when only a limited number of people know of a new way, it may remain the conscious property of these people.

But there is a point at which if only one more person tunes into a new awareness, a field is strengthened so that this awareness is picked up by almost everyone !

REFERENCES

Bhargava, Rajeev 2002 'India's majority-minority syndrome' http://www.opendemocracy.net/conflict-india_pakistan/article_691.jsp accessed on 19th May, 2010.

Editorial, *EPW* April 10, 2010, Vol. XLV, No. 15.

Guha, Ramachandra. 2010. 'Ambedkar's Desiderata' in *Outlook*, 1st February, 2010, pp. 22-30

Multiculturalism a symposium on democracy in culturally diverse societies 484. December 1999 http://www.india-seminar.com/1999/484/484 accessed on 15th April, 2010.

Nanda, Meera 2010. in *Himal March* 2010, Vol. 23, No. 3.

4

Multiculturalism and Minorities in India

Irfan Engineer

Multiculturalism and minority rights have always been a hotly contested subject in India. Sir Syed Ahmed Khan called Hindu and Muslim communities as the two eyes of a beautiful lady with both eyes being necessary for her beauty. However, he opposed the formation of secular Indian National Congress branding it to be a representative of the majority community and advised Muslims to keep away from it. The British colonialists played an important role in honing the communal identity that emerged during the period through selective concessions and privileges. Competition for political concessions and communal privileges strengthened the communal identities and challenged secular nationalism.

The ethno-communal nationalism defined on the basis of religion—Hindu nationalism and Muslim nationalism—was against the principles of liberty, equality and fraternity. The All India Muslim League initially negotiated the rights of Minority Muslim community demanding separate electorates and weightage to the representation of minorities in legislative bodies. Although it cooperated in the freedom movement intermittently, it slowly veered round to defining communal nationalism arguing that Muslims constitute a nation and, therefore, need a separate state. However, ironically, Muslim League was not the first to argue that Hindus and Muslims constituted different nations. Vinayak Damodar Savarkar in his pamphlet on *Hindutva* published in 1923 "*Hindutva: Who is a Hindu?*" gave a political and nationalist identity to Hindu community.[1] Lala Lajpat Rai wrote a series of articles in the *Tribune* from December 1924 to January 1925.[2] In the 11th article in the series, Lala Lajpat Rai wrote: "My suggestion is that the Punjab should be partitioned into two provinces, the Western

Punjab with a large Muslim majority, to be a Muslim-governed Province; and the Eastern Punjab, with a large Hindu-Sikhs majority, to be a non-Muslim governed Province".

Ultimately partition was accepted by the Congress and the Muslim League as a solution to the problem of minority question. The rights of minorities were debated in the Constituent Assembly of India. Members of Constituent Assembly from the Christian community readily agreed not to press for separate electorates or political representation. Some members from the Muslim community argued in favour of continuing the separate electorates but in the end were persuaded by Sardar Vallabhbhai Patel not to press their demand.

Inspite of the partition, the rights extended to the minorities in the Indian Constitution are in accordance with the International law. However, in practice, religious profiling, discrimination and exclusion of minorities are the order of the day. Amiya Bagchi argues that Indian business communities, partly under the compulsion of authoritarian foreign rule, partly under a traditional dissociation from the mechanics of the exercise of political power, and partly under the influence of such leaders as Mahatma Gandhi and Jawaharlal Nehru, practiced uninvolved multiculturalism, although a few of them became militantly Hindu or Muslim at critical political junctures. So long as Nehru was alive, the state in India adopted a neutral stance in conflicts over religion. The Indian business community acquiesced in this democratic multiculturalism even when privately they might have shared a different view of how the Indian state should behave.[3]

Constitution of India

The Constitution of India does not define the term minority, but indicates who the minorities are. Article 30 of the Constitution states that "All minorities, whether based on religion or language, shall have the right to establish and administer educational institutions of their choice". The Constitution of India, therefore, recognizes only religious and linguistic minorities. A majority of 7 out of 11 Judges of Constitutional Bench of Supreme Court of India in their recent judgement have ruled that Since the states in India have been carved out on the basis of language of majority persons of that region, minorities—both religious and linguistic—should be determined at the State level (and not whole of India).[4] Justice Quadri in his separate judgement but concurring with the majority defined the word minority as "a non-dominant group" or a numerically inferior group.[5] The ethnic minorities are also subsumed as linguistic minorities. The official stand of the Government of India in its report to the Human Rights Committee is that there are no ethnic minorities in India.[6]

The linguistic minorities in India do not suffer the same degree of exclusion, disabilities and discrimination as do the religious minorities. The reason is that after independence, the States (as provinces are called in India) were reorganised on linguistic basis. At present, both English and Hindi both are the official languages of the Union. Of the 22 languages mentioned in the Eighth Schedule of the Constitution, except Sindhi, Santhali and Bodo, all the others are official languages of at least one State, being language of the majority of the people of the State. However, the linguistic majority in one State may be linguistic minority in another State. When Hindi was sought to be imposed as the only official language (i.e., withdrawing English as additional official language), there was massive opposition in South India. The Union of India learnt its lessons and has made no attempts to impose any one language as the only official language, and its policies have been inclusive.

The right wing Hindu nationalists do not base their politics on linguistic fault lines but see Hindu religion and culture as the common bond and uniting factor. The regional parties that exist in some of the States base their politics on development of the State and for State's rights *vis-à-vis* the Central Government rather than basing their politics on exclusion of linguistic minorities.[7] It is the religious minorities that are disadvantaged, marginalised and discriminated and are subjected to exclusionary treatment in India and, therefore, we propose to examine the socio-economic situation of the religious minorities in India.

Hindu[8] religious community constituted about 80.5 per cent at the 2001 Census. Muslims accounted for 13.4 per cent of the population (1,38,188,240), Christians for 2.3 per cent (24,080,016), Sikhs 1.8 per cent (19,215,730), Buddhists 0.8 per cent (7,955,207) and Parsis formed a negligible percentage (69,601). Jains are not yet recognized as a minority community, although they are demanding to be recognised as a religious minority. At the 2001 Census, Jains were 4,225,053, and constituted less than 0.4 per cent. Other minorities were in negligible numbers.[9]

Ideology of the Cultural Nationalists

The right wing majoritarian communal organisations which follow the *Hindutva* ideology, like the Rashtriya Swayamsevak Sangh (RSS), Bharatiya Janata Party (BJP), Vishwa Hindu Parishad (VHP), Bajrang Dal (BD), Akhil Bharatiya Vidyarthi Parishad (ABVP) and others are collectively referred to as the *Sangh Parivar.*[10] The *Sangh Parivar* and its *Hindutva*[11] ideology has always problematised Islam and Christianity as religions from foreign land whose holy land is outside the geographical region extending from River Sindhu to Arabian Sea. The other minority religions, viz., Buddhism, Sikhism, and Jainism were considered as Hindus on the ground that followers of these religions consider India as their fatherland as well as their holy land.

Hindutva ideology seeks to convert India into "*Hindu Rashtra*" (Hindu Nation) rather than a Secular Democratic country.[12] It perceives Islam, Christianity and Communism as the main obstacles in the creation of *Hindu Rashtra*, being religion or ideologies form outside the fatherland. M.S. Golwalkar, the ideologue of *Hindutva* wrote, "The foreign races in *Hindustan* must either adopt the Hindu culture and language, must learn to respect and hold in reverence Hindu religion, must entertain no ideas but those of glorification of the Hindu race and culture or may stay in the country wholly subordinated to the Hindu nation claiming nothing, deserving no privileges, far less any preferential treatment not even citizens rights."[13] *Hindutva* ideology always perceived history as an incessant war between the Hindu nation and the pan-nationalist Muslims, and Christians and viewed the loyalty of Muslims and Christians to the nation with suspicion and in essence advocated second class citizenship for Muslims and Christians. The *Hindutva* ideology has permeated considerably amongst the middle class of the majority community and, in turn, amongst the bureaucrats. Due to the influence of the *Hindutva* ideology, Muslim and Christian minorities are most discriminated, deprived of human rights and suffer violent attacks of Sangh Parivar organisations.

Muslim minority is particularly singled out for exclusionary treatment because of the peculiar history of the country. South Asia witnessed incursions by Muslim Rulers right from 711 A.D. beginning with Muhammad bin Qasim. Muslim Rulers ruled South Asia from 1206 A.D. till the advent of the British. The Sultanate period followed by Mughal period went through various phases. Many wars were fought by the emperors to extend their boundaries, and some of the wars were with the Hindu kings. Memories of these wars provide ample opportunity to the Sangh Parivar to project communal understanding of history, demonising not just the Muslim rulers, but Islam in general. The extremists among the Sangh Parivar seek revenge on the present generation Muslims for acts of Muslim Emperors, accusing them of carrying the "mentality" of Muslim Emperors. Hindu kings are projected as heroes who resisted Islam. The entire History is projected as a continuum of struggle between Hindus and Islam. Muslim Emperors are charged with Islamic mission to destroy all cultural symbols of Hinduism and convert the Hindus forcibly. The Colonial rulers too communalised the history of South Asia and periodized history into Hindu period, Muslim period and finally the British period. The British Colonialists deliberately communalised history with the objective of dividing the two main communities in India—Hindus and Muslims—in order to deepen the communal identities, setting one against the other, and in order to facilitate and perpetuate colonial rule. The British Colonial rulers also encouraged politicians who thrived on communal mobilization by granting communal rights and concessions, including separate communal electorates, triggering off competitive communal mobilization, undermining the nationalist freedom movement.

Competitive communal mobilization deepened and strengthened the communal identities on the one hand and sharpened the prejudices against the "other" community on the other. This led to frequent riots, ultimately leading to creation of Pakistan.[14] Communalisation of history, competitive communal mobilization during colonial period leading to violent riots, partition of the country along communal lines leading to the exchange of population and displacement of millions, death, and sexual assaults has deepened prejudices within a section of the majority community against Muslims. Another factor which strengthens and deepens communal prejudices against Muslims is their significant presence in a number of districts to matter politically. There are 25 districts in the country with one million or more of Muslim population and 51 districts with Muslim population between 500,000 to 999,999; 104 districts with Muslim population between 250,000 to 499,999 and 125 districts with Muslim population between 100,000 to 249,999. According to percentage, there are 20 districts with more than 50 per cent Muslim population and 220 districts with more than 10 per cent but less than 50 per cent Muslim population.[15] While, the

Congress and some regional parties try to mobilize Muslim votes with token and symbolic gestures,[16] the *Sangh Parivar* tries to whip up feelings and popular sentiments against them, and direct their hate propaganda against Muslims, claiming to represent the interests of the majority community in an effort to consolidate their votes. Muslims thus willy-nilly become victims of communal violence, discrimination and exclusion.

In spite of secular Constitution, the minorities, particularly the Muslims and the Christians are discriminated by those manning the administration of the State in day to day governance. Communal forces like the *Sangh Parivar* target the minorities, restrict their religious freedom and human rights and reduce the minorities to second class citizens taking advantage of the political tolerance to discrimination and exclusion of minorities, or at times even complicity of the State.

The Muslims in India have been stigmatized by *Sangh Parivar* and other followers of *Hindutva* ideology as terrorists,[17] *jehadis*, habitual offenders (a community with very high proportion of criminals), violent and aggressive (as Islam is alleged to be a violent religion), religious fanatics, and practitioners of polygamy (and because of polygamy, Muslims multiply like rabbits with a design to out-populate the Hindus and thus Islamize the only Hindu country). Muslims are further stigmatized for the acts of demolition of Hindu temples by Muslim rulers. Muslims are stigmatized as dirty, socially and educationally backward and their backwardness is alleged to be only because Islam teaches them to remain backward and shun education. The stigmatization campaign has permeated deep down and these myths have become quite popular. The discrimination, exclusion and stigmatization of Muslims is particularly heightened in north India. The Christians are stigmatized to be involved in conversion activities and posing a threat to Hindu majority of the country.

Human Rights are universal. Civil, political, economic, social and cultural rights belong to all human beings, including members of minority groups. Members of minorities are entitled to the realization of all human rights and fundamental freedoms on equal terms with others in the society, without discrimination of any kind. Minorities—both the individuals belonging to minorities and the minorities as groups—also enjoy certain human rights specifically linked to their minority status, including their right to maintain and preserve their culture, religion, and language free from discrimination.

We will first examine India's International commitments and then proceed to review the Constitutional measures to protect the rights of the minorities. Finally, we will examine the functioning of the Constitutional measures and special laws and incidents of violations of Human Rights of minorities.

Constitutional Provisions: Prohibition against Discrimination and Equal Opportunities

India is considered as the largest democracy in the world. India is also a signatory to The Universal Declaration of Human Rights.[18] Though the Indian Constitution was framed after the painful partition of the country along religious lines, Indian leadership stuck steadfast to the principles of secularism.[19] The Preamble of the Indian Constitution proclaims India to be a sovereign, socialist, secular, democratic republic. The words secular and socialist were added in the preamble *vide* Fortysecond Amendment of the Constitution in 1976. However, even before the Fortysecond Amendment, the Supreme Court of India had ruled that the basic structure of the Constitution was secular. Article 14 of the Constitution[20] provides that all citizens are equal before law. In fact, even non-citizens are to receive equal protection of law. Article 15[21] prohibits the state from discriminating against any citizen on the grounds only of religion, race, caste, sex, place of birth or any of them or be subject to any disability on anyone of the aforesaid grounds. Article 16[22] guarantees equality of opportunity in the matters relating to employment or appointment to any office under the state. Both the Articles 15 and 16 do provide positive discrimination or affirmative action favouring the Scheduled Castes, Scheduled Tribes, socially and educationally backward classes in the form of reservations of seats in educational institutions, in public employment and in matters of promotions with seniority.

The Mandal Commission was appointed by the Government of India in January 1979, to identify the socially and educationally backward classes and to consider the question of seat reservations and quotas for them. The Commission submitted its report in 1980, and identified various castes which were backward. (also referred to as Other Backward Classes or OBCs). The Commission estimated that 52 per cent of the total population (excluding SCs and STs), belonging to 3,743 different castes and communities were 'backward'.[23]

About eighty Muslim and Christian castes (wherein members of the former backward castes converted en masse to Islam or Christianity but their social, economic and educational condition did not improve much) were also included in the list of Backward Classes. Subsequently, the lists were expanded and names of backward class communities, including those belonging to the minorities identified by Commissions appointed by some of the States. As a result of inclusion in the list of Other Backward Classes, the castes belonging to the minorities also become entitled to 27 per cent reserved seats in educational institutions along with other OBCs.

Andhra Pradesh, a southern State, legislated to provide for 5 per cent reservation for the entire Muslim community. However, the Andhra Pradesh High Court struck down the legislation as unconstitutional and violating Article 15 and 16 of the Constitution. The Andhra Pradesh legislation provided for reservations for all Muslims on the ground that the entire Muslim community was socially and educationally backward and, therefore, was covered under the provision for affirmative action in Articles 15 and 16 of the Constitution. The Andhra Pradesh High Court opined that the affirmative action of reservation was for socially and educationally backward classes and not for a religious community, and, moreover, there was no data on which the Andhra Pradesh Government could have come to the conclusion that the entire Muslim community in Andhra Pradesh was socially and educationally backward. The overall aggregate percentage of reservation, according to Supreme Court could not exceed 50 per cent. However, after providing for 5 per cent reservations to Muslims, the overall aggregate percentage of reservation would exceed the 50 per cent benchmark. The order of 5 per cent reservation for entire Muslim community was struck down on this ground as well.

Thereupon, the Andhra Pradesh Government asked the AP Commission for Backward Classes to examine the social, educational and economic status of the Muslim community. Based on the Commission's findings, the Andhra Pradesh Government decided to create group E called "Socially and Educationally Backward Classes of Muslims" in the list of Backward Classes. 15 specific classes of Muslims were included in the list. Those excluded from the list of backward class Muslims were—Syed, Musahik, Mughal, Pathan, Irani, Arab, Bohra, Shia, Imami, Ismaili, Khoja, Cutchi-Memon, Jamayat and Navayat.[24] The quota of reservation was brought down to 4 per cent to meet the criteria that not more than 50 per cent of total seats could be reserved. The Supreme Court initially stayed the law passed by the Andhra Pradesh Government granting 4 per cent reservations for some sections of the Muslims. However, later, in March 2010, the Supreme Court restored the quota for Muslims. The United Muslim Action Committee had opposed reservation for Muslims[25] on the basis of categorization of only some of them as backward using the criteria of castes. They maintained that there was no caste system in Islam and, therefore, the reservations should be for the entire Muslim Community in Andhra Pradesh or not at all.

The Tamil Nadu Government promulgated an ordinance to introduce reservations for Christians and Muslims of backward caste denominations to the extent of 3.5 per cent each from September 14, 2010. In the year 2009, the State's Backward Classes Commission, headed by a retired Judge, Justice M.S. Janarthanan had examined the issue and recommended the possibility of extending separate quotas to religious minorities on the basis of caste denominations. The Muslim communities covered under this 3.5 per cent sub-quota are Lebbais, Marakkayars, Moplahs, Sheikhs and Sayyids (those who trace their lineage to Prophet Mohammad).[26]

Presidential Order on Declaration of Scheduled Castes: Discrimination against Christian and Muslim Minorities

Article 341 of the Constitution[27] provides for including certain castes, races or tribes as Scheduled Castes. The Scheduled Castes (SCs) are those castes which were treated as untouchables by the upper castes as they did manual scavenging work considered impure and polluting. Socially, educationally and economically, they were completely excluded and in fact considered less than human beings. Dr. Bhimrao Ambedkar, the Chairman of Drafting Committee of the Constitution was also from *Mahar* caste listed as SC in the Constitution. As an affirmative action, certain Parliamentary and State Legislature constituencies are reserved for SCs and only SC candidates can contest from those constituencies.[28] The SCs have reserved quotas in Government employment, public sector, and educational institutions. They are also entitled to relaxation in qualifying marks for reservations in matters of promotion to any class or classes of services or posts in connection with the affairs of the Union or of a State.[29]

The Constitution provides for National Commission for the Scheduled Castes to investigate and monitor all matters relating to the implementation of the safeguards provided for the Scheduled Castes and to inquire into specific complaints with respect to the deprivation of rights and safeguards of the SCs and perform other similar duties in the interests of the SC and ST.[30] Being covered under the Scheduled Castes and Scheduled Tribes (Prevention of Atrocities) Act, the SC have much better Constitutional safeguards as compared to the OBCs who only enjoy 27 per cent of reservations of seats in educational institutions and in government employment, far less than their proportion in the population, which is 52 per cent.[31]

But, Minorities are discriminated under Article 341. The Presidential Order of 1950 notifying Scheduled Castes mentions that those of only Hindu caste could be notified as SCs. Thus the *Arzals*[32] (SCs who have converted to Islam) and SCs who converted to Christianity are deprived of the Constitutional and statutory safeguards and protections mentioned above, though their socio-economic and educational conditions continue to be the same, the stigma and attitudes associated with untouchability remain unchanged, and they continue to suffer same deprivation, social exclusion and sanctions within the community as well as by the other communities. It was initially argued that only Hindu religion had caste system, and Christianity as well as Islam did not believe in caste system and, therefore, there could not be SCs amongst them.

But the Presidential Order was amended in 1956 to include SCs who have converted to Sikh religion and in 1990 even the SCs who had converted to Buddhism were included. Even Buddhism and Sikhism do not believe in caste system and stand for social equality. There is, therefore, no justifiable ground now to exclude SCs practicing and professing Islam and Christianity. This often leads to a situation where a Christian or Muslim members of SC have to hide their religion from the public if they want to avail of Constitutional and statutory safeguards available to SC. Members of SC who publicly profess and practice, or convert to Christianity or Islam, lose their SC status. This is clearly a discrimination of minorities belonging to Christianity or Islam.

In Chapter 10 of its Report submitted to the Prime Minister on 22 May, 2007, the National Commission on Religious and Linguistic Minorities headed by Mr. Justice Ranganath Mishra former Chief Justice of India and Dr. Tahir Mahmood said:[33]

> "To be more specific, we recommend that all those social and vocational groups among the minorities who but for their

> religious identity would have been covered by the present net of Scheduled Castes should be unquestionably treated as socially backward, irrespective of whether the religion of those other communities recognizes the caste system or not.
>
> "We also recommend that those groups among the minorities whose counterparts in the majority community are at present covered by the net of Scheduled Tribes should also be included in that net; and also, more specifically, members of the minority communities living in any Tribal Area from pre-independence days should be so included irrespective of their ethnic characteristics."

At para 16.3.5 of the Report, the Commission *recommended that Para 3 of the Constitution (Scheduled Castes) Order should be wholly deleted by appropriate action so as to completely de-link Scheduled Caste status from religion and make the Scheduled Castes net fully religion-neutral like that of the Scheduled Tribes.*

The Commission also recommended (Para 16.3.6) that all those groups and classes among the Muslims and Christians, etc., whose counterparts among the Hindus, Sikhs or Buddhists, are included in the Central or State Scheduled Castes lists should also be covered by the Scheduled Caste net. If any such group or class among the Muslims and Christians, etc., is now included in an OBC list, it should be deleted from there while transferring it to the Scheduled Castes.

In view of the provisions of the Constitution on freedom of religion, the Commission recommended (Para. 16.3.7) that once a person has been included in a Scheduled Caste list, a wilful change of religion on his part should not affect adversely his or her Scheduled Caste status.[34]

Obstacles in Converting to Christianity or Islam

Article 25[35] of the Constitution guarantees freedom of conscience and free profession, practice and propagation of religion. The only reasonable restriction on the freedom of conscience is that the said right is subject to public order, morality and health. The state can nevertheless regulate or restrict any economic, financial, political or other secular activity which may be associated with religious practice. Not only all Indian citizens, but citizens of other countries are also entitled to practice, profess and propagate their religion.

In spite of the above, the *Sangh Parivar* often violently and vociferously objects to Christian missionaries from other countries coming to India and propagating their religion. When American Evangelist Benny Hinn wanted to hold prayer meeting in Bangalore, the *Sangh Parivar* opposed it. However, the Karnataka State Government gave permission for the meeting on the condition that no law and order problem would be created. When, the *Sangh Parivar* contested the impugned permission in Karnataka High Court, the High Court ruled that even non-Indians could propagate their religion under Article 25. The meaning and import of the freedom of Religion under Article 25 was further expounded by the Supreme Court of India in *Bijoe Emmanuel* vs. *State of Kerala*.[36] When students belonging to Jehovah's Witness sect refused to sing National Anthem on the ground that it went against their religious beliefs, the school expelled them and handed them school leaving certificates. The Supreme Court held that "*the real test of democracy is the ability of even an insignificant minority to find its identity under the Constitution*".

As the freedom of Religion in Article 25 is subject to three reasonable restrictions on the ground of public order, morality and health, a number of States have passed legislations making religious conversions extremely difficult if not impossible. The anti-conversion legislations have been justified on the basis of maintenance of public order. Ironically, these laws passed by various provinces are called Freedom of Religion Act. The first anti-conversion law in independent India was passed in the year 1967 and 1968 in Orissa and Madhya Pradesh respectively. In fact, for the first time in some States, including in Orissa and Madhya Pradesh, non-Congress Governments were formed. The Hindu Nationalists and right wing elements were also sharing powers with other non-Congress Parties in a coalition. The Freedom of Religion Acts in Orissa and in Madhya Pradesh required that any conversion from one religion to another take place after due notice to the District Magistrate who in turn was to file a report of such conversions. Any person desiring to convert to any other religion was required to file an affidavit before the Judicial Magistrate First Class that he was converting voluntarily. Conversion using coercion, force, fraudulent means or by any inducement was made a cognizable offence. The terms coercion or force, or fraudulent means or inducements were not well defined and left the scope open to bring most conversions, if not all, under the scope of the Act. The Act made conversions very difficult if not impossible. These legislations were subject matter of challenge before the Supreme Court in *Rev. Stainislaus* vs. *State of Madhya Pradesh.*[37] The Supreme Court in the impugned judgment held that the Madhya Pradesh and the Orissa Act were meant to avoid disturbances to public order by prohibiting conversions in a manner reprehensible to the conscience of the community. . . . Freedom of religion does not include freedom to convert any person to one's own religion. . . .conversion would impinge freedom of choice granted to all citizens alike. Dissenting from the majority judgment, Justice P. Jaganmohan Reddy opined that it was equally the right of the person sought to be converted to follow the new religion of his choice.[38] Thereafter, the Arunachal Pradesh Freedom of Religion Act 1978 was enacted to provide for prohibition of conversion from one religious faith to any other by use of force or inducement or by fraudulent means. On October 5, 2002 the Tamil Nadu Governor promulgated an Anti-Conversion Ordinance, which was subsequently adopted by the State Assembly. The Act was, however, withdrawn after the then ruling party AIADMK realized that its failure to secure a single seat in the 14th Lok Sabha elections was due to the anti-conversion law.

Himachal Pradesh, Gujarat, Rajasthan[39] and Chhattisgarh are the latest provinces to come up with anti-conversion laws. The later versions of the law have made conversion even more difficult, by placing a number of hurdles. The Gujarat law was amended to permit conversions from one sect of a religion to another sect of the same religion, but not to another religion. There was an exception to that rule, viz., that the Hindus, Jains, Sikhs and Buddhists, though they are different religions, could convert each other's followers to their religion without any restriction. There was an indirect implication that Jains, Sikhs and Buddhists are sects of Hindu religion. Therefore, the only conversions that came under bureaucratic regulation and for all practical purposes undeclared ban, was conversion from Hinduism (including Jainism, Sikhism and Buddhism) to the two religions—Christianity and Islam, which according to the Sangh Parivar, are foreign religions. The Governor of Gujarat refused to give his assent to the amended law and referred it to the President of India. As a result, the unamended law continues to be in force. The District Magistrates have absolute discretion to grant or refuse to grant permission for conversion as these acts do not lay down any guidelines for them to consider giving or refusing to give permission for conversion.

Legislations that give arbitrary powers and discretion to any authority have been held to be violation of Articles 14, 15 and 16 of equality and are, therefore, anti-constitutional. The definition of conversion is also sought to be made arbitrary and discriminatory to the minorities to exclude "re-conversion" to the religion of one's forefathers. Thus, conversion to Hinduism from Christianity or Islam would not be considered as conversion being religion of one's forefathers but conversion to Christianity or Islam from Hinduism alone would be considered conversion.[40] In spite of the religious freedom granted under the Constitution, if a person has to seek bureaucratic permissions and depend on their whims and fancies, Article 25 would practically be reduced to a dead letter. Keeping in view the fact that coercive and forcible conversions or conversions by fraud and inducements are covered by the provisions of the Indian Penal Code, such unnecessary restrictions make a mockery of the Constitution.

The Sangh Parivar has always stigmatized that the Christian Missionaries are converting lower caste and Scheduled Tribe members in large numbers. They often attack the missionaries falsely accusing them of indulging in conversions.[41] We shall consider the attacks on Christian minorities a little later. The oppressed lower castes have often taken recourse to conversion to renounce the religion which treats them as untouchables, excludes them and discriminates them. Their conversion is on the one hand, a protest against their oppression and a hope on the other hand, that they would be treated as equals in the new community they seek to enter through their conversion. The anti-conversion laws seek to make it more difficult for the oppressed lower castes to register their protest and facilitate their upward mobility.[42] The anti-conversion laws would easily be, and are being, misused by the Sangh Parivar and other anti-minority forces to harass church and even secular leaders of minorities who serve the lower castes and oppressed sections through their institutions and struggle for human rights and human dignity of all. The BJP uses anti-conversion law as a tool to institutionalize the ideology of Hindu nationalism, i.e. *Hindutva*, which envisions a "Hindu nation" where the religious minorities are allowed to live but in subordination to the majority community.[43]

Special Religious Zone in Tirumala

By an ordinance, the Andhra Pradesh Government declared the seven hills surrounding the temple town of Tirumala, the abode of Lord

Venkateswara and the roads and footpaths leading to the temple as "*Tirumala Divya Kshetram*" and banned all religious activities other than what was traditionally practiced. The Government notified the places of worship covered by the ordinance to include 10 *theerthams* within the Tirumala Tirupati Devasthanams (TTD) limits and 20 temples elsewhere in the State. The ordinance also banned all political activities, including election of local body for self-governance. The total area of Tirumala Region is 332 sq. km. consisting of seven hills. Tirupati Balaji Temple is on the seventh Hill. However, the *Tirumala Divya Kshetram* extends to all the seven hills and the roads and footpaths.

The Andhra Pradesh Ordinance outlaws not only all conversions, including those which are not by force, inducement or by adapting fraudulent means, it also bans all religious activities that were not traditionally practiced. Even prayers and other religious ceremonies come within the purview of the Ordinance if they were not being traditionally practiced. The Chief Minister justified the ordinance on the grounds that religious activities of 'other' religions were posing a threat to public order. Except for empty threats by a lunatic fringe, no imminent threat was perceived by anybody, including the Chairman of the TTD, who said no significant non-Hindu activities had come to light. Instead of placing reasonable restrictions on the rights guaranteed by Article 25, the Ordinance deprives the citizens of the right altogether. In *A.K. Gopalan* vs. *State of Madras*[44] case, the Supreme Court had held reasonable restriction did not mean deprivation and that the interference must be reasonable. The reason for restricting the rights guaranteed must also be clear and present threat to public order and not an imagined and remote threat. The Andhra Pradesh Government's logic seems to be that if a lunatic fringe threatens the public order, then the State must restrict the rights of those stigmatized by the lunatic fringe instead of meeting the threat to public order by putting reasonable restrictions on the lunatic fringe. This would only encourage the lunatic fringe further.

Discrimination against Non-Hindu Religions under Family Laws

In India, the family laws are largely based on religion and are community specific. Hindu, Muslim, Christian, Parsis, all have their community specific, religion, tradition and custom based family laws. Part of the family laws is codified. There are gender-based discriminations in each community's family laws. However, the family law applicable to the majority Hindu community discriminate against minorities, particularly if a family member wants to convert to a non-Hindu religion. A Hindu, who wants to convert to a non-Hindu religion, is put to a severe disadvantage with respect to his/her right to family property, maintenance, child custody, etc.

Under the Hindu Marriage Act 1955, post-marriage conversion by either spouse gives to the other spouse ground for divorce, even without mandatory judicial separation. Children born to a Hindu after she/he has converted to another religion (and their descendants) are disqualified from inheriting their property, unless any descendant re-adopts Hinduism before opening of succession. If a father or mother has renounced Hinduism, he or she is deprived of the right to act as the natural guardian for his/her child. Husband who has renounced Hinduism cannot be guardian of his minor wife, even if she so desires.[45] Wife's consent for adoption of a child is necessary only if the wife remains Hindu. A Hindu wife cannot directly adopt a child if her husband is also a Hindu. She can only be a consenting party. However, a married Hindu woman can directly adopt a child without the consent of her non-Hindu husband. Natural father of a Hindu child can give it in adoption without the consent of his non-Hindu wife; while Hindu wife's consent is necessary. If the father has changed his religion, a Hindu wife can give the child in adoption without his consent. Only a Hindu child can be adopted. Right of adopting a son is denied to a person having a Hindu son, grand-son or great grand-son but the existence of a non-Hindu son, grand-son or a great grand-son is not a bar. Non-Hindu wife cannot claim maintenance from a Hindu husband but a Hindu wife has a right to live separate from non-Hindu Husband on the ground of his conversion without losing her right to maintenance. A widowed daughter-in-law must be maintained by her father-in-law, but not if she is a non-Hindu. Every person legally entitled to maintenance from any Hindu relative loses that right on conversion to a non-Hindu religion. As Sikhism, Jainism and Buddhism are by definition considered Hindu religions, conversion to these religions does not disentitle one from any rights but conversion to any other religion will disadvantage him/her in regard to the aforesaid rights.[46] On marriage under Special Marriage Act, a Parsi, Muslim, Christian or Jew will lose coverage of their personal laws for succession and will be covered under the Indian Succession Act of 1925, but a Hindu, Buddhist, Jain or Sikh will retain their personal laws for succession except when it is inter-religious marriage.

Constitutional Rights of Religious Denominations or Sub-groups or Sections thereof

In addition to freedom of religion granted to all individuals, Article 26 of the Indian Constitution grants collective rights to a religious denomination or any sub-group or section thereof to establish and maintain institutions for religious and charitable purposes; to manage their own affairs in matters of religion, to own and acquire movable and immovable property and to administer such properties.[47] The importance of Article 26 is tremendous for the minorities as the State cannot curtail rights of religious denominations or sections thereof belonging to minorities from acquiring properties and maintaining their religious institutions.

Prohibition on Religious Tax and Expenditure on a Particular Religious Denomination

Article 27[48] of the Constitution is about separation of religion and the State. The State is prohibited from compelling any person from paying taxes, proceeds from which are spent on any particular religion or religious denomination. However, Indian Government extends a subsidy of Rs. 12,000 for each Muslim undertaking Hajj pilgrimage, which covers about 50 per cent of the air fare. Every year there are about 127,000 pilgrims from all over India. The Sangh Parivar has used the Hajj subsidy to castigate secularism, which according to them has only meant appeasing Muslims. The Muslim political leaders would not seriously object if the subsidy is withdrawn as performing Hajj is not obligatory if it is not within the pilgrim's means. Muslim leadership further argues that if there was no compulsion to take AIR India flights, the rush for Hajj is so much that Muslims would even otherwise be able to bargain with various Airlines and bring down the fare to the level of subsidized fare.[49] This is a clear anomaly to the secular Constitution of India. However, the United Progressive Alliance II Government has announced in April 2010 that Hajj subsidies will be phased out gradually without evoking any protest from the community. It is important to note that not only Hajj pilgrimage is subsidized, the Government of India also subsidizes pilgrimage of Hindus to *Kailash Mansarovar* in China and of Sikhs to *Nanakana Saheb* in Pakistan.

Prohibition on Religious Education in State Funded Educational Institutions

Article 28 of the Constitution prohibits religious instructions in institutions wholly maintained out of State funds.[50] Education is important for any political ideology and for control over minds. However, most of the textbooks prescribed by the State have anti-minority bias. Most History textbooks do not mention the name of the assassin of Mahatma Gandhi, who was member of Hindu Mahasabha as well as RSS. Muslims are portrayed as invaders who demolished temples and enslaved Hindus. Aryans (with whom the upper the caste Hindus identify) and who migrated a couple of thousand years ago are shown as peaceful and indigenous people. "The Standard. X textbook in Social Science which had the first edition in 2006. . . .has a whole chapter XXI. . . .entitled 'Social Problems and Challenges.' Most of this chapter is devoted to communalism, casteism and terrorism. Several statements in this chapter and elsewhere in the textbook cast very serious aspersions on the minority community."[51]

Referring to the Muslim community, the Std. X Social Science textbook states, "when a community works intentionally to safeguard its narrow interests, it creates social tension".[52] In the section on terrorism, the textbook categorically states "Making full use of Muslim fanaticism, Osama Bin Laden organized die-hard Muslims and founded the International Jihad Organization in the name of the *Jehadi* movement".[53] The textbook lists all the terrorist actions in the world where Muslim terrorists have been alleged to be responsible and the North East terrorist actions from amongst the tribal people, but makes no mention of the pogrom in Gujarat in 2002 where more than 2000 people were killed. The Std. IX Social Science textbook (2006) states that the Governor Albuquerque of Goa, allowed the Portuguese to plunder the natives and to convert and to enslave people, insinuating bias against and responsibility of the Christian community. The Std. X textbook on Social Science justifies and even glorifies the caste system. The "Indian" festivals and culture described lays a disproportionate emphasis on festivals and culture of a small elite section of upper caste Hindus with festivals and cultural heritage of minorities and lower caste Hindus getting mentioned only occasionally and in passing.[54]

In a National Consultation organized by the *Centre for Study of Society and Secularism*, on "Minorities and Biases In Textbooks" in New Delhi on 13th and 14th January, 2007, attended by experts on education and pedagogy from all over India, the following resolution was passed :

> "We have, however, witnessed distressing action by the Central and State governments over the years of violating the fundamental aspects of nation building, through the preparation of teaching—learning materials, both formal and supplementary made for our schools and children. The attempt to impose a particular religion as NATIONAL and to indoctrinate the young minds which results in promotion of hatred to other religions, cultures and communities must be deplored. Apart from textbooks and supplementary materials, systematic recruitment of teachers espousing such views has considerably enhanced this condemnable destruction of Indian composite culture. . . .
>
> "The Madhyamik Siksha Board, Rajasthan, Ajmer has published School Textbooks from class 8 to class 12 in the years 2005-06 which contain highly objectionable content which are blatantly in conflict with the Constitution of India, especially the provisions of Articles 15, 28, 21, 51A. These textbooks have been written with an underlying assumption of Indian culture being synonymous with Hindu and Aryan culture. Manu has been described as the father of humankind and *Brahma* as the creator of this Universe. An obsession with religion, an enthusiastic advocacy of the superiority of Hindu religion over other religions and defining Indianness in Savarkarite terms declaring those who do not consider their fatherland as their holy land as people with no entitlement as citizens are only some of the objectionable features of these books which range from History, Sanskrit to Science, Economics and Social Sciences. Fascism has been described as significant as it removes the ills of democracy. . . . All secular and rational Indians, in particular *adivasis*, dalits, minority groups cannot allow their tax and other money to be used to propagate and impose a violent world view on their children through school textbooks."

When BJP-led National Democratic Alliance was in power in the year 1998-2004, the then Education Minister, Mr. Murli Manohar Joshi introduced astrology and Vedic Mathematics in the University syllabus. The syllabus and the content of the education alienate the minorities.

The textbooks used in Saraswati Shishu Mandirs, a chain of schools run by the Sangh Parivar are even more anti-Minority. It is stated in their textbooks that Hindus made several hundred attempts to liberate *Ramjanamabhoomi* temple. They use communal symbols to teach mathematics for example, in one of the mathematical exercise, the problem posed is that if 100 *karsevaks* (Hindu volunteers who demolished the Babri Masjid in Ayodhya) can demolish Babri Masjid in 2 days, how many *Karsevaks* would be necessary to demolish the Masjid in 1 day?

Cultural and Educational Rights of Minorities in the Constitution

Articles 29 and 30 of the Constitution pertain to educational and cultural rights of the minorities.[55] Article 29 provides that religion, race, caste or language cannot be the only ground for denying admission into educational institutions maintained by the State or out of State funds. Minorities, whether based on religion or language have a right to establish and administer educational institutions of their choice. The Article further provides that the State shall not discriminate against the educational institution in giving grants-in-aid on the ground that they are run by the minorities. By virtue of Article 30, minorities enjoy a certain degree of autonomy in establishment and administration of educational institution run by them, particularly in matters of admission of students, recruitment of staff and in appointment cf Head of the educational institution. A majority of 7 out of 11 Judges of Constitutional Bench of Supreme Court of India in their recent judgement have ruled that since the States in India have been carved out on the basis of language of majority persons of that region, minorities—both religious and linguistic—should be determined at the State level (and not whole of India).[56] Justice Quadri in his separate judgement but concurring with the majority defined the word minority as "a non-dominant group" or a numerically inferior group.[57] Justices Ruma Pal, Variava and Bhan in their dissenting judgement on the other hand argued that "if the protection (of Article 30) is limited to State action, it will leave the group which is otherwise a majority for the purpose of State legislation, vulnerable to Union legislation which operates on a national basis. When the entire nation is affected, surely the question of minority status must be determined with reference to the country as a whole."[58] After the judgement of the Constitutional Bench of the Supreme Court, there are no minorities at national level.

National Commission for Minorities

Based on Section 9(1) of the National Commission for Minorities Act 1992, the Commission's priorities would fall under the following broad categories; (a) evaluation of progress of development of minorities, (b) monitoring the Constitutional safeguards in place *vis-à-vis* the minorities, (c) redressal of grievances of minorities and (d) getting research and evaluation studies conducted and appointing consultants to advise on specific minority related issues.[59]

Unlike the National Human Rights Commission, which has powers to award compensation to the victims whose human rights have been violated by the State, the NCM's recommendations are not binding on the government, even though it is a statutory body. Consequently, the NCM's role after the anti-Muslim pogrom in the year 2002 in Gujarat was not visible and far less effective, while the NHRC could play proactive role, approach the Supreme Court of India and get some reliefs for the victims, and could reopen and retrial of the cases like the Best Bakery case and Bilkis Bano's complaint and getting important cases related to Gujarat pogrom outside the State for justice. The Gujarat Government's complicity in the pogrom has been pointed out by several Fact Finding missions, and naturally it has completely disregarded the recommendations of the NCM.

The NCM also monitors the Prime Minister's New 15-Point Programme for the Welfare of Minorities.[60] However, the NCM's recommendations are more of an advisory nature and are not binding on the government.

Hate Crimes Against Muslims in India

Muslims and Christians have been victims of hate crimes. Muslims constitute the second largest religious group in India and in terms of population next only to Indonesia. It was estimated that by the year 2006, Muslim population in India would be over 150 million.[61] Muslims reside across the country and yet their concentration varies substantially across regions and from State to State.[62] Muslims are more urbanised as compared to others. In Tamil Nadu, Maharashtra, Karnataka, Andhra Pradesh, Madhya Pradesh, Gujarat and Chhattisgarh, majority of Muslims live in urban areas.[63] Christians on the other hand constitute 2.3 per cent of the total Indian population and constitute a majority only in Nagaland, Mizoram and Meghalaya.[64]

The Sangh Parivar and other organisations following *Hindutva* ideology are inevitably behind hate crimes against Muslims and Christians, though the offenders enjoy near immunity in spite of indictment by several official commissions appointed by the government to inquire into the causes of communal violence in various parts of India. Justice B.N. Srikrishna Commission appointed to inquire into communal riots in Mumbai in 1992-93, indicted Mr. Balasaheb Thackeray, the Chief of Shiv Sena, a political party which follows the ideology of *Hindutva* in the State of Maharashtra. He is found to have led his army of rioters like a military general. The Central and State governments have appointed 31 Commissions of Inquiry to report about various communal riots, from Jabalpur in 1961 to Aurangabad in 1999.[65]

Although during the years 1950 to 2002, 11,850 persons have been killed in 370 incidents of communal rioting (80% of those killed were Muslims and the rest were Sikhs, Hindus, Christians and others),[66] none of the major recommendations of the Commissions of Inquiry have been implemented and the guilty have gone scot free. In all the communal riot related cases, the police either do not record the complaints of the victims or when compelled to register a few FIRs, they deliberately do not record the FIRs accurately (to help the accused) and often do not record the name of the accused even though the victims name the accused. Thereafter, the cases are closed as true but undetectable.

A number of studies by human rights organizations have highlighted the partisan role of the police during riots. The police are also known to use excessive force on the members of the minority community during communal riots. Over the years, the frequency of riots has increased and the number of deaths in each riot also has increased considerably. Of late, sexual assaults on women are increasingly used. The near impunity of the rioters has led to a situation where, what Paul Brass describes as a 'institutionalized riot system' has come into existence. In the words of Paul Brass, "where riots are endemic, what I call 'institutionalized riot systems' exist in which known persons and groups occupy specific roles in the rehearsal for and production of communal riots. In such systems a central role is played by what I call 'conversion specialists', those whose task is to decide when a trivial, everyday incident will be exaggerated and placed into the communal system of talk the communal discourse, and allowed to escalate into communal violence."[67]

For paucity of space we shall very briefly examine the 2002 anti-Muslim pogroms in Gujarat. The BJP-led Gujarat Government allowed dead bodies of 59 Hindu Nationalists, burnt when miscreants burnt S-6 compartment on Sabarmati Express train near Godhra Railway Station on 27th February, 2002 to be carried in a procession several kilometres along with emotional speeches on the way. The Sangh Parivar alleged the incident to be a conspiracy by Muslims. The Chief Minister, Narendra Modi justified the pogrom that followed calling it a natural reaction of Hindus to the burning of S-6 compartment of Sabarmati Express (calling it Newton's Law). The Report of Indian People's Human Rights Tribunal headed by Retired Supreme Court Judge, Justice Krishna Iyer, quotes a Minister of Modi Government's cabinet and concludes that the police and administration at highest level were called to CM's residence and instructed to allow the 'natural reaction' of the 'people of Gujarat'. Two Ministers took personal charge of the police control room. In the anti-Muslim pogrom that continued for over a month, most districts in Gujarat except some districts in Kutch and Saurashtra were affected. The pogroms were led by Sangh Parivar mobs armed to the teeth and the complicity of the Government has been established by several fact finding bodies and Human Rights organisations, both national and international and even the National Human Rights Commission. Officially 1,071 people were killed but unofficial conservative estimates put the figure at about 2,500. Those killed included Ehsan Jaffri, a former Member of the Parliament. Two High Court Judges Justices Kadri and Divecha belonging to Muslim community felt unsafe in their official quarters and had to shift with their family to safer Muslim ghettoes.

Deployment of the Army was delayed until the hoodlums on the street had decimated Muslims in their area. Tens of women were sexually assaulted and even a few months old babies were not spared. Hundreds of thousands were displaced from their homes and are not able to return even today after nearly six years, some are living in refugee camps and others had to be resettled in ghettoes far away from their livelihoods and on the outskirts of the concerned cities.

Although some districts withstood the dangers far more firmly than did others thanks to local factors and players, "the widespread reports and allegations of groups of well-organized persons, armed with mobile telephones and addresses, singling out certain homes and properties for death and destruction in certain districts—sometimes within view of police stations and personnel—the further question arises as to what the factors were, and who the players were in the situations that went out of control.[68]

Taking cognizance of the allegations that FIRs have been poorly or wrongly recorded and that investigations are being 'influenced' by extraneous considerations or players, the National Human Rights Commission stressed on the need to restore the integrity of the process and recommended the entrusting of certain critical cases to the CBI. . . .The Commission also asked the State Government to identify the players who were influencing situations that had gone out of control. It had come to the Commission's knowledge that well-organized persons, armed with mobile telephones and addresses, were singling out certain homes and properties for death and destruction. The Commission also noted that public servants who had sought to perform their duties diligently had been transferred at short notice. These findings led the Commission to observe that there was a widespread lack of faith in the integrity of the investigating process and the ability of those conducting investigations.

After every communal riot wherein the minorities are targeted, minorities are forced to migrate to 'safer' ghettoes. Muslim ghettoes are then prone to attack in the next round of communal violence and are also useful to spread prejudices and fear about Muslims in absence of daily interaction which reduces to a great extent due to gheottoisation. Attack on Muslims is followed by stigmatization campaigns through the media, holding them responsible for the violence and their way of life which allegedly poses threat to the "Hindu nation". With reduced interactions and exaggerated sense of insecurity during violence, the stigmatization campaigns are deeply internalized. Muslims are then sought to be punished by open calls for complete social and economic boycott by circulating leaflets and pamphlets.

Hate Crimes Against Christians

The hate campaign against Christians has heightened since 1997.[69] Piggy-riding on the issue of Ramjanamabhoomi-Babri Masjid hate campaign against the Muslims in particular and minorities in general throughout the 1980s, the BJP formed its government in several States in North India and was confident of capturing power at the Centre at the XII Lok Sabha Election in 1998. The BJP, a dominant constituent of National Democratic Alliance finally, formed their government in the year 1998. In order to expand its social base amongst the Scheduled Tribes and Scheduled Castes, the organisations belonging to the *Sangh Parivar* took advantage of their government and led a wide and virulent campaign against the missionaries, and church leaders working for empowering the STs and SCs in particular and against the Christians in general, alleging them to be indulging in reckless conversions through force, coercion, fraud and inducements. They further widely campaigned that soon the Hindus would be in minority due to conversion activities which was increasing the Christian population exponentially. Together with the high pitch hate campaign against Christians, the *Sangh Parivar* led violent attacks on the church leaders and Christian converts from SCs and STs.

In one of the recent attacks on Christians in Phulbani and Kandhamal Districts of Orissa State, at least six people died, 400 Christian homes and 60 churches were burnt down. While the young and healthy Christians could flee for their lives, children, women, old and sick were attacked. Those left behind had to starve for days, and sick suffered without medical attention. Some were forced to convert to Hinduism to get food, medical attention and shelter. With the State Security Forces being under the influence of *Sangh Parivar*, no complaints from the victims and Christian communities were filed by the police.[70] According to an eye-witness report,

> "it was as if the miscreants were determined to inflict the deepest possible wounds on the religious psyche of the people. . . .the rioters went about their task with meticulous care, desecrating the church, vandalizing the cross and breaking statues and other religious items. They systematically destroyed the records pertaining to Baptism, births and deaths, marriages, etc., maintained in the church and then burnt the edifice down after making away with all

> items of value. The desire to trample on the rights of other citizens and to cause as much pain as possible to their religious sentiments is only too apparent. The same picture emerges when one sees the burnt out shells of churches and other religious structures in different parts of the district".[71]

To add insult to the injury, the State Government denied compensation for the destruction of religious places on the plea that such compensation has not been given in other riots. Though the National Commission for Minorities was unable to obtain official estimate of damages suffered by religious places, non-official estimates assessed the damage suffered by the churches, presbyteries and seminaries at about Rs. 2 crore.

According to a report tabled in the Parliament, there were 116 incidents of attacks on Christians across the country between January 1998 and February 1999. Most of the attacks have taken place in the north and the west where the Christian populations are smaller and Hindu nationalist sentiments are stronger. The increase in violence has paralleled the rise of the Hindu right in India's political arena and the undermining of communal harmony by Hindu extremists, a trend that had been noted by the United Nations special Rapporteur on religious intolerance in a 1997 report.

John Dayal, founder of *United Christian Forum for Human Rights* points out that the real number is much higher in as much as many cases of attacks on Christians go unreported for fear of reprisals.[72] When the BJP Prime Minister, Atal Behari Vajpayee visited Dangs after attack on Christians in 1998, instead of condemning the attack, he called for a "national debate" on conversions, supplying justification for the attack. Needless to say that the offenders did not have any reason to remotely suspect that they will be held accountable to law as the police and the government were known to be complicit. Even if the police were forced to arrest some offenders, some insignificant foot soldier who was mobilized for the attack would be arrested while the inciters, the abettors and the conspirators who caused the attack would roam around freely to incite and plan other attacks.

Discrimination of Muslims

Social, Economic and Educational Status of the Muslim Community of India—A Report by Prime Minister's High Level Committee chaired by Justice Rajender Sachar,[73] also known as Sachar Committee Report, has brought out what was obvious to all those who cared to know that the Muslim Community was backward in all respects. The Sachar Committee has compiled voluminous data which points out that the Muslims are under-represented in all the fields in all States. The literacy rate among Muslims was 59.1 per cent which is far below the national average of 65.1 per cent. Only 6 per cent of the graduates are Muslims. Only one out of twenty Post Graduate Students are Muslims, whereas the figures are better for SCs/STs, in as much as one out 13 Post-Graduates are from SCs/STs. Muslims are found more as self-employed workers. 61 per cent of the total Muslim workforce is self-employed as compared to 55 per cent of Hindu workforce. As employees, Muslims generally work as casual labourers. While 25 per cent of Hindu workers are engaged in regular jobs, only about 13 per cent of Muslim workers are engaged in regular jobs. Only about 27 per cent of the Muslim workers in urban areas are engaged in regular work while the share of such workers among SCs/STs, OBCs and Hindu workers is 40 per cent, 36 per cent and 49 per cent respectively.

The Sachar Committee has similarly compiled figures of Muslims having access to Bank credit, access to social and physical infrastructure, including village amenities, government employment, etc. The data so meticulously collected by the Sachar Committee points out to the fact that not only the Muslims are a backward lot, but also that they are discriminated. The Report of the Sachar Committee states, "The villages with large Muslim populations are located in States/areas with poor physical and social infrastructure. This has resulted in Muslim households being poorly served by amenities compared to other Socio-Religious Communities. Improvement of rural social infrastructure in these States will provide Muslims better physical access to key amenities such as education, health, transport and communication." The Report gives similar instances of decreasing medical facilities, post and telegraph facilities, *pucca* (concretised or bituminised) approach roads and bus stops, availability of tap water, electrification, piped potable water, etc. With the size of Muslims in a village or a locality increases, the facilities provided by the State decreases.

One of the reasons why the Muslims have continued to be backward even after nearly 60 years of independence is their gross under-representation at all levels in the political structure of the country. The number of Muslim MPs in Parliament has never crossed the 50 mark, which is about 5 per cent of the Parliamentarians. One of the reasons identified in the Sachar Committee Report for under-representation of the Muslims in the political structure of the Indian State at various levels is the way the constituencies have been delimited. As a result, minorities in India lack effective agency and political importance and they do not have the necessary influence or the opportunity to either change or even influence events which enables their meaningful and active participation in development process. Though Muslims according the last Census constitutes 13.4 per cent of the population, they are less than 2 per cent in private sector employment and about 4 per cent in government employment.

We would like to conclude with the observation of the Sachar Committee, "The need for equity and inclusion in a pluralistic society can never be overemphasized. But the mechanism to ensure equity and equality of opportunity to bring about inclusion should be such that diversity is achieved and at the same time the perception of discrimination is eliminated. This is only possible when the importance of Muslims as an intrinsic part of the diverse Indian social mosaic is squarely recognized".

NOTES

1. http://indianchristians.in/news/images/resources/pdf/Rajasthan Freedom of Religion Bill 2008 only. pdf
2. All the data are according to 2001 census. See the Report of Prime Minister's High Level Committee on *Social, Economic and Educational Status of the Muslim Community of India* (popularly called as the Sachar Committee Report), published by Government of India in November 2006.
3. Article 14 reads: Equality before Law—The State shall not deny to any person equality before the law or the equal protection of the laws within the territory of India.
4. Available at http://en.wikipedia.org/wiki/Mandal_Commission
5. Available at http://indianchristians.in/news/content/view/2094/1/
6. Available at http://ncm.nic.in/annual_programe_action.html
7. Available at http://ncm.nic.in/points_programme.html
8. Available at http://www.hindusarise.com/
9. *Available at http://www.indiaedunews.net/Andhra_Pradesh/Supreme_Court_order_on_Muslim_quota_a_relief_for_ students_ 11075/*

10. *Available at http://www.indiaedunews.net/Tamil_Nadu/Now_caste-based_reservations_for_Tamil_Nadu_minorities_2046/*
11. Available at http://www.mfsd.org/mishrareport/NCRLN%201E.pdf
12. *Available at http://www.worthynews.com/christian/india anti-conversion-laws-linked-to-higher-persecution/*
13. Bagchi, Amiya Kumar. Multiculturalism, Governance and the Indian Bourgeoisie in *Multiculturalism, Liberalism and Democracy*, (Eds.) Rajeev Bhargava, Bagchi Amiya Kumar and R. Sudarshan, Delhi (1999), Oxford University Press.
14. Brass, Paul R. *The Production of Hindu-Muslim Violence in Contemporary India*, Seattle (2003), University of Washington Press.
15. Engineer, Asghar Ali. *Communal Riots after Independence—A Comprehensive Account*, New Delhi (2004), Shipra Publications.
16. For creation of Pakistan, the British Colonial powers, communal leaders of both the communities and to some extent even the secular nationalist leaders were responsible. Due to limitations of space, we are unable to cover this aspect in any detail.
17. For details, see http://tamilinfoservice.com/manitham/faq/5.htm
18. From e-mail circulated by John Dayal, General Secretary, All India Christian Council, founder of *United Christian Forum for Human Rights* and a Sr. Journalist, on 30-12-2007. John Dayal was also member of the Fact Finding Team that visited the affected areas.
19. From the Affidavit filed on behalf of the Government of India in Writ Petition No. 16 of 2004 (*Janhit Manch* Vs. *Union of India*, pending before the Bombay High Court.
20. Government of India, *Census Report, 2001.*
21. Government of India, Registrar General and Census Commissioner, India, *Census of India*, New Delhi (2001), Available at http://www.censusindia.net/
22. Government of India, Social, Economic and Educational Status of the Muslim Community of India: A Report by Prime Minister's High Level Committee, New Delhi, November 2006. The Committee was chaired by Justice Rajender Sachar and is referred to generally as the Sachar Committee Report.
23. Hindu Adoptions and Maintenance Act 1956.
24. *Hindutva* ideology and Hindu religion are entirely different. Vinayak Damodar Savarkar who wrote his treatise on *Hindutva* in 1923 in his book *Hindutva: Who is a Hindu?* and coined the word for the first time, stated that *Hindutva* and Hindu religion were different. Savarkar writes, "*Hindutva is not a word but a history. Not only the spiritual or religious history of our people as at times it is mistaken to be by being confounded with the other cognate term Hinduism, but a history in full. Hinduism is only a derivative, a fraction, a part of Hindutva. ... Hindutva embraces all the departments of thought and activity of the whole being of our Hindu race*". See *http://www.hindusarise.com/*

25. *Ibid.*
26. *Ibid.*
27. *Ibid.*
28. *Ibid.*
29. See htp://www.hindusarise.com/
30. *Ibid.*
31. *Ibid.*
32. *Ibid.*
33. *Ibid.*
34. *Ibid.*
35. In his dissenting judgment, Justice P. Jaganmohan Reddy opined that since the court did not comment on the definitions in the two Acts of the expressions, namely, allurement, fraud, force, inducement, fraudulent means, etc., it was not possible to say whether these definitions affected the fundamental rights of the minorities to propagate their religion. Moreover, the court significantly overlooked the freedom of religion of the person getting converted. Conversion is equally the right of the person who is sought to be converted, as such it is of no consequence to him if it is not a part of the freedom of propagation of the religious group to which conversion is made, provided he is not subjected to force/fraud and inducement.
36. In one of his election speeches, Mr. Narendra Modi, the BJP Chief Minister of Gujarat said that it was true that all Muslims were not terrorists but it was equally true that all terrorists are Muslims. This is quite contrary to the fact that persons of other religions are also known to have indulged in acts that states would usually brand as terrorist acts. I am deliberately refraining from naming any group as those who are terrorists for one section are liberators for other sections. Such statements encourage racial and communal profiling of Muslims in popular perception.
37. Islam, Shamsul, *Golwalkar's We Or Our Nationhood Defined: A Critique* New Delhi (2006), Pharos.
38. Muslims in India are broadly classified into three sociological units: the *Ashrafs,* the *Ajlafs* and the *Arzals*. The *Ashrafs* trace their origin to either upper castes sections of Hindus (like the Bohras) or descendants of ruling class migrants from Arabs, Central Asia, from where the Moghuls invaded the country (e.g., Sheikhs, Sayyeds, Pathans). The *Ashrafs* were the nobles and amongst the ruling elite during the period of Muslim Emperors. The *Ajlafs* are converts from amongst the lower caste Hindus, generally by the Sufis. Their caste identities, social status and even to some extent segregation and exclusion within the community survived their conversions. The social status of *Ajlafs* and *Arzals* continued to be more or less similar to their Hindu counterparts and, therefore, have been included in the list of Other Backward

Classes. *Arzals* are converts from former untouchable castes and continue to survive in the same profession, including manual scavenging. The Hindu untouchable castes are listed in the Constitution and are called Scheduled Castes and are entitled to various affirmative actions and Constitutional protection, whereas *Arzals* are not. The list of castes compiled by the AP Commission for Backward Classes is of *Ajlaf* Muslims. There is no authentic data about the proportion of *Ashrafs*, *Ajlafs* and *Arzals* within the Muslim community as census does not collect information about caste since 1931. However, it is widely believed that with partition, Muslim elites migrated to Pakistan for greener pastures and better prospects, the community left was mainly belonging to the backward classes. *Ashrafs* form less than 10 per cent of the Muslim population; *Ajlafs* form about 75 per cent and the *Arzals* form about 15 per cent of the Muslim population.

39. National Foundation for Communal Harmony, *Commissions of Inquiry on Communal Disturbances—A Study* (4 volumes), New Delhi. The 4 volumes reproduce the findings of all the 31 Commissions of Inquiry on communal disturbances.
40. National Human Rights Commission, *Interim Report, Interim Order and Final Report on Gujarat*, (Ed.) John Dayal, 2002; Justice and Peace Commission, Delhi and All India Christian Council, New Delhi, Untold and Retold Stories of the Hindutva Lab.
41. Often their hope of receiving equal treatment in the new community is not entirely fulfilled and discrimination against them continues, though some element of human dignity is retrieved through the act of conversion.
42. *Op cit.*, n. 61.
43. Prakash, Cedric, SJ, "Gujarat Textbooks Promote Communalism and Casteism", in *Indian Currents*, Vol. XX, Issue No. 22, 26 May-1 June 2008,
44. Puniyani, Ram. Minorities and Human Rights in *Minorities in Indian Social System* (Ed.) Joseph Benjamin, New Delhi (2006), Gyan Publishing House.
45. Quoted by Ram Puniyani, *op cit*.
46. Rai, Lala Lajpat. *The Hindu-Muslim Problem* (1924), Part II, Some suggestions for political improvements. Available at http://columbia.edu/itc/mealac/Pritchett/ooislamlinks/txt_lajpatrai_19/11part.html
47. Reported in AIR 1950 SC 27; 1950 SCR 88.
48. Reported in AIR 1977 SC 908.
49. Reported in AIR 1987 SC 748.
50. Section 6 of the *Hindu Minority and Guardianship Act 1956*
51. Secularism in India has taken a slightly different meaning in as much as the state is not viewed as anti-religious but non-religious. The

concept in India is called *sarva dharma samabhava* (all religions to receive equal treatment from the state).

52. *See* Article 25 of the Constitution of India.
53. *See* Article 26 of the Constitution of India.
54. *See* Article 27 of the Constitution of India.
55. *See* Article 28 of the Constitution of India.
56. *See* Article 335 of the Constitution of India.
57. See Article 338 of the Constitution of India.
58. *See* Articles 29 of the Constitution of India.
59. *See* Judgment in *TMA Pai Foundation* vs. *State of Karnataka* reported in Supreme Court Cases, 8: 481, 2002.
60. *See* note 21 above.
61. *See* note 22 above.
62. *See* Part XVI of the Constitution of India, Articles 330 to 341.
63. *See* the Judgment in TMA Pai Foundation Vs. State of Karnataka (2002) 8 Supreme Court Cases, 481
64. *See* U.N. Doc./CCPR/c/10/Add. 8, on 13th July 1983, p. 25.
65. *See*, Article 15 of the Constitution of India.
66. *See*, Article 16 of the Constitution of India.
67. *See*, Article 341 of the Constitution of India.
68. Strictly speaking, some scholars question the use of term "Hindu" in religious sense. In ancient usage, the term "Hindu" was referred in geographical sense to refer to people inhabiting south of river Indus or Sindhu and did not refer to any religion. There are such diverse religious practices, usage, customs and traditions, deities that even the Supreme Court had to despair in determining what is essential for determining if a person is a Hindu. Taking into account these diverse religious practices and beliefs, some scholars hold that India is a country of minorities rather than inhabited by many minorities with no single community constituting a majority. The Constitution in the *Explanation* II to Article 25 (2) states that "reference to Hindus shall be construed as including a reference to persons professing the Sikh, Jaina or Buddhist religion". However, the word "Hindu" now more frequently is used to refer to a single religious community which does not follow Islam, Christianity, Zoroastrian, Jewish, Sikhism or Buddhism or Jainism.
69. The Congress party and other regional parties that have set their eyes on Muslim votes do so by agreeing to those demands of political elite of the community which help perpetuate a monolithic backward looking identity of the community that does not cost the state exchequer. For example, a symbolic gesture like declaring Prophet Mohammad's birthday as National holiday, allowing Muslims to be governed by Sharia, with spirited resistance to any change therein even within the Islamic framework. After the judgment of the Supreme

Court in Shah Bano case granting maintenance to divorced Muslim women under Section 125 of the Criminal Procedure Code, under pressure from the Muslim political leadership, the Congress-ruled government in 1986 brought in legislation to exclude Divorced Muslim women from the purview of Section 125 of Cr.P.C. and made a Divorced Muslim woman depend on her parents, brothers and other relatives for her maintenance. The Muslim political leadership resists even those changes and reforms which have been introduced within Islamic framework in other countries with Muslim majority, including Pakistan. While Samajwadi Party (one of the regional parties which has its eyes on Muslim votes) in Uttar Pradesh declared that Muslim students in schools would enjoy Friday as a weekly holiday to facilitate them to go to mosques. There was a wide protest, including from the Muslims and ultimately the government had to withdraw the order. Threats and physical assaults on Taslima Nasreen and Salman Rushdie are other undemocratic methods of a section of Muslim political leadership wherein the State has been found indulgent towards the leaders. Except the symbolic identity related issues, the Muslim Politicians have never raised substantial issues of the community like education, inclusive growth to benefit the members of the community in their political demands and agitations.

70. The population of Christians is in fact on the decline in India. The Christian community has registered a decadal growth rate (1991-81) of 16.9 per cent much below the national average growth rate of 23.79 per cent. Available at *http://www.christianaggression.org/item_display.php? type= ARTICLES &id=* 1058908736) According to Dr. Nedumpara, the downward shift in the growth rate may be due to adoption of family planning and secondly due to the conversion of Dalit Christians, in particular the tribals and Harijans, into Hinduism. This is the reason why the Christian population of 2.43 per cent in 1981 dropped to 2.34 in 1991 and 2.3 in 2001. The previous Census data also shows that among the major religions of India, Christianity has the lowest growth rate. But while conversions to Christianity is being restricted, massive re-conversions to Hinduism are being reported. Recently, some 1,793 tribal Christians reportedly reconverted to Hinduism in a ceremony in Mumbai, India. The ceremony was presided by Hindu leader Swami Narendra Maharaj, who accused Christians of "luring and misleading" methods to convert Hindus, and said that "an anti-conversion law is needed." Earlier in April, some 1,000 Dalit Christians reportedly reconverted to Hinduism in a southern district in India. (Available at *http://www.christianpost.com/article/20080501/32203_Christians_Worry_* about_Gujarat_Anti-Conversion_Law.htm)

71. The Rajasthan law passed in April 2006 still awaits the governor's consent without which it does have the force of a law.
72. The RSS is the main organization which trains the officers who man the rest of the organizations and is also respected as the ideological fountainhead. RSS exercises considerable influence over the rest of the organizations even in the day to day administrative matters. When RSS objected to certain statements of L.K. Advani, former Dy. Prime Minister of India and President of BJP, he had to resign from the post of President of the BJP. Hence, all the organizations are together called *Sangh Parivar* or Sangh Family. Ideology of the *Sangh Parivar* is also described as cultural nationalism.
73. There have been conflicts between the Kannada speaking and Tamil speaking people but central to the dispute was water sharing between Karnataka and Tamil Nadu rather than one based on language. In Maharashtra, Shiv Sena and Maharashtra Navnirman Sena (MNS) are the two regional parties which mobilize Marathi speaking Maharashtrians against North Indians. Central to the mobilization is the rights of the sons of the soil rather than opposition to Hindi. Except these occasional conflicts, the linguistic minorities are not discriminated or disadvantaged in any manner. Even in the case of North Indians being targeted in Mumbai by the Shiv Sena and Maharashtra Navnirman Sena (MNS), this writer's inquiries with Hindi speaking people in Mumbai did not reveal that they were discriminated or disadvantaged in any manner in the areas of their residence or at their workplace. North Indians were targeted in Mumbai by the MNS activists for political purposes and for public consumption and in presence of media.

5

Secularism : Concept and Indian Scenario

Ram Puniyani

The concept and practice of secularism has come under heavy criticism and attack during last decade or so. With the coming up of communal politics all over the world and also in India, the movement which aims at Religion-based Nationalism has posed various question marks on the concept of secularism as a state policy, and secularism as a cultural attitude. Also here in India it has put different question marks on the 'practice' of secularism by the ruling party in the earlier years of the republic, the Congress.

The Beginnings

Secularism as a social phenomenon emerged with the rise of industrial society. From seventeenth century discoveries of science were challenging deeply held beliefs and faiths, which were integral part of the broad canvas of religion. The application of these technologies and rise of industrial societies necessitated the change in social equilibrium, which was then prevalent. The earlier society where agriculture was the dominant production activity and 'feudal' mode of production was prevalent; the major sectors of society were tied to land as poor peasants. Demands of newly developing industries required the peasants to be freed from land. What tied them to land was feudal social structure and the concomitant ideological constructs, which were again part of the religion in the broad sense of the term. The clergy (church is the most organised form of the same but similar role is played by Brahmins, and Mullahs also) supplemented the feudal

---

(Author can be reached at *ram.puniyani@gmail.com*)

structure, 'kingdoms' and fulfilled the need to ensure firm implementation of the ideology, which supplemented the feudal production norms. This was the time when social life was revolving around the dictates of the clergy *in toto*.

With onset of industrialization process, the earlier ideological chains proved to be an obstacle to the emerging industrial society. It is in this realm that one has to understand the loosening hold of clergy and some religious traditions on the totality of social life. One has to understand the social norms developing around modern rationality, ideas from science, i.e., the beginning of 'age of reason', in contrast to 'age of faith'. The farmer having its roots in science and technology and later in the clergy's interpretation of the word of God, clergy's imposition of ideologies in the name of religion, clergy's use of emotions of people for smoothening the exploitative social system of feudalism. Historically this process first occurred in clear form in West, where the above phenomenon manifested itself in the struggle between church and the state. Church stood for the declining social force of feudal lords, stood for age of faith, while the emerging nation-state" (*vis-à-vis* kingdom) stood for 'age of reason', for industrialization process based on science and technology, concretizing newer social relations (industrialists and the workers) in the process. This process which was called 'Enlightenment' and is a part of secularization process began as radical rationalist critique of some facets of religion, especially those pertaining to the mediation between people and God by the clergy. This process assumed the undisguised role of displacing aspects of religion and faith (manufactured by clergy) to the private lives of people, freeing the social life from the constraints of orthodoxy and obscurantism towards the emerging realms of modernity.

Secularization

Thus, secularism is a product of social movement of industrial bourgeoisie and landless peasants, manifested initially (in West) as Renaissance and Enlightenment, being the expression of man's urge to live life of his own, independent of the domination by church, which was prevalent feature of medieval society. Starting from this premise secularism assumed a socio historical context in mid-nineteenth century, shaped by circumstances and philosophy of the time. Secularism was based on the values, which recognized the contribution of science as a major source of knowledge and considered technological progress, social amelioration and human welfare as the goals of life. The goals of life shifted to this world (secular, profane) from the other world (sacred). With crumbling of dogmas and supernaturalism under the wheels of science and reason, the repository of dogmas, the clergy took a back seat and modern secular democratic states began to occupy the 'drivers' seats. Secular ethos is not concerned about the other world (leaving them as a merry hunting ground for the custodians of dogmas, the clergy). In a sense secularism is the policy of modern nation-states it is philosophy of secularization process. A process through which man becomes a free person from his earlier domination by the blind faiths imposed on the society by the clergy to ensure the smooth running of kingdoms, which require divine legitimacy, conferred on them by clergy, to continue their crass exploitation of the peasantry, which is the main source of their wealth. Secularization introduces instrumental values, rational procedures and technological methods, which bring along urbanization, pragmatism, profanity, pluralism and mutual respect. Secularization process brings in the ideas of relativization, the concept that all value systems are a product of historical circumstances, without any claims of finality. As a part of the package, science replaces supernatural explanation of things with those in terms of natural laws and an intellectual attitude in which reality is accounted from worldly mode of thinking.

Secularization is a process, which relegates clergy to the background, while many other components of religion survive in modified form despite secularization and do not contradict it. Secularization process is the accompaniment of democratization, throwing the clutches of feudalism. If one is to regard religion as morality, code of conduct to fellow human beings and ethical values, there is no contradiction between secularism and religion.

As such the word secular has been derived from Latin *sacculum*, meaning span of time or age and by implication present age or the world. Thus, the word secular stands for this world or concerned with the affairs of this world. As such its antonym is 'other worldly' and not religion or religious. In societies which have undergone secularization, religion does survive and state does not oppose people's faith. It occupies a place in personal life and social life and makes its presence felt in the 'social space'.

Secularism—Western or Modern

To see secularism as a principle of Christian west is a very simplistic way of looking at social phenomenon. It is true that for a brief while church possessed state power and controlled it, kings of Europe were subordinate to it for some time and then they revolted against the authority of the church to set them free. As pointed out above secularism is an outcome of secularization process, which is a comprehensive term for the changes in social values with the advent of industrialization and accompanying social relations, introduction of science, technology and rationalist thinking in society. Secularism in that sense is a marker of modernity, overcoming of feudal relationships and value system and thereby is a battle cry of newer social classes interested in overthrowing the feudal relationships and the accompanying baggage of constraining ideologies which find their vehicle in the religious clergy. It is the political expression of democratic values, Liberty, Equality and Fraternity. So secularism is a must for India. As it has entered the modern era with the introduction of industrialization and accompanying rationalism the logical values are those of secularism. Those propagating the above myth are the sections of society who stand to loose in the liberal ethos which are an accompaniment of secularism, those are the social elements who hold to religious nationalism in contrast to modern, secular democratic nationalism. No country can be a stagnant pool and with dynamic changes in society in progressive direction secularism comes in as an outcome of struggle of rising industrialist, poor peasant, worker and women against the obscurantist, dogmatic values and the feudal social system and further provides the base for enhancement of struggles of exploited and subalterns.

Indian Context

During freedom struggle itself secularism was emerging as the most dominant principle of the 'Nation in the making', India. The leaders of Indian National Congress Gandhi, Maulana Abul Kalam Azad, Nehru and others were deeply committed to the ideal of secularism though its expression was very different in all of them. It is not to be denied that some of the Hindu Nationalists also joined Congress and some other leaders in Congress were having ideologies coloured by communalism of different hue, but it is undoubted that Congress did represent secular ideology to a large extent. The constituent assembly debates made it amply clear, and secular principles were enshrined in our Constitution. The social dynamics was very complex. The process of secularization/industrialization was going on at slow pace. At this stage also though Constitution was secular, state apparatus:

bureaucracy, judiciary, army and police, was infiltrated by Hindu communal elements, Government of Congress though predominantly secular was having many leaders in important positions who were influenced by Hindu communal ideology.

Secularism in India

There are many differences in the Western/Christian social situation and the Indian situation. Hinduism is not like Christianity as far as the organization of its clergy is concerned. Since it is a collation of multiple sects it has diverse nature of its priestly class. Despite that, Hindu clergy did play a parallel role to the clergy in other religions, i.e., giving moral legitimacy to the power and authority of the king, though it may not have directly interfered in the affairs of the state. Many *Gurus* and *Acharyas* have been the guiding lights to the kings. They acquired an advisory political role to the royalty and exercised considerable influence in the court of kings. They accompanied them to the battlefield and blessed them and mediated for godly favours.

The main difference in India comes in the arena that the industrialization process. In India it began during the colonial period, initially under the patronage of colonial masters. In West secularization process accompanied the industrialization process and the culmination of this was diminution in the authority of the church. Since, India was not free, the movement for secularization was very slow. Also since the clergy was scattered, society was plural and the state was colonial, the secularization process went on in opposition to the overall hold of religious ideology and the clergy.

Freedom Movement and Secular Values

The secularization of society though slow, its political reflection in the freedom struggle and the National movement was dominantly secular, though communal (Muslim and Hindu) nationalisms also came up in the wake as a reaction to the growth of secular nationalism. Initially secularization process got reflected in movements of Jotiba Phule Ambedkar and Ramaswamy Naiker. Secular nationalism was finding expression in the politics of Gandhi and Nehru while Muslim communalism found expression in the politics of Muslim League and Hindu communalism was manifested in Hindu Mahasabha and RSS. Some of the Hindu nationalists were the part of Indian National

Congress as well. The social base of Muslim Communal nationalism was Muslim *zamindars* Landlords and moneylenders; similarly Hindu Communal nationalism had its base mainly in upper castes, amongst Hindu *zamindar* and moneylenders.

Secular nationalism was rooted amongst the nascent industrialists, newer professionals and, vast sections of peasantry and the low castes. It was the aspirations of these classes, which gave strength to freedom struggle and were translated in the foundation of Indian State and its Constitution. Thus, secularism is a principle of Indian society and not an artificial graft. It is a result of the struggles of the rising industrial class and the section of peasantry and the *shudras*.

Secularism is a marker of modernity, overcoming of feudal relationships and value system and thereby is a battle-cry of newer social classes interested in overthrowing the feudal relationships and the accompanying baggage of constraining ideologies which find their vehicle in the religious clergy. In India with dynamic changes in society in progressive direction, secularism comes in as an outcome of struggle of rising industrialist, poor peasant, worker and women against the obscurantist, dogmatic values and the feudal social system and further provides the base for enhancement of struggles of exploited and subalterns.

Secularism : Freedom Movement

India won freedom under the aegis of secular democratic movement led by Indian National Congress under the leadership of Mahatma Gandhi and Jawaharlal Nehru and Maulana Abul Kalam Azad. Secularism was the guiding principle of anti-colonial struggle and it thereby succeeded in mobilizing vast sections of this plural society. It was recognized as an essential element of platform for multi-religious, multi-caste, polyethnic population of the subcontinent, as an instrument for unity of the people at large.

The different strata of society, which were the main bulwark of this movement, were modern, i.e., industrial bourgeoisie, urban proletariat, poor peasants, women, *shudras* and modern intelligentsia. This core was able to mobilize sections of other population after Independence.

Constituent Assembly: Indian Constitution

Constituent Assembly was formed which framed the Constitution, which was diverse in nature, and represented the aspirations of majority of population. The Constitution thus framed after prolonged debates made different provisions, which formed the base of secular practice. These secular provisions of the Constitution of India are, state by itself shall not espouse or establish or practice any religion, public revenues will not be used to promote any religion, the state shall have the power to regulate any economic financial or other secular activity associated with religious practice [Article 25 (2) (9) of the Constitution], every individual person will have, an equal right to freedom of conscience and religion.

Indian State

Ours is a secular state which has no particular religion of its own and must observe neutrality and equality in respect of all religions prevalent in the country. The state cannot discriminate between one religion and the other, or between their respective followers—regardless of their numerical strength in the country. At the same time Constitution guarantees to individual and groups/sections of citizens the fundamental right to religious freedom in all its facets. Thus, secularism, equality of religions and neutrality of state to various religions within the constitutional limits are the basic features and part and parcel of unalterable basic structure of Constitution of India.

Thus, though the Constitution makers had not used the word secularism in the explicit fashion, the Constitution of India was standing on the firm foundations of secular principles. Indira Gandhi merely added a descriptive word for something, which was already ingrained in the Constitution. The spokesmen of Hindu Right taking advantage of the fact that the word was added during the much-dreaded 'emergency' are trying to throw mud on the very concept of secularism, which is anathema to their political interests.

Communalism

This resulted in a social development, which was mixed; on the one hand, secularism thrived and on the other, communalism though remained dormant, was never dead. With social changes during late 70's and early 80's communalism got a strong boost and it started attacking secularism in a big way. Its expression surfaced first through the policies of Indira and Rajiv, but in due course, the *Ramjanmabhumi* was taken up by BJP and during the course of this secularism came under severe attack.

BJP rose rapidly around the issue of *Ramjanmabhumi* and the concept of Religion based Nationalism, Hindu Rashtra came up challenging the secular democratic nationalism. During this campaign for temple at the site of mosque an attack on secular ethos, syncretic culture and composite nationalism was also launched. It is in this backdrop that one has to understand as to why for so many decades after the independence 'secularism' was never on the firing line, as to why only during last decade and a half secularism has come under cloud and the concept of Hindu Rashtra is being asserted aggressively.

Indian Political Scene

Congress began as a secular party with the inclusion of people of all religions, and their continued association with this party during freedom movement. At the same time, many a communalist formed the part of its leadership, Lala Lajpat Rai, Madan Mohan Malaviya and Dr. Moonje. Even the founder of RSS, K.B. Hedgewar was associated with it till 1934. At medium and grassroot level many a Hindu communalist in particular remained and are part of this party. It is this which made Nehru to warn that Congress should be cautious of those members who sound secular but are communal in the real sense. At the level of policies Congress took quite a principled secular path till the demise of Pundit Nehru, after which it was compromised regularly. The problem became apparent with Indira Gandhi's election speeches in, Rajiv Gandhi's 'when a big tree falls'; Shah Bano, shilanayas, and Narsimha Raos' afternoon siesta when the Babri was being razed to the ground. Many a riot took place during its regime when the ruling Government either acted as the silent witness or colluded with the rioters.

While evaluating this it has to be kept in mind that the riots take place due to three major factors, the instigator and conductor, which according to the inquiry commissions, (Jagmohan Reddy, Justice Madon, Vithayathil, Shrikrishna and Venugopal) mostly has been some organization which is a offshoot of RSS. The second factor is those who are supposed to control it, the political leadership. In this case, the Congress when in power has been weak and ineffectual at places and active colluding at other. Mostly it has been lacking the political will to control it effectively. The third force is the police and bureaucracy, which has been regularly communalized and been force providing the umbrella to the rioters or been the active participant in the execution of the pogroms. Communalism is not the programme of Congress, its basic programme remains Secularism, but its execution of those values has been lacking in will power.

Left and CPM, has come this arena of discussion after Nandigram, when in order to execute the global economic agenda, they used their cadres to settle the point by 'paying its opponents back in the same coin.' Its programme remains essentially secular, while the proactive will to counter the communal issues is not visible at all, be it the plight of minorities or the worsening hate against minorities in the States ruled by the left parties. The communism prevalent in the minds has not been tackled at all.

BJP is the political child of RSS, which has the agenda of Hindu nation. Irrespective of its temporary mask of Gandhian Socialism, it does lapse into the 'Hate minorities' mind set at the drop of the hat. It has the patriarch RSS and associates; VHP, Bajrang Dal, Vanvasi Kalyan Ashram, etc., who have been communizing the mind set, which is the base of communal violence. This RSS combine has been actively initiating situations which bring in violence. It has led many a carnages and with the help of certain elements of Congress and the helpful state machinery, has been polarizing the communities along religious lines. The scholars of communal violence have made the observation that in the aftermath of most of the communal violence RSS combine becomes stronger in the areas, where the violence has taken place. Communalism, in overt and covert language is its political vehicle towards the Hindu nation. Its communalism is programmatic.

In our semi-secularized society, where the values of liberty, equality and fraternity are not fully rooted, where the transformation of the caste and gender equations are not fully achieved, one can classify the secular formations, individuals into four broad categories on the scale of secularism. The first category exists as a rarified group. This category belongs to the party/individual who proactively strives to bring in caste and gender equality in a substantive way. Here, land reforms are the key and the endeavour to bring in the unity between communities is the hallmark of this group. Some *dalit* formations, gender right groups, groups working for communal harmony fall here. A synthesis of values of Bhagat Singh, Gandhi and Ambedkar can best describe this group, which today is not in a very good state of its health.

The formations like Left are genuinely secular but they have ignored the proactive measures to pursue this. Congress is mired by too many power seekers to be able to stand firmly to oppose the communal elements and lands up being the accomplice, in part or in full, of the phenomenon. BJP is the aggressive, intimidating opponent of democracy and secularism, whatever its expression. Its biggest 'achievement' is that some of the political workers compare it with other electoral formations. That's the bankruptcy of our times and cleverness of this party. It is effectively using the electoral space to do away with democratic values in due course. It is the Indian face of fascism.

The anti-Sikh violence was a sort of single phenomenon, which had more to do with the ethno-regional factors. The Nandigram carnage is more of economic massacre, while the BJP-led pogroms are targeted at the minorities as minorities, to consolidate their political hegemony. To be sure none of the violence can be condoned. The subtleties of these differences point out that while we do not have the real good choice for electoral arena, we will have to keep putting the civic pressure for bringing in better and better political policies through the grassroot campaigns. All the same to compare BJP with other electoral formations will be undermining the threat of the agenda of RSS, which seeks to abolish democratic space and build a society in the image of glorious Hindu past.

One can very well say, today in electoral arena we do not have a choice between good better and the best. We are riddled with bad, worse, worst and BJP !

Challenges to Secularism

Today the scenario is very complex. The communal forces in the form of various organizations doing politics in the name of religion have become dominant. The threat of attack to secularism is not only from the communal political party but it is deeper. It operates through communalization of social space, by spreading myths and stereotypes against minorities, and by practicing a divisive ideological propaganda and politics. It also operates through different cultural mechanisms, through attack on rational values and culture, through increase of blind religiosity. The section of media and the continuation of many textbooks based on communal historiography and sociology is also a big threat to secular values.

If we wish to strength the secular ethos, it has to be an all round effort, through all platforms of society with a multilayered approach. The issues which undermine the secular values, like Article 370, Uniform Civil Code, allegation of appeasement of minorities, all these need to be handled at humane level by putting across the honest attitude to all sections of society. It has to be firmly aligned with the values of freedom movement and the values of Indian Constitution. The attacks on secular values are the determined attempts by section of society to do away with the rights of the weaker sections of society, *dalits*, women, workers and *adivasis*. We have to ensure that their self-assertions, their rights are preserved and strengthened.

6

Dilemmas of Secularism in France and India

Nalini Rajan

The aim of this essay is to show that secularism is a matter of negotiation in the context of any democratic nation-state. I attempt to demonstrate the point that—in a multi-religious environment—all democracies, whether developed or developing, face dilemmas. In this essay, I discuss the difficulties of maintaining secularism in both India and France, in the present day.

Since secularism is our primary concern here, let us conceptualise this notion as triadic relations between religion, state, and individuals or groups in society. In an ideal or classical secular state, we may envisage these relations in the following manner: between the individual or group and the state (where religion is excluded), between the individual or group and religion (where the state is excluded), and between the state and religion (where the individual or group is excluded). The corresponding three principles, namely, equality of citizenship, freedom of religion, and state neutrality or wall-of-separation doctrine, have to be considered closely.

A common mistake in considering such a model is that the ideal is to maximise all three principles of equality, freedom and neutrality. The truth is that in any secular state certain principles need to be sacrificed for safeguarding certain other principles. There are, in reality, different degrees of freedom, equality and neutrality, depending on the socio-cultural institutional framework (comprising the judiciary, the electoral system, the media, and so on) in any specific context.

Another common mistake is to pit the values of a secular state against those of a communal state, that is, one characterised by conflicts between religious groups, covertly or overtly encouraged by the state apparatus. The fact of the matter is that a secular state is capable of exhibiting communal traits, when it is not adequately neutral with regard to different religions within the polity. If one is to name the antonym of a secular state, it would be a theological state, which clearly favours one religion above all others.

A theological state cannot honour the principles of state neutrality or equality of citizenship. However, depending on the benevolence of the head of state, it is capable of according to certain forms of religious freedoms. For instance, in the fifteenth century, Deva Raya II of the south Indian Vijayanagara kingdom placed a *Quran* on a stool in front of his throne, so that his Muslim subjects could pay their respects to him, without a sense of violating their belief that it is sinful to bow before an infidel ruler. In the sixteenth century, there is the celebrated example of the Mughal Emperor Akbar who abolished the hated *jiziya* tax on Hindus and established a form of religious syncretism called Din-i-Illahi. In fact, examples of religious tolerance in theological states abound all over the world, particularly in post-Inquisition Europe.

Freedom of Religion in European Monarchies

In France—which is seen as being closest to the idea of a secular state—the Edict of Nantes was passed in 1685. With the passing of the Act, Roman Catholicism became the official religion in France. Why was it necessary to pass this law?

The French people had been influenced by events in neighbouring Britain and Germany.

Johannes Gutenberg's work on the printing press began *circa* 1436, and William Caxton's approximately around 1446. The printing press enabled the first success of a heretical doctrine in the history of the Roman Catholic Church in 1517, when Martin Luther pasted his response to papal indulgences on the door of the Wittenberg chapel in Germany. This notice was called the "Disputation of Martin Luther on the Power and Efficacy of Indulgences", which came to be known as The 95 Theses and sparked off the Reformation.

The English Church, for its part, was under papal authority for nearly a thousand years, before separating from Rome in 1534 during the reign of King Henry VIII. These events had repercussions in France, in the form of doctrines like *Deism* (a religious philosophy and movement that derives the existence and nature of God from reason and personal experience) and *Jansenism* (as expounded by Cornelius Jansen, 1585-1638), which challenged the power of the Vatican. Voltaire (1694-1778) was an influential Deist, whose ideas favouring reason and progress influenced both the American and the French Revolutions.

The Edict of Nantes ensured that the poorest Roman Catholics in France—as much as the richest—got a priest to give them the last rites before they died, in order to ensure a safe passage to heaven. It was the job of Roman Catholic priests to record every birth, marriage, and death among the followers of the faith.

In 1787, two years before the French Revolution, the French state (sensing the mood of the populace) passed a law, ensuring that priests of all Christian denominations performed these duties.

The French Revolution took place in 1789. On August 27, 1789, the French Republic passed the Declaration on the Rights of Man ensuring toleration of all Christian and Deist denominations. A few days before the dissolution of the National Assembly, on September 27, 1791, a member of the Jacobin Club, formerly a Parliamentary councillor, named Duport, pointed out that freedom of worship did not permit any distinction in the political rights of citizens on account of their creed. The question of the political existence of the Jews had been postponed two years earlier in the Declaration on the Rights of Man. Still, if the Moslems and the men of all sects were admitted to enjoy political rights in France, why should not a decree passed that the Jews in France enjoyed the privileges of full citizens? This proposition was accepted amid loud applause.

By 1991, the Jacobins even started worshipping Reason and during the Reign of Terror, 1793-94, some extremists went to the extent of degrading Roman Catholicism. Such acts were condemned by Maximilien Robespierre, who was the principal architect of the Reign of Terror, and who was himself guillotined in 1794.

The French Constituent Assembly drafted a civil code between 1800 and 1804, which more or less initiated the severance of the authority of the Roman Catholic Church over French legislation. This step logically led to the establishment of a religiously neutral state. Exactly a century later, in 1905, the Law of Separation of Church and state was passed, and secularism or *laicite* of the state was formally put in place.

Religion in the Modern Day

As early as 1791, the First Amendment of the US Constitution stated, among other things, that "Congress shall make no law respecting an establishment of religion, or prohibiting the free exercise thereof" (Jefferson's Virginia Act for Establishing Religious Freedom). This put in place Jefferson's oft-quoted words of "a wall of separation between the church and the state" (in a letter to the Danbury Baptists in 1802). We are informed that "the framers of the (Indian) Constitution did not write the word secular or secularism into it despite the efforts of one member (K.T. Shah) to have this done. But it also did not accept the suggestion of another member (H.V. Kamath) to open the document with an invocation to God. Words apart, the spirit of the Constitution breathed the ideal of freedom of religion. It was only in 1976, during the "Emergency' regime of Prime Minister, Indira Gandhi, that the word 'secular' was introduced into the Preamble of the Constitution by the Fortysecond Amendment. It was thus, that India came to be characterised as a 'Sovereign Socialist, Secular, and Democratic Republic'. The precise sense in which the word secular is used is clarified by the corresponding term '*pantha nirpeksha*' (denominationally neutral) in the Hindi version of the document".

While the logic of left-liberal secularism in India is undeniably—even constitutively—defined by opposition to the public face of religion, there is also a further sense of the crisis that it faces today that complicates this dialectic. Religion's role in the modern world has been vastly reconstituted, so much so that religious debates and conflicts are no longer primarily waged over matters of belief, the true God, salvation, or other substantive issues of faith, as they once were. Religion has now become a matter of cultural practices and of identity politics. These forms of religion have been appropriated by the 'majoritarian-minded' Hindu right.

There are two basic understandings of the 'crisis of secularism'. One is that secularism is a cultural or ideological phenomenon and its very basis is jeopardised, beset by religious forces external to it. The second is that, owing to the crisis of the state, secularism suffers a functional breakdown and cannot achieve its ends. Communitarians like T.N. Madan, Ashis Nandy, and Partha Chatterjee, endorse one or the other position. Adopting an anti-state or anti-modernity viewpoint, Indian communitarians believe that the left-liberal's non-contextual secular agenda has pushed the country to the brink of Hindu fundamentalism.

The conflict, then, is between communitarians who oppose coercive state secularism on the ground that secularism is alien to Indian culture, advocate a pluralist, decentralised polity with fuzzy boundaries, and support autonomy for religious communities, and left-liberal secularists, who support egalitarianism, uniformity of law, and the separation of religion from politics, or the 'private' from the 'public'. In India, both sides would be pitted against *Hindutva* or majoritarian Hindu right politics, or again, religion-as-ideology. This does not mean that secularists are necessarily against any form of religion-as-faith.

When non-Western nations make claims to secular modernity, it is not republicanism alone but national unity that is at stake. The two major controversies in India, pertaining to the subject of secularism, are the right to religious conversion and the relevance of a uniform civil code in family matters across all religious faiths (Article 44 of the Constitution of India).

The topic of religious conversion raises many anxieties in India, partly because of the persecution of Indians of all faiths by the Portuguese in the sixteenth century, particularly during the Goa Inquisition, and partly because an influential figure like M.K. Gandhi believed that freedom of religion should be a matter of freedom of conscience and not of choice. Since all religions lead to godhood, a deeper knowledge of one's own religion was preferable, Gandhi felt, to shifting allegiance from one religion to another. B.R. Ambedkar argued from the other end of the ideological pole that religious freedom, especially for oppressed untouchable castes, should be a matter of freedom of choice, so that they could escape the tyranny of Hinduism. At the time of Indian Independence, it was decided that not only Christians and Muslims, but also Hindu Arya Samajis, should be given the religious freedom to proselytise. Despite this allowance, many State governments with large *dalit* or *adivasi* populations, like Madhya Pradesh, Orissa, Gujarat and Himachal Pradesh, have passed anti-conversion ordinances.

More interestingly, in the context of a court case pertaining to a Hindu male converting to Islam in order to indulge in bigamy (*Sarla Mudgal* versus *Union of India*, 1995), Justice Kuldip Singh mourned the fact that the uniform civil code had not yet been passed in India. The Hon'ble Judge was less concerned, in this case, with the travesty of gender justice than with the polygamous practices of Muslim men. Indeed, Indian Judges have usually invoked the necessity of a uniform civil code, when dealing with Muslim litigants, as did Justice Y.V. Chandrachud in 1985, while delivering his judgement on the Shah Bano case pertaining to maintenance after divorce.

The confrontation between Hindus and Muslims would be far less intense if the former were to make an attempt to understand the culture and philosophy of Islam.

Headscarf Controversy

The same observation may be made with respect to secular France which has exhibited a crass inability to deal with its Muslim population during the last twenty years or so. One of the most egregious examples of the so-called failure of French secularism has been in the context of the *hijab* or Muslim headscarf worn by women.

To begin with, it may be useful to recapitulate some of the background and elements of the debate surrounding the headscarf controversy.[1] In the autumn of 1989, a problem arose at a secondary school in Creil, near Paris, when the principal, himself originally from the Caribbean, forbade three Muslim women students from attending classes because they refused to remove their headscarves. In defence of his action, the headmaster cited a 1937 French law prohibiting religious symbols in school. In this particular case, the then French Socialist Minister for National Education, Lionel Jospin, ruled that the students could not be prevented from attending classes, even if they flatly refused to remove their headscarves. In response to this ruling, a polemical article appeared in 'Le Nouvel Observateur', denouncing the Minister for having 'succumbed' to the religious fundamental forces, in spite of a commitment to a policy of what the French call *laicite* or what can be loosely translated as 'secularism'.

This article would have been ignored but for the fact that it was signed by respected leftists and feminists, like Elisabeth Badinter. In the view of Badinter and the other signatories to the article, the headscarf is a sign of Islamic women's total domination by their patriarchy. Women in headscarves, then, are seen as making an inchoate plea for rescue by the French secular state, and from their oppressive families. From this viewpoint, no doubt, Islamic practices are primitive and barbaric, and those who adhere to such practices must be civilised with the aid of ideas of *laicite*. The problem with this perspective is that it denies the possibility of 'Islamic feminism', and views gender emancipation solely through Eurocentric lens.

Studies have revealed that Muslim women's motivations for veiling can vary dramatically—between expressing their belief in the *Quran* and expressing their contempt for Western values. After all, women are peculiarly vulnerable when their men are most threatened, as under colonial occupation. The veil or the *burqa*, by attempting to render invisible the woman, makes her more visible. The veil imprisons and liberates. Zaynab al-Ghazali, the only prominent woman in the Muslim Brotherhood of Egypt, strongly recommends the veil for Muslim women, in the name of opposing secular and Western values. She also calls for a strange mix of political action and domesticity, which calls to mind the similar ideology of the *Durga Vahini*, the women's wing of the Hindu fundamentalist group, the *Vishva Hindu Parishad*.

The veil appears to have been pre-Islamic in origin and in use among the Greeks and the Persians. The relevant verses in the *Quran* recommending the use of the veil on the basis of enhancing female modesty are the following: "And when you ask them (the Prophet's wives) for anything you want to ask them from before a screen (*hijab*); that makes for greater purity for your hearts and for them" (S. 33:53); "O Prophet ! Tell your wives and daughters and the believing women that they should cast their outer garments over themselves, which is more convenient that they should be known and not molested" (S. 33:59).

Modesty, however, is a relative term. Some women who wear headscarves may believe that the hair and neck form part of feminine beauty, while those who wear the *burqa* may believe that every part of the female body needs to be covered. Those who wear neither the headscarf nor the *burqa* may feel that feminine arms, legs, head and neck may be exposed without immodesty and that modesty requires merely avoiding revealing clothes like miniskirts, halter-necks and bikinis.

Arab feminists like Fatima Mernissi points out that the 'screen' is not the veil.[2] Some go on to maintain that the relevant verses in the *Quran* only apply to the Prophet's wives. Finally, they point out the instance of gender egalitarianism in the *Quran* (S. 33:35) that refers to vast rewards Allah has prepared for both "men who guard their modesty and women who guard their modesty". A few Islamic feminists attempt to turn the gender tables by castigating Muslim men for not adhering to Quranic principles of morality, like wearing *galabiyyas* and growing beards.

Wearing of the veil has been put to the test primarily by the Muslim diaspora in Western countries. The 1989 exclusion of the three Muslim girls of North African extraction from their school in Creil precipitated a major debate in France among the estimated 2.7 million Muslims presently residing in France, which is still governed by the Jacobin ethos of uniform citizenship in "*la Republique, une et indivisible*".

The events in Creil were mirrored in 1990 in Cheshire, England, when two pupils at Altrincham Grammar School for Girls were sent home by the head teacher for wearing headscarves. The current Muslim population in the UK is believed to be 1.5 million. In the UK, by the late nineteen-sixties, it was realised that identical treatment to citizens, irrespective of their cultural differences, was an inappropriate legal response.

On the face of it, it would seem that pluralist Britain would allow school girls to wear headscarves, whereas republican France wouldn't. Actually, the reverse has happened.[3] In France, substantial inroads into Jacobin doctrine have occurred in three respects. First, despite opposition from the ideological left, private Catholic schools receive substantial funding from the state. Second, there has been some decentralisation of secondary school administration and considerable power has been handed over to local authorities. Third, teaching of history, geography and 'civics' in France has recently moved away from the inculcation of patriotism to an appreciation of cultural plurality and diversity.

In Britain, the Race Relations Act 1976 has focused on racial, not religious, discrimination. "A key question, however, under the Act is whether the proportion of pupils of the plaintiff's racial, ethnic or national group who can conscientiously comply with the regulation is 'considerably smaller' than the proportion of pupils not of that group who can comply with it."[4] Since very few Muslim girls in the UK wear the *hijab*, it would be very difficult for them to win a case on this ground. Thus, the Act does discriminate against the interests of religious minorities. The only way in which such cases can be resolved—as happened both in Creil and in Cheshire—is by schools reaching a speedy and sensible compromise on the matter of allowing religious symbols in class.

Despite its controversial status for having collaborated with right-wing governments, an organisation in France like *Ni Putes, Ni Soumises* (Neither Whore nor Submissive) headed by Fadela Amara, appears to broaden the terms of the debate as far as the Muslim veil is concerned. Muslim women in the ghettoes of Western Europe are now saying to the men in their community: "Just because we do not wear the veil, we are not whores." And to the French secular state, they are saying: "Just because we do wear the veil, we are not submissive".

What is most important is that it is now being recognised that there are various modes of being a woman within the Islamic world.

Although, the French state, throughout the 1990s, has vacillated between a policy of tolerance for the presence of religious symbols in schools and one of banning all ostentatious religious symbols, including Christian, Jewish and Sikh ones, it has now clearly opted for the latter, in the name of *laicite*, in the form of a proposed law to this effect. The French policy of *laicite*, which originated in the heady days of the French.

Revolution, when the Roman Catholic Church was viewed with deep suspicion, has had a long and troubled trajectory—from the uneasy compromise with the Church under Napoleon Bonaparte, leading to the Concordat system and culminating in the Law of Separation between the church and the state in 1905. Since then, although the French Government has alternated between emphasising religious freedom under right-wing governments, and insisting on a wall of separation policy under the socialists, there has been an overall commitment to *laicite* in the French polity.[5]

The western or Christian bias involved in the French policy of *laicite* has been exposed by several analysts, who point out that the "secular schools, which the French Left so passionately defends, are only secular in that they are not doctrinally Christian".[6] Confining the weekly holiday in schools to Sunday, which is convenient to Christians for attending church but not to Muslims or Jews, or tacitly allowing Jewish parents to pick up their children from school on Friday afternoons in order to prepare for the early Sabbath on Saturdays, forcing all girl students to wear a uniform of knee-length skirts—are these practices not skewed in favour of the Judaeo-Christian tradition and discriminatory against the Muslim community?

For some[7] opting for a less religiously skewed and more neutral state policy will not do. The reason is that there will always be other layers of discrimination in liberal democracies. After all, it is easy to point out the reactionary or irrational practices of Muslim immigrants to the west; it is much harder to demonstrate the existence of equally irrational practices of non-Muslim westerners. Indeed multiculturalists claim that—putting aside the thorny idea of agency—there is not that much difference between the genital mutilation of young girls in Islam and the painful cosmetic surgeries (breast enlargement or reduction, liposuction, facelifts) and the bodily alterations (tattooing, body-piercing) undergone by westerners, between Islamic polygamy and the present practice of western serial polygamy, and so on.

Inevitably, too, there are opponents of this view who insist on maintaining differences, rather than establishing similarities, between cultures. In this battle over representation, they would rather look for opinions on the matter among the 'insiders' of the targeted community, like Muslim feminists (who are divided over the issue of the ban on headscarves in schools) or the likes of a Tariq Ramadan, a Swiss-based Muslim philosopher, grandson of the founder of Egypt's Muslim Brotherhood, who is seen in different quarters as a promoter of moderate Islam and as a demagogic anti-Semite. In other words, this position suggests the impossibility of the French secular state to represent the Muslim immigrant community, owing to the mutually irreconcilable values of the two cultures. Curiously—albeit for very different reasons—this is also the left-wing feminist Elisabeth Badinter's view, as we have seen.

However, the headscarf controversy itself is embedded in a context that drastically reduces options and limits the scope of this spectrum. And this context of course is the school.

It is important to be aware of the fact that the French educational system itself has a long history of *laicite*. Jules Ferry, the Minister for Public Education from 1879 to 1883, introduced a new educational system that became fully operational during his tenure. Free education in primary schools was adopted in June 1881 without much difficulty. It was considerably more difficult to counter the power of the Roman Catholic Church and adopt a policy of *laicite*. Finally, the law of March 28, 1882, made primary school education compulsory and *laique*. A few years after Jules Ferry's departure, two other laws according a purely secular status to the teaching personnel were passed.

The question was posed: what kind of value education in terms of moral principles would French school children receive in lieu of religious teaching? The answer was given: all school children, irrespective of gender, social class, or religious affiliation, would receive the same education, thus promoting the unity of the Republic. Thereby the Republic itself was the bearer of values.

This claim, however, has not been without problems. The initial dilemma was: is *laicite* to be understood in the positive sense of promoting secular values in schools, or in the negative sense of maintaining strict neutrality and not referring to any values at all within the educational framework. Given the powerful presence of the Roman

Catholic Church in France, Jules Ferry was forced to push the negative ideal of value neutrality in schools. So where is the space for value education in the French school system? We turn to this issue in the final section.

Public Sphere

If value education is not to be reduced to a system imposed from above, it would appear that schools would have to impose some limits on the authority of both the family and the state, in order to create the conditions for the emergence of a public space for debate and dialogue. This space should engage the participation of students as well as teachers or resource persons and is expected to promote the ideal of active citizenship among high school children between the ages of 14 and 18. The importance of this public space lies in the fact that our public interests as citizens are quite distinct from our private interests as individuals. The ideal of citizenship involves the morality of association which, in turn, involves not the liberal virtue of impartiality, but the more substantive democratic values of tolerance, mutual respect, and civic virtue. The public sphere in school education may be neutral on religious beliefs (such as the Christian faith in divine redemption), but it cannot be neutral on political values (such as the headscarf controversy), since, by definition, a certain set of these values constitutes its operational basis.[8] It is obvious that even those who adhere to the Kantian principles of impartiality and neutrality must reframe their ideology in the context of school education, and subscribe to a more substantive, even paternalistic or perfectionist version of liberalism.[9]

By the same token, post-modernists will realise that an extreme form of pluralism, according to which all differences, opinions or interests are equal, could never provide a framework for a political dialogue in the public sphere of school education. Some sort of evaluative criteria should exist to decide what is admissible here and what is not. Children cannot be told that class, ethnic or gender-based prejudices are no better or worse than emotions like sympathy, kindness or benevolence.

At the same time, it is important to realise that emotions themselves—related as they are to what we call the voice of conscience—form a poor basis on which to constitute a genuinely political sphere. After all, the voice of conscience directs the attention of school children inwards, towards the self-rather than outwards, towards the world.[10] This, indeed, may be the dilemma of introducing Gandhian values—to the exclusion of all others—in the Indian education system, for it is unlikely to foster public or civic virtue among school children.

Thus, on the whole, entering the public sphere of school education for the social scientist is analogous to what it means to enter a school zone for a motorist—you have to slow down considerably. The wide range of options available to the social scientist in the academic world is drastically reduced to a narrow tunnel of possibilities for promoting the values of citizenship, political participation, debate and dialogue among school children on the threshold of adulthood. In other words, we may find that the public space in the school system will require a set of substantive values that are somewhat independent of the teacher's or resource person's views in a larger framework of the outside world. The separation of different kinds of the public and the private is by no means easy.

In actual terms, the manner in which the public sphere is promoted in schools is delineated by some analysts[11] in the form of three principles:

1. In order to promote tolerance among school children, they must be exposed to other cultures.
2. In order to be tolerant, it is important that school children are taught to possess some measures of detachment from their own personal commitments. That is to say, they should learn to situate their commitments in a context and thus perceive them to be contingent.
3. There should be a common commitment among school children to a public sphere.

Schools in liberal democracies are generally faced with the conflict between the demands placed on education by liberalism, namely, that the state or school authority should not interfere with the private beliefs of individuals, and the demands on education by democracy, namely, the maintenance of democratic institutions, like the public sphere in schools. How do French schools promote the public sphere? No doubt there are regional variations—as well as considerable differences between state-owned and privately-owned schools. However, if we were to consider the question from the viewpoint of a Weberian ideal-type French school, we may be able to reach certain conclusions.

With its republican emphasis on the inculcation of a unified national consciousness, the French school is likely to eschew pluralism as a public good. Given its rejection of private religious symbols and beliefs, the French school system promotes a principle of equal exclusion of the private from the public, rather than a principle of equal accommodation of the private in the public, as does the more multicultural American school system. Whereas, the American school model is likely to blur the distinction between the public and private realms by emphasising the need to respect others' private beliefs—which raises different kinds of problems like the inability to create a public space for debate—the French model is entirely committed to promoting the public sphere and to keeping the private realm out of it. At the same time, it would be very difficult to conduct a meaningful discussion in this model on a difficult subject, say, like the headscarf controversy, given the context of an all-embracing 'us' and the annihilation of 'them'. In brief, the French model performs fairly well in terms of (3), but fails to take (1) and (2) to their logical conclusions.

The Indian school ideal-type has had a very different trajectory. Under this model, parents are in theory permitted to separate themselves into more-or-less homogeneous groups based on common interests and commitments—like gender, class, language, caste, or religious community. The Indian State then fully or partially funds the schools that cater to private interests—although it is true that there are also some fairly pluralistic State-run and private schools in existence. On the whole, however, parents are encouraged to ensure that their children are educated in a school whose ethos explicitly favours the particular commitments and values held by the family. Thus, the 'privatisation' of the public school system seems well on its way here. This system fulfils the ideal of political liberalism more effectively than that of democracy.

Such a system may foster 'divided pluralism'—that is, a pluralist community of literates at the national level, but multiple units of mutually uninterested mono-economic, mono-religious, mono-cultural, mono-linguistic sub-communities in civil society.[12] In such a context, pluralism cannot be part of public culture and school children cannot be easily encouraged to examine values other than their own. In a way, Indian schools—with very few exceptions—fail to honour all the three criteria enumerated above in order to create a public sphere.

Indeed, if schools are to be imagined as a democratic public sphere, then the teacher's role, too, must be conceived in a much more dynamic fashion. At the same time, we must realise that schools are not 'out there'—outside of us. They clearly implicate us in our prescribed roles within the family structure and in civil society. In other words, we face the formidable task now of bridging the gap between 'us'—and 'them'—defined as the insider-cum-school teacher. The articulation of this task is likely to take different and paradoxical forms and directions in the future—but that has always been the positive challenge of the discipline of social science.

NOTES

1. I prefer to use the term 'headscarf', since I hold the view that this is already a modified version, adopted by Muslim immigrant women in the west, of the more traditional 'hijab'.
2. *See* Mernissi's *The Veil and the Male Elite: A Feminist Interpretation Of Women's Rights in Islam*. Addison-Wesley Publishing Company, 1991, The University of Michigan, for further elaboration of this point.
3. For a detailed analysis of religious minority treatment in the UK and in France, see Sebastian Poulter's *Muslim Headscarves in School: Contrasting Legal Approaches in England and France*, Spring 1997, Volume 17, Number 1, pp. 43–74.
4. This pertains to Section 1(1)(b) of the Act and is quoted in Poulter, 1997, p. 65.
5. *See* Jean Bauberot's 'The Two Thresholds of Laicisation' in Rajeev Bhargava (ed), – Secularism and its Critics, Oxford University Press, 1998, for an elaboration of this theme.
6. *See* Norma Claire Moruzzi's 'A Problem with Headscarves: Contemporary Complication of Political and Social Identity', Political Theory, Volume 22, No 4, November 1994.
7. For a defence of multicultural values, I refer to 'Muslim Minorities in Liberal Democracies: The Politics of Misrecognition' by Joseph H. Carens and Melissa S Williams, in Rajeev Bhargava (edited), *Secularism and its Critics*, Oxford University Press, 1998.
8. For a deeper discussion of the ideal of citizenship, see the Preface: Democratic Politics Today and Maurizio Passerin d'Entreves' 'Hannah Arendt and the Idea of Citizenship' in Chantal Mouffe (ed), *Dimensions of Radical Democracy: Pluralism, Citizenship, Community*, Verso, 1992. On the subject of education, see Amy Gutman's Democratic Education, Princeton University Press, 1987.
9. John Rawls endorses this position on page 250 of A Theory of Justice, Harvard University Press, 1971.
10. On page 156, Maurizio Passerin d'Entreves, *op. cit.*, makes this point in reference to Hannah Arendt's notion of citizenship.

11. Meira Levinson's '*Liberalism* versus *Democracy*? Schooling Private Citizens, Volume 28, No 3, June 1987. in the Public Sphere', *British Journal of Political Science*, 1997, Volume 27, No 3, pp. 333-60.
12. Meira Levinson, *op. cit.*, makes this point with respect to the British school system, broadly on which the Indian system is based.

7

Multiculturalism and Secularism in India: A Study

S.A. Palekar

Important dimension of the democratic state in India is its secular nature. The important relationship between the state and the nation in India is constitutionally defined in 'secular' or better 'multicultural' terms. The secular ideology of the Indian State appears as a paradox in view of the deeply religious orientation of the Indian society. This phenomenon must be understood in terms of the nature of Indian nationalism. The imagined Indian national community[1] came to be conceived in a way that both the nation and the state were closely intertwined. The civic-territorial conception of the nation in India was conceptualized in terms of aggregation of the various cultures and communities that had co-existed within the same territorial and social space. There was no lag between the projected national community and the projected state that the Indian nationalists in the latter half of the nineteenth century and early decades of the twentieth century envisioned, notwithstanding the cancerous growth of communalism between Muslims and Hindus between 1930 to 1940 largely due to colonial "divide-and-rule' policy that both the nation and the state remained in the making in British India and were born together in 1947. Indian secularism/multiculturalism was a product of this imagined national community.

The modernizing elites of India evolved, during the freedom movement against the British Raj, a concept of secularism that was premised on the crystallization of: (i) a common focus of national allegiance to the nation in the making, and (ii) the development of rule of law and a common Indian citizenship. They did not visualize a state that would maintain a wall of separation between the state and religion. This was not only because Indian religions lacked the institution of an autonomous corporate church.[2] This was also because of the felt-need for reforms in Indian religious traditions, especially the rituals, behaviour patterns and family laws offensive to modern/ rational sensibilities. But the nationalists were also sensitive to religious cleavages in Indian society. The Indian National Congress, therefore, either abdicated the field of social reforms in favour of reform organizations and movements within various religious communities, or else it took up an issue of communal import only when it perceived a substantial concurrent consensus for it in society, including within the minority communities.

However, the nationalist leadership in colonial Indian encountered two formidable hurdles to national integration. Soon after the establishment of the British Raj on the ruins of tottering Mughal State, the British rulers adopted the policy of "divide and rule" that led to the politicization of communal and caste consciousness on an unprecedented scale. For, the communal segregation and splendid isolation of communities in the traditional society came to an end with the onset of the process of modernization. And the colonial rulers manipulated the emerging ethnic cleavages by playing one group against the other to their own advantage. Besides, a section of Indian Muslims perceived political change in India in an essentially historically rulers' mindset and reverse "majoritarian" mode of thought. To them, Hindu majority in the society automatically meant a Hindu majority in the polity. Intermediation by liberal political institutions between society and the polity whereby the Hindu majority—more categoric than real in any case—would be broken into cross-cutting political allegiances and alliances did not make much sense to them. From Sir Syed Ahmed Khan's exhortations to Muslims to keep away from the Congress to Mohammed Ali Jinnah's demand for a separate homeland for Muslims was logical culmination of this counter-majoritarian but sectarian mode of thought. The more intimate familiarity of Indians with the majoritarian Westminster model of Parliamentary Government rather than other political systems based on consensus or concurrent plural majorities was not very helpful in this context. And the communal safeguards and revolutionary and federal measures introduced by the British to modify the majoritarian model in India did not have much positive impact either. These measures only fanned the fires of paranoia of separatism among the Hindus and fuelled the embers of insecurity and communalism and secessionism among the Muslims. In the normal course of national evolution in India without a colonial intervention, these measures might have had more positive results in terms of classical Indian syncretic and coexistential cultural construction. And in India today, despite the bitter historical memories and paranoia about fissiparous tendencies, some institutional reforms towards federalizing India's predominantly Parliamentary system appear to be necessary. In the process, we must combine a responsible Parliamentary Government with responsible federalism.

Nehru and Gandhi represented two major models of secularism in modern Indian political thought. Both stood for Indian national unity and a common legal basis for Indian citizenship. But, whereas Nehru emphasized the liberal-individualist foundation for Indian citizenship and national identity, Gandhi patronized an approach that sought to aggregate the primordial pluralities and communitarian-ethnic identities into a larger composite national communitarian consciousness. Thus, the Nehruvian stance came closer to the Western liberal-individualist view of secularism drawing sustenance from rationalism and scientific temper. The Gandhian approach, on the other hand, adhered to the traditional Indian ideal of *sarvodharma samabhava* (equal empathy for all religions). Nehru was quintessentially liberal while Gandhi was primarily communitarian.

The concept of secularism adopted in the Constitution of India combines the Nehruvian and the Gandhian approaches to Indian citizenship. The Constitution first guarantees a series of Fundamental Rights—right to equality before law; right to political, civil, occupational and religious freedoms and protection of life and personal liberty; right against exploitation, and right to constitutional remedies—to all Indian citizens irrespective of religion, race, caste, creed, sex, place of birth or any of them. It then extends some cultural and educational rights to religious institutions of their choice. However, no educational institutions maintained by the state or receiving aid out of state funds shall deny admission to any citizen on grounds only of religion, race, caste, language or any of them. Moreover, the constitutional granting of freedom of conscience and free profession and practice of religion under Article 25(1) does prevent the state from legislating regulation or restriction of: (a) economic, financial, political or other secular activities which may be associated with religious practice, and (b) provision for social welfare and reform or the throwing open of Hindu (Sikh, Jain or Buddhist) religious institutions of a public character to all classes and sections of these religions [Article 25, Clause 2(a) and (b) and Explanation 11]. Furthermore, the freedom of a religious denomination or any sect thereof to manage its own affairs in matters of religion, including the establishment and maintenance of institutions for religious and charitable purposes is "subject to public order, morality and health" (Article 26). In addition, State-aided educational institutions shall not provide any religious instruction (Article 28, Clause 1). Thus, the secular state in India is essentially a "rule-of-law secular state", though it does not abjure an absolute jurisdiction over matters of religion. Indeed, it considers the securing of a uniform civil code for all its citizens so desirable as to incorporate it as one of the Directive Principles of State Policy (Article 44). Similarly, the overriding importance of promoting national integration is underlined by inclusion in the Constitution of Fundamental Duties of citizens, among others "to abide by the Constitution and respect its deals and institutions, the National Flag and the National Anthem" (Article 51a).

In addition to economic and religious factors exacerbating communal conflicts and silent discrimination against Muslims by Hindus and against Hindus by Muslims, another major factor fomenting communalism in India is the political variable. And here it is not only the communal parties like the Bharatiya Janta Party, Shiromani Akali Dal, and Muslim League that are the villains of peace but also the secular parties. If the former indulge in overt communalism, the latter take recourse to covert communalism, with an electoral axe to grind. All parties, including the communal ones, loudly profess their commitment to secularism or travel some distance on the secularist path when it electorally suits them. If this is largely true of the secular parties like the Congress, Janta, CPI (M) and CPI, this has also been true in some measure of communal parties like the BJP and Akali Dal, both of which underwent a perceptible process of decommunalization in the 1960s and 1970s[3] before being overtaken by a new phase of Hindu revivalism and Sikh fundamentalism. Nonetheless, even secular parties enter into electoral alliances with communal parties or hobnob with Rashtriya Swayamsevak Sangh (RSS) chief or go to the Imam of the Jama Masjid for an appeal for Muslim votes. From one point of view, a greater degree of commensality among secular and communal parties should be welcome. For, it must have at least some secularizing and integrating impact on the party system in general.[4]

Whether, the steep rise of Hindu and Muslim and Sikh fundamentalism in the 1980s and 1990s was the driving wedges of fascism in India? Or does it mean that India has come of age as a secular state and hence can withstand the beginning of a more natural political expression of religious identities? Will the tumult of mighty disharmonies now rocking the ship of the Indian multicultural state subside to the normal levels of electoral politics typical of multi-religious Western democracies or will it lead to the excavation of its foundations? When the Hindu communal backlash gave the Congress in 1984 its unprecedented electoral landslide victory before it finally shifted to effect the mighty revival of BJP in 1989 and later in the decade, it was well within the bounds of Parliamentary politics. In a perceptive interpretation of the Hindu vote in 1984, Kothari had remarked[5].

> "While everyone seems to sense this one way or another, it is necessary to see how this happened and how it represents a basic reversal of India's political culture (as also of the core of Hindu identity). A long period of plural segmented existence was leading to a slow sense of uneasiness with mainstream politics to a sense of being cheated a feeling that the very spirit of accommodation and tolerance on which the Hindus pride themselves was being misuse, that the 'minorities'—from Muslims and Sikhs to *dalits* and *adivasis*—were being pampered. They had the reservations, they owned the arms, they got the benefits of state patronage, and here were we, the so-called majority, left high and dry".

This electoral realignment was preceded by long periods of Congress predominance bases on an electoral winning coalition of Brahmins, Muslims, Sikhs, Harijans and *adivasis*. The Hindus, then, were more an artifact of categorization than a homogeneously conscious religious community. This made possible the cross-cutting electoral coalition of minorities and *dalits*. This radically changed over the years to prepare the ground for the tremendous upsurge of BJP in 1989 in the Hindi heartland in general and in 1991 in Uttar Pradesh in particular. The Rudolphs[6] attempt to explain the phenomenon in the following terms :

> "Religious performance, celebrations, and demonstrations began to transcend localities and to acquire national

> dimensions. As they did so, they became more strident and militant. The agitations and *yatras* (pilgrimages) of the Hindu solidarity and unity movements, such as the Vishwa Hindu Parishad, were no longer the local phenomena they had been in the 1880s when Bal Gangadhar Tilak aroused Hindu political solidarity around the Ganesh festival at Poona. Aided by the proliferation of religious symbolism in the print and electronic media, Hindu themes and organizations crossed State boundaries and helped diverse sects, castes and classes to acquire the consciousness of a popular and more homogeneous Hinduism".

The *Hindutva* ideology of the RSS-BJP combine has been dubbed by some as an Indian variant of fascism. This characterization is made on the supposed similarity of the *Hindutva* political forces with inter-war fascist parties and movements in terms of religious-ethnocentrism, stigmatization of minorities, authoritarian monolithic nationalism, and simultaneous emphasis on Hindu *Sangathan* as well as plebiscitary mass appeal with religious nationalist motives and charismatic leadership. Yet Indian variants of fascism are also supposed to have some specific indigenous features. For example, Ahmad[7] opines:

> "The striking feature of *Hindutva* fascism is that unlike the German or Italian or even the Irani variants, it speaks relatively rarely of the economic instance and fashions its ideological discourse along categories, of 'nations' and 'community'—through the methodical use of violence as a political instrumentality. That communal violence draws upon many other kinds of routine violence in our society is a central part of my argument; at the same time, however, it is this single-minded politicization of violence—even a certain rationalization of violence as a means for capturing state power—that distinguishes *Hindutva* fascism from other kinds of violence as well as from other forms of authoritarian populism".

Ahmad[8] goes on to point out that Hindu fascism decries secular Indian nationalism as a failed nationalism and employs an upper-caste Hindu revivalism in a distinctly non-class mobilization strategy.

However, some degree of caution and circumspection is called for in blanket characterization of Indian religious communalism as downright fascist. For one thing, religious communalisms in India do not outrightly reject the Indian Constitution and the liberal-democratic regime. The BJP, for example, formally subscribes to what it calls "positive secularism", distinguishing it from what it decries as "pseudo-secularism", or "minorityism". Its "integral humanism" privileges the claims of the collectivity over those of the individual, but it is society-centric rather than statist and the protagonists of Hindu Rashtra have been at pains to clarify that this conception is coterminus with Indian territoriality inclusive of all communities residing here rather with Hindu religious group in its narrow sense. It must, however, be pointed out that the term Hindu Rashtra does alarm and frighten the minorities. However, compulsions of electoral politics in India's diverse society and polity have led to a palpable degree of moderation of Hindu militancy. The BJP leadership apparently realizes that to win power at the national level and to promote secular nationalism in Pakistan, it has to become a more liberal and pluralist political formation. Its departure from the ideology of revocation of the 1947 Partition of India (*Akhand Bharat*) is underlined by the visit of Prime Minister Vajpayee in 1999 to Minar-e-Pakistan Resolution in 1940 and reference by former BJP President and leader of the opposition L.K. Advani to Jinnah's secular vision in his inaugural speech in the Pakistan Assembly during the 2005, visit to Pakistan.

India's secularism was invented for integrating the multicultural pluralities of the society into a common nation-state as well as for containing the explosive potentialities of the imperial 'divide and rule' policy and the Muslim League's "two-nation" theory in British India. Indian secularism is different from Western versions of secularism of which two broad models are (a) the *de facto* British secularism where the state has become secular in spite of the conventional association of the Anglican Church of England with the state, and (b) *de jure* American and French models where the Constitution puts a formal wall of separation between the state and church/religion. What then, are the basic features of the secular state in India? These may be summed up as follows: (a) no formal state religion and a prohibition on taxation on religion, (d) no separation between state and religion evident in the grant of legislative and judicial jurisdictions of the state over religious matters such as reforms of family laws and practices and enabling legislation for management of religious shrines and estates. Besides, the state in India has formally and persistently endeavoured to free education and election from the use of denominational instruction and religious electoral campaigns. Even if there have been attempts on the part of some governments, e.g., the BJP-led NDA regime, these have been restrained by the political opposition, the press and universities, and the judiciary.

What has been India's successes or failures as a secular state? Again, a clear-cut positive or negative answer is difficult to offer. Perhaps the most significant indicator of the success is that there is no political party in India that has formally rejected the constitutional ideal of secularism. Even the BJP that is considered to be the greatest challenge in divided India to the secular state says that it is not opposed to secularism *per se*, only to "pseudo-secularism" or "minorityism". It professes what it calls "positive secularism" and clarifies that for it, cultural nationalism or 'Hindu Rashtra' and 'Bharatiya' of the Constitution of Indian are not contradictory. Yet, the fact remains that the greatest Indian dilemma today is religious communalism and fundamentalism that led in the past to the partition of India. The practitioners of this brand of politics on both majority and minority sides strut the land with injured psychies of historical and imperial victimhood, demanding cultural autonomy, ethnic identity, and right to history and, therefore, to the future. Hindus, Sikhs and Muslims alike have critiques the "pseudo-secularism" or "minorityism" (*a la* BJP) of the Congress regime (though no party can be fully absolved of indulging in covert or overt communalism), the homogenizing and hegemonizing policies of the Indian aggregate State(s) and the attendant discriminations and disparities. Frequent communal riots, chain-bombings, and other kinds of sabotage, often carried out with foreign connivance, seemed to have become the standard machinations of the Government, opposition, and terrorists alike at least until 1993 when the National Human Rights Commission, judicial activism and activities of civil rights groups made their presence felt. Punjab, in the latter half of 1980s, and Jammu and Kashmir, in the early 1990s, remained infested with terrorist violence and religious fundamentalism. Hindu fundamentalists worked up in the latter half of the 1980s a powerful mass movement for the restoration of a Ram temple in Ayodhya on the site of the Babri Masjid to rectify a historical wrong by Mughal invaders; and the medieval structure was demolished by a frenzied mob on 6th December, 1992. Narsimha Rao-led Congress minority Government at the Centre, which was having an informal rapprochement with the BJP in the preceding period, finally reacted by dismissing the BJP Governments under Article 356 of the Constitution not only in Uttar Pradesh (where Ayodhya is located) but also in Madhya Pradesh, Rajasthan and Himachal Pradesh for the failure of the Uttar Pradesh Government to carry out administration according to the provisions of the Constitution and apprehended failure of the Governments in other three States to implement the ban on some Hindu (and Muslim) communal organizations. The Supreme Court made judicial history by reviewing presidential proclamation of emergency in States for the first time in the *S.R. Bommai and Others vs. Union of India and Others*[9] and upheld the dismissal of the BJP Governments in UP, MP, Rajasthan, and Himachal Pradesh. In the same judgement, earlier dismissal of State Governments in Karnataka in 1989 and Meghalaya in 1991 were found to be unconstitutional. The Court went so far as to observe that but for the fact that new elections had since been held in those States, it would have formally struck down the proclamations and directed the revival and restoration of the respective governments and legislative assemblies. The Supreme Court in the above judgement also appropriately declared that democratic form of government, federal structure, unity and integrity of the nation, secularism, socialism, social justice and judicial review are "basic features" of the Constitution and hence beyond repeal by the amending power of the Parliament.

The recent challenges to the secular character of the Indian State strike at the very foundations of composite national culture and multi-cultural nature of the Indian nation-state. The nation in India was born with democracy and secularism as its integral constituents. BJP's advocacy of what it calls "cultural nationalism" implies that secular Indian nationalism is anti-cultural. This is untenable and strikes a deadly blow to multi-cultural State and nationalism born in the throes of the anti-colonial nationalist struggle and founded on the eve of Independence. May be the BJP itself does not reject what we are calling here multi-cultural Indian nationalism; for it has gone on record that it seeks to remove distortions of Indian secularism by putting in place what it calls "positive secularism". It augers well for the future of Indian nationalism. There is no doubt that despite the recent stresses and strains, India continues to be a secular State. Elucidating the nature of Indian secularism, Bhargava aptly observes:

> "India was never intended to be either a hyper-substantive or an ultra-procedural secular state. It was never meant to exclude every religious practice or institution from the domain of politics. The dominant justification of the policies and practices of the Indian State was done by appealing to contextual secularism of the principled distance variety, exclude religion for some purposes and include it to achieve other objectives, but always out of non-sectarian consideration."[10]

Some observers have taken a serious alarmist view of the rise of *Hindutva* forces in the 1990s. To be sure, the destruction of the Babri Masjid in 1992 by a frenzied mob mobilization by Hindu communal organizations was most shocking. In its wake, a number of Hindu and Muslim communal organizations were rightly banned, but the BJP was not one of them. It "responded by appearing less militant and dissociating itself from the Vishwa Hindu Parishad (VHP), which had been weakened by the ban and ebbing of emotions after the demolition of the mosque, which it had previously portrayed as a symbol of Hindu humiliation".[11]

In his study, Jaffrelot analyses the BJP in particular and Hindu nationalist movement in general as oscillating between two partly contradictory and partly complementary strategies of mobilization, namely, the moderate and the militant. The former relied on electoral strategy of *Hindutva* identity formation by simultaneous stigmatization. The BJP has indeed swung from militancy to moderation. An earlier phase of moderation had culminated in the merger of the Bharatiya Jan Sangh, BJP's former namesake, in the Janata Party in 1977. "(T) he real challenge before Janata", writes Rajni Kothari, "was to bring the Jan Sangh within the democratic framework just as the Communists had been under Nehru."[12]

As a result of religious fundamentalism, nonetheless, the secular state in India has come under tremendous strain. However, the future of secular state in this country should never be in doubt. This is so not only because of the millennial tradition of "high tolerance and low integration" in the Indian society[13] but also because both secular and religious nationalists have stake in the multicultural secular state, which is the only viable framework for civilized well-being and national unity[14]. Again, the immense possibilities of pluralist and federal politics in India are unfolding in electoral politics and coalition/

minority Governments that tend to promote secular politics. Another point also needs emphasis. Despite their calls for Hindu and Sikh hegemonies (*dharma's* supremacy and Khalsa's *bolbala*),[15] neither the BJP nor the Akali Dal has ever demanded the abolition of the secular state in India. BJP leaders have ridiculed what they derisively call "minorityism" of the secular parties[16], but their call for "positive secularism"[17] does not jettison the secular ideal *in toto*. The increasing levels of conflict in the Indian society and polity, coupled with insufficient integration of regional sub-cultures with the mainstream, mean that the principle of supremacy of the Constitution would move to the centre-stage in the years ahead. The principle of parliamentary supremacy was already modified in the Constitution on account of India's effort to combine it with federalism and judicial review. The processes of secularization and political reconciliation would be greatly helped if it becomes a constitutional convention that the Supreme Court verdict in religious matters would not be sought to be overridden by the executive and the Parliament (as it was done by the Rajiv Gandhi regime in the Shah Bano case) without an all-party consensus behind the parliamentary majority. This needs to be incorporated into the Republic's Constitution. And secularism needs to be reoriented as multiculturalism.

NOTES

1. Achin Vanaik, *The Painful Transition: Bourgeois Democracy in India,* Verso, London, 1990, pp. 171-2.
2. Aijaz Ahmad, "Radicalism of the Right and Logics of Secularism", in Praful Bidwai, Harbans Mukhia and Achin Vanaik (Eds.), *Religion, Religiosity and Communalism,* Manohar, New Delhi, 1996.
3. Benedict Anderson, *op. cit.,* theorizes the origins and evolution of nationalism as a modern phenomenon largely produced by print (media) capitalism and democracy. This theory—somewhat oversimplified—can also explain the Indian case.
4. Bharatiya Janta Party (BJP): *Election Manifesto, Lok Sabha Elections 1989,* Central Office, New Delhi, 1989, p. 7.
5. Donald E. Smith, *India as a Secular State*, Princeton University Press, Princeton, 1966.
6. *Ibid.*
7. Jaffrelot Christophe, *The Hindu Nationalist Movement and Indian Politics 1952 to the 1990s* Viking-Penguin India, New Delhi, 1996, p. 529.
8. L.K. Advani, *"Fallouts of Minoritysm"* in M.M. Shankhdher & K.K.

Wadhwa (Eds.), *National Unity and Religious Minorities,* Gitanjali, New Delhi, 1991.

9. M.P. Singh, "Ideological Spectrum of Indian Party System: A Middling Pattern with Persisting Multipolarity" in M.P. Singh & Rekha Saxena (Eds.), *India's Political Agenda: Perspectives on the Party System,* Kalinga, Delhi, 1996.
10. M.P. Singh, "Whither Indian Pluralism", in Urmila Phadnis (Ed.), *Domestic Conflicts in South Asia, Vol. I, Political Dimensions,* South Asia Publishers, New Delhi, 1986.
11. Rajiv Bhargava, "The Secular Imperative" in M.P. Singh & Rekha Saxena (guest-editor for this volume) in *Political Science Annual* 1997 edited by Subrata Mukherjee & Sushila Ramaswamy, Deep & Deep, New Delhi, 1998.
12. Rajni Kothari, "The Problem", Special Issue on the 1984 General Elections, *Seminar,* No. 306, February 1985.
13. Rajni Kothari, "Towards a Politics of Intervention", in his *Politics and the People: In Search of a Humane India,* Ajanta, Delhi, 1990. Harish Puri, "The Akali Agitation: An Analysis of Socio-Economic Basis of Protest", *Economic and Political Weekly,* Vol. XVIII, No. 4, 22nd January, 1983.
14. Rajni Kothari, "Towards Intervention", *Seminar,* New Delhi, No. 269, January 1982, p. 23.
15. Rudolph, Lloyd and Susanne Rudolph, "Confessional Politics, Secularism and Centrism in India", in J.W. Bjorkman (Ed.), *Fundamentalism, Revivalists and Violence in South Asia,* Manohar, New Delhi, 1988.
16. S.C. Dube and V.N. Basilov (Eds.), *Secularization in Multi-Religious Societies: Indo-Soviet Perspectives,* Concept Publishing Company for ICSSR, New Delhi, 1983.
17. Supreme Court, *S.R. Bommai & Others* vs. *Union of India & Others, Judgements Today,* Vol. 2, No. 8, March 1994.

8

Prospects of Secular Society in India : Looking for a Subaltern Avenue . . .

G. Patrick

Secularism in a Post-Secular World ?

A section of western social theorists, especially from the North American context, have begun to speak about emergence of a post-secular world today.[1] The world, at least the western world, is turning out to be post-secular, they argue, not due to any maturation or saturation of the secular or the process of secularisation,[2] but precisely due to its failure.[3] They believe that the classic secularisation thesis implied in the works of a proto-sociologist like Karl Marx, or in those of the masters of sociological thought like Auguste Comte, Herbert Spencer, Emile Durkheim, Max Weber[4], Sigmund Freud, etc., that "as modernisation progressed, religion increasingly became privatised and ultimately faded away" has miserably failed. They instead point to a "resurgence of religion" or as Peter Berger would put it a "desecularisation"[5] taking place during the contemporary era of advanced modernisation, known in different names as post-modern, late-modern, liquid modern,[6] etc. Harvey Cox who spoke about the *Secular City*,[7] makes a reversal and speaks today about *Fire from Heaven*,[8] Jose Casanova, a leading sociologist of religion, dwells upon "deprivatisation" and emergence of "public religion" today.[9] They base their arguments on the thick presence of religion not only in individual's personal life but in public sphere as well, with the facility provided by the advanced Information and Communication technology. They also point to the emergence today of *New Age Religions / Spiritualities / Movements* as witness to the dismaying of the secular and the return of the religious.[10] While these phenomena are more or less positively premised, we also find the emergence and public dominance of such phenomena as religious fundamentalism and communalism, which are negatively oriented. In any case, religion has come to occupy the public space quite consequentially.

A question then comes to our mind: Are we not on an anachronistic project in endeavouring to make of a secular society? Are we not engaged in something with a mistaken notion of its relevance?

The questions prod us to take a more concerted look at the debate on the secular or the process of secularisation. We find that there are other social theorists, from the same western context, who take a more nuanced look at the reality and observe that "resurgence of religion" is not, pure and simple, an indicator of the failure of the secular; but an expression of the contemporary transformations wherein secularisation as much as religion adapt to newer conditions of life. For example, Pippa Norris and Ronald Inglehart, based on a huge survey covering 80 nations across the world, argue that "rich societies are becoming more secular but the world as a whole is becoming more religious".[11] They opine that the sense of security an individual acquires right from his/her formative years is a vital ingredient in making or unmaking his/her secular outlook. Charles Taylor, another prominent social theorist, speaks about a new "condition of belief" in which believing becomes one of the strong possibilities for a "buffered" self, which, unlike the "porous" self of the traditional era, has capacitated itself with such abilities as faith, knowledge, instrumental rationality, and so on.[12] Taking cue from Charles Taylor, Jose Casanova and others speak of a *secular immanent frame* to denote the fact of the secular vision or approach becoming an embedded frame of vision, without, however, obstructing the practice of religion in the practical empirical realm.[13] Interestingly and paradoxically though, Gianni Vattimo, a post-modern votary of Christianity, claims that secularisation is the very process, a process of kenosis, by which religion, Christianity in particular, is becoming relevant and meaningful today.[14]

Neither the secularisation nor the resurgence theses seem to apply to the Indian context in the same manner in which they apply to the west.[15] Indian sub-continent and the countries of South Asia have not undergone a process of "secularisation" as it took place in the west under the aegis of industrialisation, modernisation, rationalisation and urbanisation. The process of modernisation did not weaken the practice of religion in the public sphere, and neither did it produce as strong a secular outlook or a wall of separation as it occurred in the west. The Indian public sphere, and the everyday life-context—the Habermasian "life-world" of the people, remained and remains symbiotically integrated with the practice of religion. It would be more factual to say that India, due to the impact of globalisation, is witnessing an accentuated practice of religion in a new mode. It is experiencing, with the facility of Information and Communication Technologies, an invigorated practice of religion, in an ever-growing *reflexive* mode of religious consciousness.[16]

We are then witnessing two simultaneous developments, apparently paradoxical: Institutions of public character—education, medicine, politics, health and medicine, etc., are increasingly growing independent of religion on the one hand, and, on the other, religion is increasing becoming a public phenomenon. As Peter Beyer, a leading theorist of religion of the global era, proposes, religions are changing their roles from "functions" to "performance", i.e., from traditional religious functions involved in mediating salvation and grace to making a contribution to other societal sub-systems like economy, society, politics, etc.[17] He cites the development of liberation theology in Christiánity as one of the good examples of his theory of performance.

In the Indian context, religion, among other things, is turning out to be a powerful identity-marker in today's context. Needham and Sundar Rajan point out that, "[R]eligion's role in the modern world has been vastly reconstituted, so much so that religious debates and conflicts are no longer primarily waged over matters of belief, the true god, salvation, or other substantive issues of faith, as they once were; it is instead religion as the basis of *identity* and identitarian cultural practices—with co-religionists constituting a community, nation, or "civilization...".[18] We in India, or South Asia, are witness to the currents of identity politics, wherein religion serves as a very potent resource in the process of politicisation.[19]

It is, therefore, not a failure of secularisation pure and simple, but a context-specific transformation, involving religion and secular modernisation in a differential manner. This very transformation is sufficient ground for pursuing an exploration of it in today's world, and especially in our Indian context. Our concern of exploration is not so much on the sociological process of transformation in a disinterested manner; but on secularism and secularisation as values for us today. What is the prospect of the secular/secularism/secularisation in terms of empowerment of the subalterns of this country?—is our preferential question. The secular state in India, for some, came with opportunities, but for the lowly (including the minorities), it came with a promise. It came with a promise of real freedom (of conscience, of religion, etc.), of social dignity, of removal of structures of age-old oppressions, and of alleviation of systemic poverty and exclusion from socio-economic opportunities. The secular came not merely as a modernising process, but also as a catalytic agent of empowering transformation. What happens to that promise? A look at the secular with these questions is, then, the primary focus of this exploration.

This essay has three parts: first part takes a look at some salient ingredients of Indian secularism; second dwells upon the contemporary debate; and, third probes the possibility of a subaltern approach to secularism.

Contours of the Secular in India

It would do well to briefly take a look at some of the salient ingredients that went into the making of Indian secularism at its initial phase.

Secular Propensities of the Subcontinent

Indian subcontinent, even in its pre-modern context, had features which evinced secular potentials. Following are some among them:

1. Indian subcontinent had teachers of Lokayata and Charvaka who philosophised upon the well-being of this world, opposing other-worldly religiosity. Most important of all, we have the non-transcendental shramanic religious traditions (Jainism, Buddhism, Ajivakam, etc.) emergent and vigorously operative throughout the subcontinent for about a millennium, and then became one of the subterraneous components of our religious oeuvre. History is marked with their regional variations across the regions. The Dravidian South had a specific type of religiosity (whose traces are found in *Sangam* literatures) which was uniquely characterised by humanistic traditions centring round *akam* (internal world marked by love, family, etc.) and *puram* (external world

marked by war, conquest, etc.) corresponding to the five landscapes (*Inthinnaikal*).

2. Religion in the Indian subcontinent was, as pointed out by Romila Thapar and others, performing a down to earth societal function, often times involved in negotiations between different social groups for their social status.[20] Though this has its dark side of legitimising social hierarchies, it can serve to show that religions here had a strongly this-worldly character. These religious traditions (beliefs and practices) very rarely made a distinction between sacred and secular along the line of platonic soul-body dualism.
3. *Embodied Religiosity*: The innumerable cults surrounding male and female deities considered the body as the medium of religious experience, as evident in the shamanic practices. The body was not domesticated or treated as polluting. This primary datum of religious experience deterred the development of a separate class of people known as 'sacred' as against 'profane' or 'religious' as against 'secular'. (The development of a priestly class in India, the brahmanic class, relied less on treating the human body *per se* as impure than treating the bodies of labouring class of people as impure.)
4. There was an absence of anyone absolutist imperial religious universe, holding sway over the entire subcontinent. Perhaps the tradition that came closer to such universal claim was the Sanskritic religious universe, which was spread through the length and breadth of this continent through the active agency of princely states[21] and itinerant religious personnel. However, this was resisted by regional and counter religious traditions, and so it stood relativised.
5. Diversity and religious disputes, born of the disputative and 'democratic' impulse of Indian psyche, as argued by Amartya Sen, remained a strong feature of the religious terrain of the Indian subcontinent.[22] This feature can well be said to serve as the bulwark of Indian variant of secularism.

These were/are some of the salient secular propensities present primarily at the grassroots of the Indian society. Apart from these, we can also note the presence of open and pluralistic outlook among some rulers of this subcontinent. We have examples of Ashoka, Akbar, etc., who evince openness and sense of equality of traditions. In addition to these emperors, we also find several local kings or chieftains who exhibited great sense of appreciation and accommodation towards other religious traditions, by donating lands or building religious worship centres or instituting endowments, etc., for people of religions other than their own. (This is not to deny the prevalence of religion-related violence during the pre-modern era. Religious clashes, however, remained confined to the circle of religious leadership. It is only now we see the people being mobilised for religious violence.)

Western Stirrings...

As we all know, the western stirrings of modernity and secularism were mediated through the colonial dispensations. Their initial contributions should be traced back to the time of introduction of print culture in India. Though printed material was introduced during the sixteenth century itself, printed literature was available to the wider public only by the eighteenth century. Initial printed material was, as elsewhere, religious scriptures or classics. Paradoxically though, this was the beginning of the emergence of a secular public sphere. As opined by Dilip Menon, "The missionary journals democratised access to a literate sphere of debate and knowledge, and also provided an alternative sphere of reflection on self and society." (Menon, 13) Public debates, though on religion, began to constitute a public sphere.[23] It was in sharp contrast to religious orations that took place within precincts of temples, wherein sections of people were not allowed and, therefore, remained systemically paralysed from shaping up to be public spheres. Soon enough such secular materials as linguistic commentaries, grammars, translations of Indian classics into European languages, anthropological commentaries, and the like began to circulate. Innovative popular literary genres, like for example, the novel, appeared on the scene. Emergence of such literatures engendered good public debates, and began to create a public sphere, a free space, away from the control of political rulers. The kind of public debate Caldwell's *A Comparative Grammar of Dravidian Languages* created is a case in point. Contributions of the Orientalists and the Vernacularists in coming up with reading materials for the public is yet another milestone in the development of a public debates, which was different from royal court debates and temple-centred discourses.[24]

Another significant western stirring came in the form of introduction of the western style 'modern' education. In a context wherein education, restricted to a privileged few, was imparted in esoteric 'sacred' languages, it came to be available in a secular language, and that too in modern subjects like mathematics, history, philosophy, literature, etc., to a wider public. Due to this process, a certain massification and democratisation took place, which broke the exclusive monopoly of the ritual hierarchy upon education. This was a milestone in the development of a secular subterraneous layer for India. Though the immediate beneficiaries happened to be the *bhadralok* type of people, who came to constitute the middle class of India, it indeed was the beginning of democratising the educational sphere, nay, the civil sphere as well. In a cascading effect, other strata of the Indian society too began to participate in modern education during subsequent phases. It was then a step-by-step progressive incorporation of the wider public into the secular sphere.

In due course of the colonial intervention, several factors as mass education, urbanisation, industrialisation, competitive market, etc., came to induce a mass mobilisation among the people, and that ensued in a course of assertion by subaltern sections of people. A current of interrogation of the religiously sanctioned caste-system set in and it was manifest in varieties of 'transitional' and 'acculturative' socio-religious movements, as explored by Stephen Fuchs, Kenneth Jones and others,[25] that emerged during the nineteenth and twentieth centuries. These were people's movements which put forward, in religious idioms, the case for social equality, economic parity, cultural autonomy, and political liberty. They had the unique distinction of having a religious form, with secular contents. To the extent they succeeded, depending on the context, to that extent, they advanced certain important ingredients of modern secularism too. They came up with a religious language of dissent, whose implications were primarily social, economic and political. Resisting the operation of a certain hegemonic tradition, contesting its supremacy, and weakening its forces were the dynamics with which the socio-religious movements operated. In and through them, the Indian subalternity got enlivened, and began to gradually enter into the public sphere. It is revealing to note that Ambedkar, a vanguard intellectual for the emancipation of *dalits*, began his struggle through the 'secular' constitutional medium, but finally, almost losing hope with that, took recourse to a religious medium.

Capitalist Modernisation

Capitalist modernisation was an important ingredient in the making of secularism. It was introduced to India with the joint ventures of the East India Company initially and subsequently the British Empire on the one hand, and the Indian propertied class of people, like the feudal lords, on the other. The colonial dispensation brought a capitalism that had enveloped itself in the liberal democratic thought of the west, the Enlightenment values being its predominant constituent. This capitalist modernisation, with its liberal political economy, depended on a rational common public sphere for its operation. In an important way, it was this need that was at the heart of the 'modern secular' political dispensation in India. The capitalist market needed a 'secular' morality, independent of the religious moralities of different religious communities of India.[26] As Himanshu Roy notes: "The notion of secularism was primarily an offshoot of market morality that began to unfold as capitalism progressively expanded. It was premised on the necessity of individual freedom required for manoeuvre in the market, that would not be hampered by one's religion, nor would religion obstruct the functioning of the market". (Roy, p. 158)

Modernisation of India was indispensable both to the British and the Indian capitalists; perhaps more so for the Indians who ardently welcomed the modernising process for India. This class of Indians, primarily the Indian elites, were so enamoured of the prospects of capitalist modernisation that they wished for the removal of any obstacle in the name of religion, community, and the like. For them, secularism came as a worthy instrument to wade through the messy religious and cultural world. As pointed out by Nivedita Menon, secularism was the "term that (had) has stood in for the entire modernizing project of the Indian elites..." (130) and this project "intimately tied secularism to a notion of 'development' that (was) is predicated on the large-scale sacrifice of sectional interests in the greater interest of the Indian citizen..." (Nivedita Menon, 131)

Early Indian Nationalism

It was within this framework of the capitalist modernisation process, Indian nationalism took shape and arose as an ideology of modern state making. The pioneering Indian nationalists were persons who had been imbued with a modern vision of state for India, without however getting 'denationalised' from their traditions. Modernity and tradition converged differentially, and produced various strands in nationalism. It may well be surmised that the so-called Indian variant of secularism too emerged depending on the way modernity and tradition cohered differentially in the modern makers of India.

Scholars point out to at least two groups of Indians, who faced up to modernity either by reforming or defending the Indian traditions. They were also the forerunners of Indian nationalism and secularism. One group, represented by such persons as Raja Rammohun Roy, Keshab Chandra Sen and their Brahmo Samaj, was appreciative of the liberal modernity of the west and looked up to it to reform India, especially of its obscurantist practices like *Sati*, slavery, child-marriage, etc. Raja Rammohun Roy said, "the greater our intercourse with the European gentleman, the greater will be our improvement in literary, social and political affairs." (Roy, H. 160). Keshab Chandra Sen seems to have said in London (1870) in a speech that "your philosophy is ours, 'we are your thought', 'we are intellectually united' " (Roy, H. 160). Such was the manner in which this group had been impressed by the liberal modernity. This group, as in the words of Roy, "supported the religious neutrality of the colonial state but also sought its intervention in religious reforms as part of the modernising project of the country". (H. Roy, 160)

The other group was represented by persons, who, being challenged by the liberal modernity of the west as well as of the missionary rhetoric, took an aggressive posture towards it and worked towards preserving the Indian traditions, by cleansing or purifying them. Dayananda Saraswathi's Arya Samaj was the vanguard institution of this trend. A little later, there were also others like Sri Aurobindo and Vivekananda who sought to combine the Vedantic traditions and the western modernity and presented a 'Hinduism' of universal appeal as an alternative to the material west. This group was "for religion playing a public role as communicator and mobiliser. It was to be religion that was rational bereft of unnecessary rituals and orthodoxy . . . They believed in individual religious freedom and believed that religious worship was concern of the individual who cannot be forced upon for unitary path either by community or state". (H. Roy, 160)

These were the two dominant 'Neo-Hindu' trends within which the Indian National Movement took shape. We also had the modernising group within Islam, centring around Sir Sayyad Ahmad and his Aligarh movement, which sought to make the Muslim youth to benefit out of the English education and the reformist modernity. Persons emerging from this movement too became significant contributors to the Indian National Movement. All these trends, in the estimation of Gerald James Larson, finally converged into the Indian National Movement.[27]

These early nationalist streams, as observed above, also laid the basic framework for Indian secularism. Generally, they all stood for the freedom of the individual as regards his/her religion, and wanted the state to be neutral to different religious communities, even while protecting community rights.

Gandhi and Nehru

As we all know, Gandhi and Nehru were two stalwarts in the making of a secular nation. Gandhi was known for his religiosity, and for his religious egalitarianism rendered in the words of *sarva dharma samabhava*. Gandhi expressed himself and his vision for this country very much in religious idiom. He considered the practice of Truth as his religion, and took this religious value to be the ultimate goal of any human being and also of any political pursuit. He is known for his statement, "those who say that religion has nothing to do with politics, know neither what religion is nor what politics is". Politics for him was religion, and religion was politics. His political mobilisation under the religious ideal of *Ramrajya* was propelled by his integrated understanding of religion and politics. As in the words of Gerald James Larson, "his aim was the religious regeneration of India and Indians". (192) He imagined the Indian nation to be one where religious values sustained the practice of politics. He welcomed the presence of religion in the public sphere too. However, when it came to the necessity of keeping the country united, he looked for the viability of religious co-existence and wanted the state to be neutral to all religions.

While this account is true from one angle, as Larson states, "[H]is was a thoroughly Neo-Hindu reformist and nationalist vision, influenced by the older Neo-Hindu traditions . . . but influenced also by English education, liberal democratic ideas, enlightenment rationalism, liberal humanism, socialist ideology, the practice of parliamentary democracy..." (Gerald James Larson, 193). When he came over to India to lead the Indian National Movement, he was faced with the dire need of mobilising the masses against the colonisers. And as Larson puts it, "he could not in his time have become the political leader of the majority group in India, fortified by mass support, without being religious, he could not be religious without being Hindu . . . " (192).

Nehru, the maker of modern India, was for neutrality of state to all religions. However, his secular stance was less characterised by a positive estimation of religions. It was more informed by the western Enlightenment 'prejudice' that all religions would one day fade away. However, Nehru stated that: "A secular state does not mean an irreligious state: it only means that we respect and honour all religions giving them freedom to function". (Ronojoy Sen, xxiv) On another occasion, Nehru defined a secular state as one where there is 'free play for all religions, subject only to their not interfering with each other or with the basic conceptions of our state." (Ronojoy Sen, xxiv) Nehru's state secularism was perhaps impregnated with the hope that the country needed to be economically developed, in which no religious or cultural hurdle should impede. Like Gandhi, Nehru too embodied the aspirations of the Indian bourgeois class which wanted to modernise and develop India.

Ambedkar and E. V. Ramasamy

Ambedkar was also a product of western liberal modernity. However, it is quite revealing to see how his secular vision for the country differed from Gandhi and Nehru. While the latter emphasised the *sarva dharma samabava* ideal, Ambedkar considered the emancipation of 'untouchables' from the 'Hindu' religion as of primary importance, because he thought that the sufferings of the untouchables were the "result of the cold calculating Hinduism". (6) He looked up to the modern secular state, whose constitution he was involved in framing, to perform this task. Therefore, he demanded affirmative actions from the state for the 'untouchables'. A western liberal secular state, he knew would not permit this. But he envisaged the secular state in India as radically different, because of its different history. He looked for the freedom of the country, primarily to address the problem of the 'untouchables'. In his own words: "If there is any cause of freedom in this Indian turmoil for independence it is the cause of the Untouchables. The cause of the Hindus and the cause of the Mussalmans is not the cause of freedom. Theirs is a struggle for power as distinguished from freedom". (6) He considered the Congress, the vanguard of the Indian National Movement, as "a body of middle class Hindus supported by the Hindu Capitalists whose object is not to make Indians free but to be independent of British control and to occupy places of power now occupied by the British". (6) Ambedkar, therefore, had less faith in the Congress or its leaders like Gandhi,[28] but relied heavily on the secular state of India to achieve emancipation for the 'untouchables'.

However, when Ambedkar realised that the secular State too was not achieving what it could, he looked for a religion that would provide an egalitarian ethics for the emancipation of the 'untouchables'. He thought, as surmised by Shabnum Tejani, that "as long as the secular State was dominated by caste Hindus, Dalits would never be able to secure their dignity and human rights..." (Shabnum Tejani, 61) He, therefore, found in Buddhism, "the potential for what social and political reform had failed to provide." (61) Ambedkar's interest in Buddhism was, as Tejani states, "preeminantly secular, focused on the provision of an ethics of Dalit emancipation." (62-63). He, thus, considered religion to be a positive player in the secular society to achieve emancipatory ends. He did not consider its public presence as anti-secular.

While Ambedkar was active in central India,[29] we had another powerful person, namely E.V. Ramasamy, involved in a thorough critique of religion for the cause of emancipation of the subalterns from caste oppression. He found 'rational critique' to be a powerful instrument to achieve this. He also comprehended that there was an unholy nexus between religion and caste oppression. Therefore, he sought to liberate the people from caste oppression by undertaking a ruthless critique of religion. Interestingly, he wanted the secular state to ensure the freedom to freely critique and challenge religious faith, instead of being preoccupied with the maintenance of tolerance, co-existence, etc. His vision of a secular State is one which was a rational public sphere where dissent and disputes even on religious matters would take place. Paula Richman and V. Geetha make a relevant point on E.V. Ramasamy's contribution:

> Ramasamy's political practice, his commitment to enhancing dissent that would counter collision between religion and state, his faith in the value of submitting all issues to discerning examination—all these remain useful contributions to civic debate. He sought for himself the right

> to disagree with matters of religious belief and likewise extended this right to all. He had great trust in conversations and polemic, and in fact the grand historical success of his movement lay in this—that he did not seek to vanquish his opponents but to engage them in arguments." (Paula Richman and V. Geetha, *Crisis of Secularism,* 85)

It may reasonably be surmised that E.V. Ramasamy's contribution has a lasting impact until this day. There are political parties vying with each other to share his legacy in order to mobilise the people politically. And his influence is still to be seen in the kind of inability communal parties are facing in Tamil Nadu relative to their easy success in northern regions. Thus, we see that Ambedkar and E.V. Ramasamy introduce a different approach to the understanding of the secular state and secularism.

Constitutional Enshrinement

The Indian constitutional enshrinement of secularism is something unique. Though it did not carry the word 'secular' right from its inception,[30] it embodied a secular vision, which was introduced into it by the modernising Indian leaders of the Indian National Movement. It was a vision born at the interjection of the specific Indian socio-cultural ethos with the Enlightenment English modernity. It had taken in several features from western constitutions, especially from that of America, but it sought to stay within its own roots. As Ronojoy Sen writes, "... the Indian Constitution [was] were greatly influenced by the American Constitution. However, on the issue of religion, the Indian Constitution is significantly different from the American one, as indeed from European models."[31]

Constitution of India delicately combined the rights of the individual and of the community. It stoutly stood for the autonomy and freedom of the individual as regards his/her right to religion, even while providing for the cultural rights of the minorities. The constitutional provisions undertake to protect the religious practice of every individual to the extent of 'practice, profess, and propagate' [Art. 25 (1)]. However, it also provides the right to the state to intervene not merely in terms of law, order and public morality, but also in view of reforming the religious space [Art. 25, (2) b], . . . *providing for social welfare and reform or the throwing open of Hindu religious institutions of a public character to all classes and sections of Hindus*]. This is something of a challenging and trying clause in the Constitution. The state takes a distance from the religious right, provides guarantee for the free practice of religion, and it also intervenes to prevent misuses. In a way, it promises to do what no other modern Constitution undertakes to do.

In the post-independent phase, the state has generally conducted itself with a rather fair sense of secularism. However, it has also unduly intervened in several cases which were beyond its purview. The case of a few regional States passing Anti-Conversion Laws to prevent conversion undertaken due to 'fraud and deceit' is a case in point. Trying to protect the citizens from fraud and deceit, though a very moral goal, is laden with serious difficulties, the very first one being the hypocrisy involved in not being able to implicate corrupt politicians who thrive on fraud and deceit while targeting the ordinary citizens on their cultural rights.

As we see from this foregoing brief account, we see a variety of factors and orientations converging into the making of Indian secularism.[32] A keen observer would note that majority of these orientations have been from the perspective of the modernising elites of our country. What Gerald James Larson points out is relevant here: "All of these traditions, it should be noted, except for Ambedkar's Neo-Buddhist movement, which does not get started, in any case, until nearly a decade after partition, were thoroughly elitist, involving not more than 2 to 3 per cent of the general population, who were overwhelmingly from the 'forward castes' (among the Neo-Hindu groups) or high-status Muslim families (among the Neo-Muslims), English-educated and English-speaking, and largely urban-based professionals (in such new fields as government service and administration, law, education, journalism, and so forth)."[33]

Contemporary Debates

The way secularism is being practiced today in India has raised heated debate and discussion about its nature and future possibility. It would do well to take a brief look at some of the salient points of the debate.

The Pseudo-Secularism Argument

Today we are aware of the forces which hold a completely negative stance towards the present-day secularism and seriously question and attempt to overthrow the secularism embedded in the Constitution, judiciary, state bureaucracy, legislature and institutions of civil society. The *Hindutva* forces brand the present-day secularism as 'pseudo-secularism' and call for revamping of the Constitution, primarily for its 'double talk' on secularism. They argue that the Constitution, while holding on to universal citizenship rights, unnecessarily tampers with it by entering into a course of concessions for minority religionists, which amount to violation of the universal rights of the citizen. And they accuse the Congress primarily for their 'trivialising' the concept of secularism. Cases like the Shah Bano ones are quoted to argue that the Congress is out to appease the minorities, and to make a travesty of secularism. Instead, they propose a religio-cultural and ethical common ground, *Hindutva* by name, to be a vision of equality of all religions, and to be the 'secular foundation' for our country.

Votaries of this proposition claim that Indian ethos is ruled by the belief in an eternal *dharma*. Vajpayee, former PM of our country, paraphrases this *dharma* as:

> The moral and material well-being of the people can be ensured by the state by acting according to *dharma* . . . *dharma* is the ensemble of the rules and regulations followed in various facets of human life of an individual and the society as a whole . . . *dharma* allows freedom of thought and faith but as long as you are following your *Dharma* or act according to your *dharma*, you are on the right track . . . *dharma* essentially means *karma* or duty. Anyone who ignores his duty i.e. *karma* cannot follow his *dharma*..."[34]

Critique: That the secular Constitution cannot have special provisions for minorities is not tenable especially in today's context of increasing awareness on the cultural rights embodied in community rights. These rights obtain significance, as the world is increasingly becoming multi-cultural, multi-ethnic, multi-linguistic, and so on. Even from a liberal theory, which usually privileges the right of an individual than that of a community, Will Kymlica argues forcefully for the cultural rights of the community by way of doing justice to minorities.[35] Charles Taylor, in his *Sources of the Self,* finds a sound reason for providing rights to the community, because an individual self is constituted with the resources of the culture, which cannot be there without a community. Moreover, the argument of Ronald

Dworkin, a political theorist, that there is a difference between 'equal treatment and treating everyone equally'[36] is a sound reasoning for providing community rights.

Again, the ideal of *dharma*, as long as it is a transcendent ideal, it could serve as a substantive ground for cultivating the Indian variant of secularism. However, when it is found to be legitimising a social practice of discrimination based on ascriptive status and duty, it falls short of being an ideal. As Romila Thapar points out, this *dharma* "referred to the social obligations and ritual duties which had to be performed in accordance with one's *varna* and *jati* and the sect to which one belonged. The duties differed in accordance with caste status. Conforming to *dharma* demarcated the upper castes from the lower . . . " (Thapar, 1999, 13) While this *dharma* had a covert referral to a hierarchical social system, its proponents began to present it as a universal ideal in a historical contingency. Dilip Menon explains this contingency as follows:

> In the face of colonial interventions in Hinduism (as in the anti-*sati* legislation) as well as the Christian polemic, public defence of Hinduism began to lay stress on its timeless character—a *Sanatana Dharma* beyond caste, creed and history. Religion was seen as the one factor that bound the Hindus together, for ruling dynasties had come and gone, while Hindu *dharma* was eternal. Thus, the Christian polemic against the inegalitarianism of Hinduism led to a closing of ranks around a revivified, all-inclusive high Hinduism forgetful of hierarchy. . . (Dilip Menon, 11-12)

Sceptical Positions...

There are a few critics today who find the present day secularism inadequate and impotent and even playing truant in today's context. It would do well to take a look at one or two of their representatives.

T.N. Madan: Secularism as Impotent

T.N. Madan, one of the sceptics, faults the present day Indian secularism as inadequate and impotent. In his words: "I believe that in the prevailing circumstances secularism in South Asia as a generally shared credo of life is impossible, as a basis for state action impracticable, and as a blueprint for the foreseeable future impotent." (298) According to him, this secularism is an import from the Christian west, and does not suit the ethos not merely of India, but of the whole of South Asia. This secularism, according to him, denies the role and significance of religion in the lives of the people, and, therefore, goes against the very grain of Indian ethos.

Instead of the present day 'impotent' secularism, Madan looks for a secularism which would be understood as interreligious understanding. It is this secularism which would, according to him, take religions as well as the responsibility of forging interreligious relationship seriously.

Critique: T.N. Madan, in my opinion, conflates his antipathy to the western (treated as Christian?) dimensions of secularism with the prevailing Indian variant of secularism. His critique of the present-day secularism is not as something that is being *practised* in the Indian context, but as something of an ideology, imported from the west and continues to remain 'unchangeable'. He does not seem to appreciate the specific character Indian secularism has obtained through the unique intermingling of the western and the Indian features.

Ashis Nandy: Modern Secularism's Hegemony and Recovery of Tolerance

Ashis Nandy, yet another fashionable sceptic, distinguishes between religion as way of life and as ideology, and accuses the present day secularism of treating every religious expression or practice as an ideology, and intending to separate it from politics. In so doing, this secularism, having been imported from the west, purports to establish the hegemony of the state, legitimising it under the labels of progress and development, which are but aberrations of the now failing western modernity. In his words, "[T]o accept the ideology of secularism is to accept the ideologies of progress and modernity as the new justifications of domination and the use of violence to sustain these ideologics as the new opiates of the masses." (S&C, 343) So, for him, it is secularism which is the culprit of the religious clashes and violence. It is so because, as he says, "[M]uch of the fanaticism and violence associated with religion comes today from the sense of defeat of the believers, from their feelings of impotency, and from their free-floating anger and self-hatred while facing a world which is increasingly secular and desacralized" (332). The way out, according to him, is to retrieve the pre-modern religious tolerance that was inbuilt into the way of life of the people in the Indian context.

Critique: The pre-modern native 'way of life, with its inbuilt tolerance' sounds highly romantic. It is quite unclear as to which 'way of life' he is referring to. The pre-modern context in India was never free of conflict—neither free of religious antagonism, nor of socio-economic conflicts. Religiously it was informed of conflicts between Vedic and shramanic traditions; between *Vaishnavites* and *Shaivites*; and even within *Vaishnavism* and *saivism*. Socially, the pre-modern context was deeply ridden with cleavages on the basis of purity-pollution rules of the caste system. Economically, it was an unassailable feudal situation which thrived on the labour of the slave-serf class of people. In such an overtly and covertly conflict ridden society, where does Nandy find a 'tolerant' way of life is not clear. It is very difficult to refute Paul Brass when he says, "[N]or can I understand how a religion such as Hinduism, based in its very essence on principles of hierarchy, discrimination, ritual pollution, and outcasting, has come to be seen as the epitome of tolerance." (Brass, 1999, 364-365)[37] Again, faulting secularism for today's religious violence is a very superficial argument, to which Thapar responds aptly: "it is less the attempt to marginalize religion through secularism that has strengthened religious fundamentalism and more the impact of globalization and concessions to dictatorial political authority that has led to a parochial retreat into religion in many parts of the world". (Thapar, 2007, 85)

The Left Camp

The Left democratic parties in India, as elsewhere, consider secularism as a bulwark of democracy and they promote it in and through their political praxis. Their understanding of secularism is born of the Enlightenment modernity combined with the Marxist approach to religion. Though they have an indifferent attitude to the role of religion in the lives of the people, they take care to protect the freedom of religion of any individual or community. They show special effort to protect the religious minorities from the onslaught of majoritarian politics. In the Indian context, they consider the *Hindutva* communal forces as well as the Muslim fundamentalist forces as enemies of democracy and secularism. As Sitaram Yetchury opines, "both the Hindu communalist offensive and the Muslim fundamentalist response today constitute a frontal assault on the very independence and sovereignty based on a secular democratic polity that defines modern India."

(Yetchury, 7). Both these forces, according to him, do not represent genuine religious aspirations of the people, but only are perpetuated for political purpose. The left party critiques the Congress as a bourgeois party which uses both communalism and fundamentalism for its own advantage.

Critique: The political mobilisation of people against communalism and fundamentalism being undertaken by the Left forces is a sure commitment to safeguard secularism in our country. It is also a fact that communal incidents have been very minimal in States ruled by the Left. However, it is also a critique on them that the Indian Left has not adapted its approach to religion contextually. H. Roy complains that " . . . the communist in India could not transcend the bourgeois paradigm either in their political demands or in their philosophical discourse except for citing repetitively the textual contents of Marx." (H. Roy, 162) It applies the same principle very dogmatically in all the countries. Religious resources are not counted as possible resources for the emancipation of people. This dogmatic stance might not allow them to look into the positive energies of religion, which can be a good ally for liberation.

Liberal Democracy (Rajeev Bhargava : Secularism as Political Ethic of 'Principled Distance')

Rajeev Bhargava, a votary of liberal democracy, dwells in detail through several of his publications, upon the promise of secular democracy in our country. (Rajeev Bhargava, 2010, xxv). He opines that secularism is under attack today, not because it has failed, but because it has succeeded to a large extent in our country. He says the critics have not understood the specific character of Indian secularism, which, according to him, is not a neat and simple import from the west. Indian secularism showed its uniqueness in undertaking to wrestle with the tension to emerge due to the way it has combined the individual and community rights and to the way it has distanced itself from the affairs of particular religions but at the same time kept the right to intervene for reform.[38] This version of secularism, he calls as 'contextual political secularism' with its own ethics of 'principled distance'[39] of the state from religions. It is not a mechanistic separation of state from religion, but a principled distance, which operates in accordance with the particular case in question. As he says, "the secularity of the state does not necessitate intervention, non-interference, or equidistance but rather any or all of these, as the case may be". (28) This principled distancing differs from the principle of neutrality in that it rests upon a distinction explicitly drawn by the American philosopher, Ronald Dworkin, between equal treatment and treating everyone as an equal. The principle of equal treatment, in the relevant political sense, requires that the state treat all its citizens equally in the relevant respect, for example, in the distribution of a resource or opportunity. The principle of treating people as equals entails that every person or group is treated with equal concern and respect. This second principle may sometimes require equal treatment, say, equal distribution of resources but it may also occasionally dictate unequal treatment. Treating people or groups as equals is entirely consistent with differential treatment. (89)

This principled distance respects the religious liberty duly. Religions are not to reel under the unilateral actions of the state, but, in turn, they too can make their critical intervention for the promotion of equality of citizenship and communities. He reflects: "Does principled distance also entail that religion intervene in the affairs of the state? In some contexts, it may certainly do so. Religion may intervene in the affairs of the state if such intervention promotes freedom, equality, or any other value integral to secularism". " . . . . unlike mainstream western secularism that appears to impose on us a choice between active hostility or benign indifference, Indian secularism brings to bear on religion an attitude of critical respect". Bhargava clarifies his theory further saying that there is a necessity for 'depoliticization' of religion in a secular state, but this should not be equated with depublicization. "Indeed, the Constitution even allows a contextual politicization of religion, for example, if such politicization advances the cause of equality and freedom. If justice ever required the local politicization of religion, then any defensible version of secularism must support it." (104)

Bhargava takes care to point out that secularism is not identical with religious tolerance: "Indian secularism must not be confused with a generally professed Hindu tolerance. It is frequently claimed that Indians have a natural, traditional affinity with secularism. In view of our traditional obsession with subtle and not so subtle hierarchies, this claim must be taken with a pinch of salt, if not pepper". (83) And, he is equally critical of such concepts as 'religious co-existence', 'inter-religious' understanding, etc. He says, "I take religious coexistence to be equivalent to peace but to identify the secular state with a state that maintains peace between religions, that allows different religions to coexist, does little justice to the rich history and conceptual structure of secularism as a multi-value doctrine. Much the same is true of the interpretation of Indian secularism as inter-religious toleration . . . . It is equally inappropriate to identify secularism with equal respect for all religions". (102-103)

Bhargava underlines the core of Indian secularism as: "the core idea of secularism then is: separation of religion and state for the sake of religious liberty and equality of free citizenship." (79) He makes a distinction between 'passive' and 'active' citizenships. While the former entails the right to physical security, material well-being, etc., of an individual, the latter refers to the protection of a citizen as he/she emerges as an active participant in a public domain. Both types of citizenships must be ensured to an individual in a secular state.

Critique: Rajeev Bhargava has a positive and dynamic understanding of secularism. His theory of principled distance can engender arbitrary exercise of power, depending on the rulers of the state. That is indeed a serious challenge to this theory. However, it breaks the dogmatism of secularism and finds sound bases for community rights, public role of religions, etc. It would do well to draw inspiration from his writings for the defence of secularism. However, I find him not relating secularism sufficiently with the quest for social justice and economic parity. He remains at the discursive level. His concern seems to be securing secularism against its elitist critics. He does not take note of the subaltern political or cultural groups which find secularism lacking because it has not ensured justice to them.

Looking for a Subaltern Avenue

We have taken a brief look at some of the salient trends, which are by no means exhaustive,[40] in the contemporary debate on Indian secularism. They are the negative stance by the *Hindutva* forces, sceptical positions of Madan and Nandy, dogmatic position of the left, and a liberal view of Rajeev Bhargava. (Perhaps the perspective of the Indian National Congress, the ruling party, could also be added to the list. Its approach is generally a liberal modern view, representing the need of the modernising upper and middle classes, but it is characterised by extreme opportunism.)

When we correlate these positions with those ingredients found in the historical trajectory of Indian secularism, we find some convergences and divergences. The capitalist modernist trend, along with the western stirrings and the Nehruvian position, broadly converge into the liberal modern view; the Gandhian position straddles between modernist and traditionalist (*sarva dharma samabhava*) positions; a strand from the neo-Hindu segment of the early Indian nationalism has swelled up into the rightist *Hindutva* forces; and, the views expressed by Ambedkar and E.V. Ramasamy, though attempted by relatively smaller political formations, are yet to be realised in the larger Indian context.

On the whole, it may well be seen that majority of the positions of the past as well as of the present follow the dominant path of treating secularism from the vantage point of the elites—the upper caste, and upper and middle class, modernising elites. Perhaps, an emancipatory view on secularism has yet to emerge from those views which have been left behind: the secular propensities of the grassroots people, the secular goals and dynamics of the counter-religious traditions and of the socio-religious movements, the initiatives of social activists and intellectuals like Phule, Iyotheedass Panditar, Ambedkar, the endeavours of the left, etc., could help us to search for a subaltern path in the woods of secular politics and politics of secularism.

Subaltern Exploration into Secularism

The subaltern studies project, initiated by Ranajit Guha in the early eighties of the twentieth century, gives us a lead.[41] It made a decisive turn in historiography, investing it with a perspective of the subaltern, which was distinguished from the elite historiography as found in the colonial and nationalist accounts. Imbued with the insight of Antonio Gramsci, it looked into the way the common sense of the subalterns was dominated over by contradictory consciousness induced by the hegemony of the dominant classes. It called for avenues to enable the awakening of subaltern critical consciousness, and create a civil society free of dominations and exploitations. This insight of the subaltern studies project gives us a good starting point. However, the subaltern studies project too has its limitation. Majority of its literature is confined to certain episodic subaltern rebellions, and resistance. As I have argued elsewhere,[42] it has, to a very large extent, failed in theorising on the question of caste and has culpably neglected understanding of its role in the operation of power or in the construction of subjecthood for the people of the lower strata. It has not emerged into a theory of practice to mobilise the subaltern people for their empowerment. In particular, the theme of secularism does not seem to find much place in subaltern explorations. It then becomes a necessity for us to re-envision secularism from the perspective of the subalterns, who hitherto have, by and large, remained excluded from the grand project of secularism. As Nivedita pleads, "we cannot reimagine secularism today without coming to terms with the violent histories of subordination and repression..." (Nivedita Menon, 132).

Religious Mechanics of Subordination

Mechanics of subordination and repression have been the chief architectonics of the Indian society. People have been held under subjection, epitomised in purity and pollution rules,[43] and been exploited of labour, social dignity and event of history. It has taken place with a symbiotic sustenance drawn from religious resources, especially of the hegemonic part of the sanskritic variety.[44] This religious component, due to its early articulation with the facility of early literacy and patronage from rulers,[45] has spread itself across the width and breadth of this subcontinent, and it continues to be one of the archetypical symbolic codes in the sub-conscious reaches of the people in India. Though several other religious symbolic systems have emerged, they have been either co-opted or relativised, confining them to certain regions or periods of history. This religious component continues to exercise its hegemonic influence over the religious consciousness of the people.

Even in today's global world, wherein the market forces have changed the face of religions, the hierarchical value embedded in this religious component reproduces itself through modern communication facilities. And it continues to spread the message and validity of a hierarchised social structure, and acclimatises the people to such hierarchical relationships. Its hegemony is one of the major factors which work against the emergence of critical secular consciousness, a consciousness to help cultivate the self with humanistic self-confidence, and, help interrogate the multiple forms of oppression.

It is instructive to listen to Nivedita Menon: "we have to recognize that 'secularism' has been implicitly marked as Hindu upper-caste and modernized upper-class all along. This is as true for secular political movements as for the state—for example, the women's movement has been criticized for tending to assume the Hindu upper-caste woman to be the norm . . . ." (134). Secularism thus, as understood in elitist circles, hides an element that needs to be problematised. This kind of elitist secularism came about, due to, as Shabnum Tejani observes " . . . . the imperative of creating a democratic majority" which, therefore, relied on "the co-optation of untouchables into upper-caste Hindu identity." (Shabnum Tejani, 2007b, 47). Thus, a religious mechanic of subordination has got integrated into the elitist secularism.

Deflection of Caste and Everyday Violence

Dilip Menon, a critical scholar, helps us in exposing and interrogating the caste dimension of secularism. He points to an amnesia imposed on us of the caste dimension of the communal clashes by inducing a deflection of the real issues that face secularism today. This amnesia enables the oppressors to displace the caste enemy with a religiously concocted enemy—be it a Muslim or a Christian. It would do well to listen to Menon:

> "There has been a reluctance to engage with what is arguably an intimate relation between the discourses of caste, secularism and communalism. That Hinduism—as religion, social system or way of life—is a hierarchical, inegalitarian structure is largely accepted, but what has gone almost unacknowledged in academic discourse is both the casual brutality and the organised violence that it practices towards its subordinated sections. What we need to explore is the inner violence within Hinduism as much as the violence directed outwards against Muslims, and acknowledge that the former is historically prior. The question needs to be: how has the deployment of violence against an internal Other (defined in terms of inherent inequality), the *dalit*, been displaced as one of aggression against an external Other (defined in terms of inherent difference), the Muslim. Is communalism then a deflection of the central issue of violence and inegalitarianism within the Hindu religion?" (2)

He continues:

> "The neatness of categories like 'Hindu' and 'Muslim' hide the porousness of identities as much as the histories of the

> inner violence of hierarchy. It is through the forgetting, and even the violent suppression of inegalitarianism within putative blocs like Hinduism and Islam, that unitary, militant identities are sought to be forged. In that sense, communalism in India may well be the return of the repressed histories of caste."[46] (25)

Menon demands that secularism should be concerned not only about the openly erupting clashes, but also about the everyday forms of violence which the caste hierarchy is imposing onto the subaltern people. The Constitution of a civic public sphere is by safeguarding it not merely from public clashes, but, more fundamentally, from the systemic violence experienced in the life-world of the people as well.

The open clashes are only stratagems to sustain 'the will to hegemonise' a society, and retain its power over a society, wherein subaltern challenges are increasingly on the rise. Communal upsurge is part of the game-plan of the erstwhile hegemonic powers of the country, who grow insecure at the growth of the subaltern classes. A secularism which does not take into consideration this societal dynamics, will fail to propose any serious solution to the apparent threat secularism is facing today. Therefore, a debate on secularism should integrally be linked not merely to the question of religion, but also that of social justice in this country.

By Way of Concluding...

This essay has attempted to point out the fact that we need a social and that too, subaltern location for secularism in the Indian context. This is something that has been ignored in the secularism discourse right from its initial days: the colonial discourse, a major part of the nationalist discourse, the counter neo-Hindu discourses, and even some of the main players in the contemporary debate are representing an elitist interest in relation to secularism. In order to be a substantive ideal and practice, secularism must endeavour also to locate its discourse in subaltern life-contexts, and explore the possibilities of emerging as an emancipatory ideal.

It would imply that we interpretatively reinvent the subaltern resources and promote them in terms of action and reflection. The secular propensities lying dormant with the religious and cultural traditions of our people at the grassroots must be promoted and cultivated; the secular potentials of socio-religious movements (starting with the shramanic movements, *Bhakti* movement, sufi tradition, regional varieties of socio-religious movements, etc.) must be tapped; socio-political initiatives undertaken by subaltern leaders like Mahatma Phule, Iyotheedoss Pandithar, Ambedkar, E.V. Ramasamy, etc., must be re-discovered; potentials of feminist movements must be promoted, and so on.

An empowering secular civil society must be open to the role of religions.[47] As pointed out by Chantal Mauffe, "As long as they act within constitutional limits, there is no reason why religious groups should not be able to intervene in the political arena to argue in favour of or against causes. Indeed, many democratic struggles have been informed by religious motives. And the fight for social justice has often been enhanced by the participation of religious groups" (Chantal Mauffe, 149). The dissent, resistance, interrogation, and weakening of dominating hegemonic forces as manifest in religious traditions are congenial to an emancipatory civil society. In today's context, we are very much in need of such liberative religious traditions to enhance our civil society.[48] Similarly, our secular society must also be able to interrogate the oppressive hold or authority religions may have on civil spheres. As Thapar would suggest, secularism should also confront "the authority of religious institutions or institutions inspired by religious identities over civic life." (Thapar, 2004, 1017) It is in building up such a healthy and emancipatory mutuality between religion and civil society that we can see the blossoming of a substantive and emancipatory democracy.

NOTES

1. *Cf.* Hent de Vries and Lawrence E. Sullivan (ed), *Political Theologies – Public Religions in a Post-Secular World*, Social Science Press and Orient Longman Pvt Ltd., 2007.
2. The cognates 'secular, secularism and secularisation' perhaps need some clarification. As per majority of sociological accounts, they had their origin in the European context, starting from the era of Renaissance humanism, running through the process of capitalist modernisation, articulated and strengthened by the Enlightenment reason and its attendant process of secularisation, serving as the bulwark of modern democratic nation-states, and so on. What is addressed as 'secular' is said to have a very ancient origin in the

Christian Augustinian literature, wherein Augustine contrasts this temporal world (saeculum) with the everlasting city of God. Secular is said to stand against or different from a spiritual or a supernatural transcendental world. The term 'secularisation' seems to have been originally used in the post-Westphalian (1648) context wherein church properties were transferred to princes as part of the peace settlement-an act denoted even then as 'secularisation'. But later on, this term came to acquire a different meaning in the sociological literature of the west: It came to stand for a range of meanings starting with total antipathy to simple indifference to religion. It was argued by sociologists that the process of modernisation would weaken the hold of religion both in private and public spheres of life. The term 'secularism' was first used during the middle of the nineteenth century (1846) by George Jacob Holyoake, leader of the English secularist and free thought movement, who used it to speak of "a form of opinion which concerns itself only with questions, the issues of which can be tested by the experience of this life". Later Holyoake explained his concept as: "Secularism is that which seeks the development of the physical, moral, and intellectual nature of man to the highest possible point, as the immediate duty of life—which inculcates the practical sufficiency of natural morality apart from Atheism, Theism or the *Bible*—which selects as its methods of procedure the promotion of human improvement by material means, and proposes these positive agreements as the common bond of union, to all who would regulate life by reason and ennoble it by service". While the cognates as terms have origin at different historical contexts, their meanings, as we see, are closely related, with different emphases.

3. C.Wright Mills summarized the process of secularization as: "Once the world was filled with the sacred — in thought, practice, and institutional form. After the Reformation and the Renaissance, the forces of modernization swept across the globe and secularization, a corollary historical process, loosened the dominance of the sacred. In due course, the sacred shall disappear altogether except, possibly, in the private realm".
4. Max Weber, unlike Karl Marx, regretted the gradual demise of religion, because he, as is known, was convinced of the positive potentialities of religion.
5. Berger, Peter (ed). 1999. *The Desecularization of the World: Resurgent Religion and World Politics.* Washington, DC: Ethics and Public Policy Centre.
6. *Cf.* Zygmunt Bauman, *Liquid Modernity.*
7. *Cf.* Harvey Cox, *Religion in the Secular City*, New York: A Touchstone Book, 1984.
8. *Cf.* Harvey Cox, *Fire from Heaven: The Rise of Pentecostal Spirituality and*

the Reshaping of Religion in the Twenty-first Century, Reading: Addison-Wesley Publishing Company, 1994.

9. Jose Casanova, *Public Religion in the Modern World*, Chicago: The University of Chicago Press, 1994.
10. Richard Dworkin, *Return of the God...*
11. *Cf.* Pippa Norris and Ronald Inglehart, *Sacred and Secular – Religion and Politics Worldwide,* Cambridge: Cambridge University Press, 2004. They argue: "Societies where people's daily lives are shaped by the threat of poverty, disease, and premature death remain as religious today as centuries earlier. These same societies are also experiencing rapid population growth. In rich nations, by contrast, the evidence demonstrates that secularization has been proceeding since at least the mid-twentieth century (and probably earlier) – but at the same time fertility rates have fallen sharply, so that in recent years population growth has stagnated and their total population is starting to shrink", p. 216-217.
12. *Cf.* Charles Taylor, *The Secular Age*, Cambridge: The Belknap Press of Harvard University Press, 2007.
13. *Cf.* Jose Casanova, *The Public Religion*
14. Gianni Vattimo takes secularisation to be a kenotic process (as found in the Christian concept of incarnation) whereby metaphysically loaded ontology is emptied out, and a more hermeneutically and dialogically experienced 'weak ontology' is at work, and that presents itself in the return of religions in the form of language events. *Cf.* Gianni Vattimo, *Belief*, Polity Press, 1999.
15. Pippa Norris and Ronald Inglehart suggest that "a growing gap has opened up between the value systems of rich and poor countries, making religious differences *increasingly* salient." *Ibid.*, p. 217.
16. Reflexivity is a concept much theorised by contemporary sociologists. They opine that the contemporary individual is gaining the reflexive capacity of monitoring one's own life, steer the life amidst varied possibilities, etc. *Cf.* Anthony Giddens, ... When it is applied to religion, it means the possibility of religious choices people can make today.
17. *Cf.* Peter Beyer, *Religion and Globalisation.*
18. Needham & Sundar Rajan, 3.
19. *Cf.* (Amalendu Misra, Identity and Religion).
20. *Cf.* Romila Thapar, 1999, 13-14.
21. *Cf.* Dick Kooiman, *Communalism in the Princely States...*
22. *Cf.* Amartya Sen, *The Argumentative Indian . . . .*
23. The missionary rhetoric could be accused of originating religious polemic in the public sphere. But, it was also the event that produced public debates on religions.
24. *Cf.* Ingleby . . . .

25. *Cf.* Stephen Fuchs, *Rebellious Prophets — A Study of Messianic Movements in Indian Religions*, Bombay: Asia Publishing House, 1965; Kenneth W. Jones, *Socio-Religious Reform Movements in British India*. Cambridge: Cambridge University Press, 1994.
26. We find Romila Thapar too reflecting along the same line: "By the mid-nineteenth century the definition of secular focused on the question of ethics. It was stated that social morality, central to the secular, should have as its sole basis the well-being of mankind to the exclusion of considerations stemming from a belief in God or in a future condition. The key elements of this morality were legal order, political freedom, individual autonomy and material well-being. These are elements endorsed even by those that find modernisation antipathetic. The emphasis, therefore, is not on a hostility to religion but on rational and moral principles governing society, principles which oppose the alienation of human beings, or the absence of social ethics." (Romila Thapar, 2004, 1017)
27. It would do well to listen to Larson on his estimation: "Overall, then, we see a variety of religious orientations and traditions interacting with one another in these formative years before and after partition: Neo-Muslim Aligarh modernists and separatists (Sayyid Ahmad Khan, the Muslim League, Muhammed Iqbal, M.A. Jinnah, and others), Neo-Muslim Deoband reformists and accomodationists (Hasan Ahmad Madani, and others), Neo-Hindu reformists and nationalists with aggressive (militant) and exclusive orientation (the Arya Samaj, the Hindu Mahasabha, the early Aurobindo, B.G. Tilak, V.D. Savarkar, Hedgewar and the RSS, Subhas Chandra Bose and his INA, and so on), and Neo-Hindu reformists and nationalists with a passive aggressive (non-violent non-cooperation, *Satyagraha*) and inclusivist orientation (the Brahmo Samaj, the Ramakrishna Mission, the Indian National Congress, the later Aurobindo, the Gandhian *Sarvodaya* movement, and so on). There were also, of course, the purely Westernising and European orientations of liberal democratic pluralism (in such early moderate leaders as M.G. Ranade and G.K. Gokhale) deriving from the intellectual traditions of the Western European nation-states, of the Nehruvian socialists and of radical socialists and communist theorizing (M.N. Roy and others) growing out of the Russian revolution and its aftermath. The Westernising orientations, however, hardly had an independent social base and were finally absorbed for the most part in the Neo-Muslim (mainly among Aligarh modernists) and Neo-Hindu traditions (mainly in the Gandhian-Nehruvian Congress ideology. One should perhaps also mention Ambedkar's Neo-Buddhist movement, largely among the Mahars in Maharashtra but also appealing to untouchables or Scheduled Castes elsewhere as well." (Gerald James Larson, 207)

28. He critiqued Gandhi and his philosophy severely. He said, "The first special feature of Gandhism is that his philosophy helps those who want to keep what they have and to prevent those who have not from getting what they have a right to get. No one who examines the Gandhian attitude to strikes, the Gandhian reverence for caste and Gandhian doctrine of Trusteeship by the rich for the benefit of the poor can deny that this is an upshot of Gandhism ... Gandhism is the philosophy of the well-to-do and the leisure class." (Gerald James Larson, 203-204)
29. We have others like Mahatma Phule, Gokhale, Ranade, and others who served as forerunners to Ambedkar.
30. The word 'secular' was formally inserted in the Preamble to the Constitution of India by the 42nd Amendment of 1976 to the Constitution of India.
31. (Sen, Ronojoy, xxvi) "As Mahajan points out, 'Independent India followed neither the English nor the American model. It chartered a different route wherein non-establishment of religion was combined with the absence of separation.' *Ibid.*
32. A more detailed account would reveal many more players and their nuanced contributions.
33. "The Gandhian-Nehruvian movement, to be sure, addressed itself to the rural and urban poor and succeeded in achieving mass mobilization, but, nevertheless, its leadership was a elitist as the other traditions in the nationalist struggle, both before partition and even more so afterwards. To put the matter differently, the freedom movements in South Asia, both the Republic of Pakistan as well as the Republic of India, were very much products of the "commanding heights." (Gerald James Larson, 207-208)
34. Vajpayee, "Secularism the Indian concept", Christopher Jaffralot (ed.), *Hindu Nationalism – A Reader,* New Delhi: Permanent Black, pp. 323-326.
35. Will Kymlica, *Multicultural Citizenship – A Liberal Theory of Minority Rights.* Oxford: Clarendon Press, 1995.
36. While the first one is a mechanistic treatment of equality, which more often than not does not amount to being equal, especially in a context of historical and systemically inbuilt discriminations, the latter is a way of ensuring equality to everyone even in the context of differences. It is the latter type of equality that the country looks for.
37. Paul Brass continues to observe: "The peaceful pursuit of interreligious dialogue through the 'recovery of religious tolerance' has no meaning for those groups who have seen themselves as oppressed and discriminated against in Hindu society: Muslims, Backward Castes, Scheduled Castes, and Scheduled Tribes. For all these groups, secularism means tolerance, acceptance, equality, non-discrimination,

not Brahmanical or Gandhian searches for transcendent interreligious truths." (Brass, 367)

38. Bhargava: "A political movement for a united, liberal, democratic India had to struggle against hierarchical and communal conceptions of community but without abandoning a reasonable communitarianism. Besides, the State had an important contribution to make in the transformation of these communities; for this reason, a perennial dilemma was imposed on it. The State in India walked a tight rope between the requirement of religious liberty that frequently entails non-interference in the affairs of religious communities, and the demand for equality and justice which necessitates intervention in religiously sanctioned social customs. Secularism in India simply had to be different from the western liberal model that does not recognize communities, and dictates strict separation between religious and political institutions." (86)
39. Bhargava: "The idea of principled distance unpacks the metaphor of separation differently. It accepts a disconnection between state and religion at the level of ends and institutions but does not make a fetish of it at the third level of policy and law." (88)
40. We can still bring in several views, especially of the minorities. I am aware of substantial work by K.N. Panikkar, Ashgar Ali Engineer, Ram Punyani, and others. Perhaps I can do it in an expansion of this work.
41. There are twelve volumes hitherto published under the Subaltern Studies series. In addition to this, we also have a number independent writers, editors, etc. on subaltern themes.
42. *Cf.* Patrick G., "Knowledge as Negotiation – A Critique of the Subaltern Studies Project", in Felix Wilfred (ed), *Knowledge-Ethics For Our Times*, (*Jeevadhara*, Vol. XXXIX, No. 229, January, 2009, pp. 60-73.
43. The work of Louis Dumont demonstrates well the structural hierarchical organisation of Indian society. *Cf.* Louis Dumont, *Homo Hierarchicus*, ... Sumit Sarkar gives an example of *Adhikari-bedha* as an organising principle based on differentiated rights, duties, powers, etc., which emerged during the seventeenth-eighteenth centuries in Bengal. *Cf.* Sumit Sarkar, *Writing Social History*, New Delhi: OUP, 1997, pp. 368ff.
44. It is instructive here to note that some of the religious themes helped in the process of subordinating the subaltern people. For example, Sumit Sarkar speaks about the workings of the theme of *Kaliyuga*: "For some two thousand years the characteristic high-Hindu dystopia of *Kaliyuga*, last and most degenerate of eras that is always imagined as the present, has firmly located the sources of evil in the insubordination of *Shudras* to upper-castes and women to men." – Sumit Sarkar, *Writing Social History*, New Delhi: OUP, 1997, p. 367.

45. Susan Bayly, "Ironically, given the widely held modern view of caste as a scheme of religious values which are unique to the Hindu cultural tradition, non-Hindu as well as avowedly Hindu rulers played a dynamic role in the process. To rule was to name, order and classify; many of the regional community titles and other reference points of the modern caste 'system' were popularised through the usages of the great state-building lords and dynasts of the Mughal and post-Mughal periods". (Susan Bayly, 1999, 369)
46. The deflection continues in different ways. The duplicity in public discourses about caste is a case in point. There are those who consider themselves as supporters of secularism brand social activists who demonstrate against caste oppression in public as casteist. This is a duplicity to which Menon draws our attention to as: "The public sphere is narrowly constructed as the sphere governed by secular categories . . . . What follows from this is the claim by the caste-Hindu secular self that s/he does not practise caste, using as s/he does impeccably unmarked categories in public discourse, while dalits and others are casteist since they deploy the language of caste in the public sphere". (3-4) "That the *dalit* self operates within a severely circumscribed range and runs the risk of attracting a disciplining violence needs to be remembered. When the question of violence does surface it is generally rendered the preserve of the state and as arising from the imperatives of governmentality. Little, if any, attention is paid to the bloodshed arising from the everyday preservation of hierarchy." (4-5)
47. Insightfully, Menon finds a parallel between the tendency to avoid disputing caste in public and the tendency to deny religion a public space. He says: "[T]his occlusion of caste in the public sphere is paralleled by the recognition of the need to eliminate public expressions of religion as part of the requirement of secularism . . . . " (4). Perhaps, it is this tendency which is also at the very root of prohibiting conversions in this land. As we know, most of the mass movements of conversion in this land have been bold public statements on the workings of caste hierarchy. Conversion cannot be hidden under the bushel of personal religiosity; its social significance should be recognised in the functioning of a healthy civil society. This civil society, built on an agonistic model of democracy, will also have a legitimate and emancipatory role for religions; and it will be both in the private and the public spheres.
48. One finds today good attempts being made by progressive movements and individuals in providing a liberative interpretation to their religious traditions. Liberation theology, contextual theology, feminist theology, etc. are good attempts within Christianity. We find progressive Islamic theologians like Asghar Ali Engineer doing yeoman's task. We need many more movements and individuals along this line...

REFERENCES

Ahmad, Aijaz. 2005. "The Making of India" *Social Scientist*, Vol. 33, Nos. 11-12, Nov-Dec.

Ahmad, Imtiaz *et al.* (eds). 2000. *Pluralism and Equality—Values in Indian Society and Politics*. Sage.

Aiyar, Mani Shankar. 2004. *Confessions of a Secular Fundamentalist*. Penguin.

Ansari, M.T. (ed). 2007. *Secularism, Islam and Modernity—Selected Essays of Alam Khundmiri*. Sage.

Asad, Talal. 2003. *Formations of the Secular: Christianity, Islam, Modernity*. Stanford: Stanford University Press.

Asad, Talal. 2007. "Trying to Understand French Secularism." Henry de Vries and Laurence V. Sullivan (eds), *Political Theologies—Public Religions in a Post-Secular World*. Social Science Press and Orient Longman.

Bajpai, Rochana. 2002. "The Conceptual Vocabularies of Secularism and Minority Rights in India," *Journal of Political Ideologies*, 7,2.

Basu, Kaushik and Sanjay Subramanyam (eds). 1996. *Unravelling the Nation: Sectarian Conflict and India's Secular Identity*. Delhi: Penguin Books.

Bayly, Susan. 1999. *Caste, Society and Politics in India—From the Eighteenth Century to the Modern Age*. Cambridge: Cambridge University Press.

Beteille, Andre. 1994. "Secularism and Intellectuals," *EPW, 29,10.*

Bhargava, Rajeev. (ed). 1998. *Secularism and its Critics*. New Delhi: OUP.

Bhargava, Rajeev. 2010. *The Promise of India's Secular Democracy*. OUP.

Bharucha, Rustom (ed). 1998. *In the Name of the Secular: Contemporary Cultural Activism in India*. Delhi: OUP.

Brass, Paul R. 1999. "Secularism out of its Place", in Veena Das *et al.* (eds), *Tradition, Pluralism and Identity*, Sage, pp. 358-379.

Casanova, Jose. 1994. *Public Religions in the Modern World*. Chicago:

Chadwick, Owen. 1975. *The Secularization of the European Mind in the Nineteenth Century*. Cambridge: Cambridge University Press.

Chakrabarty, Bidyut (ed). 1990. *Secularism and Indian Polity*. New Delhi: Segment Book Distributors.

Chandhoke, Neera. 1999. *Beyond Secularism: The Rights of Religious Minorities*. New Delhi: OUP.

Chatterjee, Partha. 1986. "Secularism and Toleration," *EPW*, 29,28.

Chatterji, P.C. 1984. *Secular Values for Secular India*. New Delhi: Lola Chatterji.

Connolly, William. 1999. *Why I Am Not a Secularist*. Minneapolis, MN: University of Minnesota Press.

Cox, Harvey. 1984. *Religion in the Secular City—Toward a Postmodern Theology*. New York: A Touchstone Book.

Crimmins, J. (ed). 1989. *Religion, Secularization and Political Thought: Thomas Hobbes to J.S. Mill*. London: Routledge.

Devi, Indira V. 2002. *Secularisation of Indian Mind—A Study of Political Ideas in India from 1885 to 1914*. Jaipur: Rawat Publications.

Engineer, Asghar Ali. 2003. *Communal Challenge and Secular Response*. Delhi: Shipra.

Engineer, Asghar Ali. *Secularism, Democracy and Muslim Experience in India—Understanding Communalism and Terrorism*. Haryana: Hope India Publications.

Esteves, Sarto. 1996. *Nationalism, Secularism and Communalism*. Delhi: South Asia Publications.

Ghurye, G.S. 1968. *Social Tensions in India*. Bombay: Popular Prakashan.

Glazer, Nathan. 2007. "Minorities and India's Democracy." K. Shankar Bajpai (ed), *Democracy and Diversity—India and the American Experience*. OUP.

Gupta, Dipankar. 2002. Limits of Tolerance: Prospects of Secularism in India after Gujarat. *EPW*, 37, 46.

Habib, Irfan *et al.* 2009. *After Ayodhya—Reclaiming the Secular*. New Delhi: SAHMAT.

Hasan, Mushirul. 1997. *Legacy of a Divided Nation—India's Muslims since Independence* in *India's Muslims—An Omnibus*, with an introduction by Mushirul Hasan, OUP, 2007.

Iyer, Krishna, V.R. 2010. "Some Tasks before the Indian Nation", *The Hindu*, 19 March, Chennai Edition, p. 10.

Jacob John, Gary Jeffrey. 2003. *The Wheel of Law: India's Secularism in Comparative Constitutional Context*. Princeton: Princeton University Press.

Jakobsen, J.R. and A. Pellegrini. 2000. "World Secularism at the Millennium," *Social Text*, 64, 18, 3.

Jalal, Ayesha. 1996. "Secularists, Subalterns and the Stigma of "Communalism": Partition Historiography Revisited," *IESHR*, 33,1.

Jayal, Niraja Gopal. 1999. *Democracy and the State—Welfare, Secularism and Development on Contemporary India*, OUP.

Kymlica, Will. 1995. *Multicultural Citizenship—A Liberal Theory of Minority Rights*. Oxford: Clarendon Press.

Larson, Gerald James (ed). 2001. *Religion and Personal Law in Secular India: A Call to Judgement*. Delhi: Social Secular Press.

Luthera, Ved Prakash. 1964. *The Concept of the Secular State and India*. London: Oxford University Press.

Madan, T.N. 1997. *Modern Myths, Locked Minds: Secularism and Fundamentalism in India*. Delhi: OUP.

Martin, David. 2005. *On Secularization: Towards a Revised General Theory*. Aldershot: Ashgate.

Mauffe, Chantel. 2007. "Religion, Liberal Democracy and Citizenship." Vries, Hent de and Lawrence E. Sullivan (eds). 2007. *Political Theologies: Public Religions in a Post-Secular World*. New Delhi: Social Science Press and Orient Longman.

Menon, Dilip. 2004. *Blindness of Insight: Why Communalism in India is about Caste?*. Navayana.

Milbank, John. 1990 (2006). *Theology and Social Theory—Beyond Secular Reason*. Blackwell Publishers.

Moore, R.J. (ed). 2004. *Critical Secularism*. NC: Duke University Press.

Nanda, Meera. 2007. "Secularism without Secularisation—Reflections on God and Politics in US and India", *EPW*, Vol. XLII No. 1, January 6-12, pp. 39-46.

Nandy, Ashis. 1983. "Closing the Debate on Secularism: A Personal Statement," in A. Dingwaney Needham and R. Sunder Rajan (ed). *The Crisis of Secularism in India*. Durham, NC: Duke University Press.

Nandy, Ashis. 1985. "An Anti-Secularist Manifesto." *Seminar 314*.

Nandy, Ashis. 2004. "The Twilight of Certitudes—Secularism, Hindu Nationalism and Other Masks of Deculturation." in Ashis Nandy, *Bonfire of Creeds—The Essential Ashis Nandy*. OUP.

Needham, Anuradha Dingwaney and Rajeswari Sunder Rajan (eds). 2007. *The Crisis of Secularism in India*. Ranikhet: Permanent Black.

Nigam, Aditya. 2000. "Secularism, Modernity, Nation: Epistemology of the Dalit Critique," *EPW*, 35, 48.

Nigam, Aditya. 2006. *The Insurrection of Little Selves: The Crisis of Secular-Nationalism in India*. New Delhi: OUP.

Norris, Pippa and Inglehart, Ronald. 2004. *Sacred and Secular—Religion and Politics Worldwide*. Cambridge: Cambridge University Press.

Panikkar, K.N. (ed). 1997. *Communal Threat, Secular Challenge*. Madras: Earthworm Books.

Rabbani, Attar. 2007. "Secular India and its Communal Challenge." *Indian Journal of Secularism*, Vol. 11, No. 3, October-December, pp. 64-90.

Rajan, Nalini. 1998. *Secularism, Democracy, Justice—Implications of Rawlsian Principles in India*. Sage.

Ram, P.R. (ed). NA. *Secular Challenge to Communal Politics—A Reader*. Mumbai: Vikas Adhyayan Kendra.

Robinson, Rowena. 2008. "Democracy, secularism and minority rights in a globalizing India." *Indian Journal of Secularism*, Vol. 11, No. 4, January-March, pp. 57-68.

Roy, Himanshu. 2006. "Western Secularism and Colonial Legacy in India." *Economic and Political Weekly*, Vol. XLI, No. 2, January 14, pp. 158-165.

Sen, Amartya. 1996. "Secularism and its Discontents," in K. Basu and S. Subrahmanyam (eds). *Unravelling the Nation: Sectarian Conflicts in India*. New Delhi: Penguin.

Sen, Ronojoy. 2010. *Articles of Faith—Religion, Secularism, and the Indian Supreme Court*. OUP.

Sharma, Arvind (ed). 2001. *Hinduism and Secularism after Ayodhya*. New York: Palgrave.

Sharma, Jyoti. 2007. *Secularism and Ayodhya Politics in India*. New Delhi: Deep & Deep Publications Pvt. Ltd.

Shefali, Jha. 2002. "Secularism in the Constituent Assembly Debates 1946-1950." *Economic and Political Weekly*, 37(30), pp. 175-180.

Smith, D.E. 1963. *India as a Secular State*. Princeton: Princeton University Press.

Sommerville, John C. 1992. *The Secularization of Early Modern England: From Religious Culture to Religious Faith*. New York: Oxford University Press.

Srinivasan, T.N. (ed). 2007. *The Future of Secularism*. OUP.

Talreja, Kajnayalal M. 1996. *Pseudo-Secularism in India*. Mumbai: Rashtriya Chetna Prakashan.

Talyabji, Badruddin. 1971. *The Self in Secularism*. New Delhi: Orient Longman.

Taylor, Charles. 2004. *The Modern Social Imaginary*. Durham.

Taylor, Charles. 2007. *A Secular Age*. Cambridge: Belknap Press of Harvard University Press.

Tejani, Shabnum. 2007 b. "Reflections on the Category of Secularism in India—Gandhi, Ambedkar, and the Ethics of Communal Representations, *c*. 1931" Needham, Anuradha Dingwaney and Rajeswari Sunder Rajan (eds). 2007. *The Crisis of Secularism in India*. Ranikhet: Permanent Black.

Tejani, Shabnum. 2007a. *Indian Secularism—A Social and Intellectual History 1890-1950*. Permanent Black.

Thapar, Romila. 1999. *Historical Interpretations and the Secularising of Indian Society*. Bangalore: Visthar.

Thapar, Romila. 2004. "Secularism and History", in Romila Thapar, *Cultural Pasts—Essays in Early Indian History*. OUP.

Thapar, Romila. 2007. "Is Secularism Alien to Indian Civilization?" in Srinivasan, T.N. (ed). 2007. *The Future of Secularism*. OUP.

Thomas, K. Toms. 2005. *Auctioning the Left Out—Christians in Civil Society Building*. New Delhi: Indian Social Institute.

Upadhyay, Prakash Chandra. 1992. *The Politics of Indian Secularism*. New Delhi: Modern Asian Studies.

Vajpayee, Atal Behari. 1969. "The Bane of Secularism", in S.S. Bhandari (ed), *Jana Sangh Souvenir*, Delhi: BJP, pp. 55-58.

Vajpayee, Atal Behari. 1992. "Secularism, the Indian Concept", *Rajendra Prasad Lecture*, All India Radio Broadcast [as found in Christophe Jaffrelot (ed), *Hindu Nationalism—A Reader*, New Delhi: Permanent Black.]

Vanaik, Achin. 1997. *Communalism Contested: Religion, Modernity and Secularization*, New Delhi: Vistaar Publications.

Veer, Peter van der. 2001. *Imperial Encounters—Religion and Modernity in India and Britain*. New Delhi: Permanent Black.

Venkataraman, T.S. 1950. *A Treatise on Secular State*. Madras.

Verma, H.S. 1990. "Secularism: Reflections on Meaning, Substance and Contemporary Practice," in B. Chakrabarty (ed). *Secularism and Indian Polity*. New Delhi: Segment Books.

Viquaruddin, Mohammed. 2008. "Secularism and Social Justice in India." *Indian Journal of Secularism*, Vol. 11, No. 4, January-March, pp. 14-24.

Vries, Hent de and Lawrence E. Sullivan (eds). 2007. *Political Theologies—Public Religions in a Post-Secular World*. New Delhi: Social Science Press and Orient Longman.

Yechury, Sitaram. 2008. *Secularism* Versus *Communalism*. Hyderabad: Prajasakti Book House.

Zakaria, Rafiq. 2002. *Communal Rage in Secular India*. Mumbai: Popular Prakashan.

9

Cultural Context of the Formation of Indian Constitution : A Review of its Achievements and Limitations After Sixty Years

S.M. Michael

Introduction

The Constitution of India grew out of the challenges and contending visions for the future of India's cultural, religious and ethnic plurality at the time of the freedom struggle. We will shortly show that the secular Constitution of the Republic of India is the outcome of conflicting views on the secular form of the modern state and various religious claims on Indian identity; between contending visions of what India should be; between the enthusiastic support for the promotion of Hindi and the fearful reticence of the non-Hindi speaking majority; and between the demands of a Centralized Government and policies defined by local needs and visions.

After sixty years of its guiding principles of the Indian nation, now it is good to take a review of its achievements and limitations from the context with which it was formed. This chapter sets out to highlight the cultural context of the formation of Indian Constitution and this chapter examines the achievements and limitations of the Constitution from its original vision of India. History may teach us a lesson that we need to learn in order to move ahead towards the future. It is my hope that knowledge of the past will help us in the present to meet the communal, ethnic and inhuman situation of our present India. Such reflections are urgent and important in a context of globalization and the present upsurge of ethnic and religious unrest worldwide, and also for us here in India who must find a way to respond to the challenges of the present times.

Indian Civilization and Indian Nationalism

India is a subcontinent with a vast population of the most diverse levels of culture. Anthropological knowledge of the people of India reveals that almost all known racial groups have migrated to India at different times in the past with their own language, religion and culture. Since, there was plenty of space, the migrating cultural and racial groups could pass on and penetrate further into the interior without much opposition. Thus, the various cultural groups did not destroy each other, but continued to live on and consolidate into the main components of the present-day population. The caste system also helped to keep the diverse racial, social and cultural groups apart, for it prevented them effectively from mixing with one another. The population of India is thus very heterogeneous. Variety and diversity permeates the whole subcontinent, every State and district, every town and village.

Indian civilization is the outcome of a confluence of various cultural, religious, linguistic and ethnic traditions. Over the years of mutual fecundation, synthesis and challenge, Indian civilization has come to be characterized by diversity of culture, religion, language, race and caste groups. According to Kothari, "in the absence of a centralized political authority it was 'the Indian civilizational enterprise' which 'over the centuries achieved a remarkable degree of cohesion and held together different sub-systems in a continental-size society'" (Kothari, 1988:2223). Thus, the unifying force of Indian civilization was the acceptance of multi-culturality and linguistic diversity rather than a political ideology of regimentation.

The Age of Nationalism in the modern sense of the word is a recent phenomenon. It developed in the eighteenth century in the West and emerged at a later period as a universal political concept. According to Kohn, it was only between 1815-1920 that the political map of Europe was redrawn, while the political map of Asia and Africa changed between 1945-1965 (Kohn, 1968:63). Before this period nationalism with its present implications did not exist; there were city-states, tribal groups and dynastic states and empires (Gellner, 1994:62).

The development of nationalism is seen as an integral part of the same historical process that saw the rise of industrialism and democracy. According to Gellner and Hobsbawm the emergence of modern nationalism is an inevitable consequence of capitalism and industrialization (Hastings, 1997:10). Partha Chatterjee expresses similar views with regard to the emergence of nationalism. In his opinion, nationalism required the replacement of a traditional, group-based culture by the culture of an industrial society, i.e., a shared culture of a larger group but where the individual and not the group was the primary unit (Chatterjee, 1986:5). Nationalism thus presupposes the existence, in fact or as an ideal, of a centralized form of government over a large and distinct territory (Kohn, 1956:4).

In India nationalism emerged in the context of colonialism (*see* Oommen, 1997; Singh, 1997:117-130). It can be traced to the political and administrative unification followed by the economic unification by the British. Politically speaking there was no India at the beginning of the nineteenth century, and for at least a century before that neither did India possess a knowledge of its own past and its ancient history (Majumdar, 1965:4). The introduction of English education, European science and philosophy, as well as the pride in India as a nation and her past culture, emerged at this historical turning point.

Cultural Context of Indian Nationalism : Contending Visions of India

What is the Cultural Foundation of Modern India ?

In its early manifestation, the struggle for nationalism, anti-colonial consciousness and the need for independence were not in the realm of politics but in the realm of ideology and culture (Pannikar, 1995:57). The first expression of this consciousness was in the form of social and religious reform movements. The important question then was—what is the cultural foundation of Indian society and how are we to reconstruct it as a modern nation on a par with other modern nation-states?

Two strands of thought emerged from upper caste Hindus: one led to an attempt at reconstructing Indian society on the basis of Western ideas originating in the age of Enlightenment and Liberalism, and the other wanted the reconstruction to take place on the basis of ancient Hindu traditions. These two visions of India developed their own ideology, leadership and organization in the course of freedom struggle in India. A third vision was voiced by oppressed and marginalized people of India. These three visions of modern India shaped the course of dialogue in India at the birth of the Indian nation and the framing of her Constitution. They are also influential in the current political debates today.

Let us concentrate on these strands of thought.

The Concept of an Indian Nation built on a Rational Approach to Culture

The Enlightenment philosophy of the West began to have its impact on the newly Western-educated Indians during the colonial period. It gave rise to the "Indian Renaissance". The spirit that was promoted by English education was usually that of British liberalism, rationalism and utilitarianism, a spirit that challenged many of the presuppositions on which the orthodox Brahminic Hindu world outlook was based. With ruthless self-criticism the new Western-educated elite sought to lay the basis for a total social transformation, to weld science and rationality to recreate India.

The beginnings of this social revolt can be easily identified in the thoughts of Raja Rammohun Roy (1772-1833). Roy vividly described the degraded state of society and acknowledged without embarrassment the virtues of Western learning, liberal legal and social institutions, and Western social ethics (see Damle and Aikara 1982:77). With a view to cleansing Hindu culture and society of its weakness and incongruities, he founded the *Brahmo Samaj* in 1828 at Calcutta. Its main ideological thrust was to transform Hinduism in the mould of Christianity. The assumption was that Hindu society could only be healed of its social evils if it adopted the Christian rejection of polytheism and idolatry.

The purpose of the *Brahmo Samaj* was to restructure Hindu culture in terms of modernity. Roy campaigned for the prohibition of *sati* until Governor-General Lord William Bentinck enacted it in 1829. His revolt against the living Hindu society and his appeal to Indians to purify their religion and reform their social institutions echoed throughout the century after his death. The Brahmo ideologues imbibed quite a bit of Christianity along with some Deism of the European Enlightenment. The third-generation Samaj leader Keshub Chandra Sen (1838-1884) professed a Christian-like veneration of Jesus of Nazareth and interiorized the Christian concept of man's basic sinfulness.

The massive all-India impact of such reform measures led to a widespread reaction to restrain its further diffusion and subsequent erosion of traditional Hindu values.

The Concept of an Indian Nation Built on Aryan Vedic Culture

While Rammohun Roy cherished held a vision of an Indian society rejuvenated by centuries of exposure to Western science and Christian morality, Dayananda Saraswati (1824-1883) urged a regeneration of Hinduism through adherence to a purified "Vedic faith". The Vedic Aryans are praised by Dayananda as a primordial and elect people to whom the *Veda* has been revealed by God and whose language (Sanskrit) is said to be the `Mother of all languages' (Dayananda, 1981:249). They migrated in the distant past, at the beginning of history from Tibet—the first land to emerge from the Ocean—towards the Aryavarta. Their territory, the original homeland of the Vedic civilization, covered the Punjab, Doab and the Ganges basin. From there the Aryans were in a position to dominate the whole world till the *Mahabharata* war, a historic watershed that inaugurated a phase of decadence. National renaissance for Daynanda implied a return of the Vedic Golden Age.

The chief object of the Arya Samaj, which he founded in 1875 in Bombay, was to bring about social and religious reform through a renaissance of early Hindu doctrines. Popular slogans were "*Back to the Vedas*" and "*Aryavarta for the Aryans*" (Smith, 1938:57). This view simply equated Indian culture with Hinduism and Hindu culture; all non-Hindu cultural traditions were regarded as contaminating influences. The Arya Samaj is probably the first movement in India to define nationalism in terms of ethnicity: in Dayananda's writings, the Hindus are the incontestable descendents of the Aryans.

Dayananda's attack on other religions as Christianity and Islam was vigorous. His book, the *Satyartha Prakash* ("Light of Truth") contains a polemical chapter against Christianity, one against Islam, one against Buddhism and Jainism, and several against allegedly degenerative trends in Hinduism. The Arya Samaj had two items in its manifesto: *Shuddhi*, the meaning of which is purification, a term for the ceremony by which non-Hindus were converted to Hinduism, and *Sangathan* which literally means union, that is the promotion of solidarity among Hindus. In short, the Arya Samaj wanted to establish a Hindu nation by propagating a common religion and culture in

India and converting others to Hinduism through the ceremony of *shuddhi* (see Jordens, 1978).

The idea of world domination by the Hindus was voiced at that time by another Arya Samajist based in the Rajasthani British enclave of Ajmer, Har Bilas Sarda (1867-1955). In the second chapter of *The Hindu Superiority* (1906), entitled "Hindu Colonization of the World", the author rejects the Central Asia theory of emigration of the Aryans to India, and asserts that Aryavarta was the birth place of a race which subsequently spread and settled in Egypt, Ethiopia, Persia, Asia Minor, Greece, Rome, Turkistan, Germany, Scandinavia, the Hyperborean countries, Great Britain, Eastern Asia and America (Sarda, 1975:109-163). According to Sarda most civilizations of the world could be traced back to the Hindu-Aryans, a race which had colonised the whole world before the *Mahabharat* war (Sarda, 1975). The ideological impact of the Arya Samaj was one among several factors that influenced the subsequent ideology of Hindu nationalism that emerged in the 1920s (Jaffrelot, 1996:17).

Vivekananda's (1863-1902) thought marked the culmination of the nineteenth century social revolt. He founded the Ramakrishna Math and Mission for the dissemination of Hinduism and for social service. He believed that India alone had a spiritual message whereas the West was steeped in sensuality: "Up, India, and conquer the world with your spirituality" (Vivekananda, 1957:600).

There are thus two predominant versions of nationalism in India: Indian nationalism and Hindu nationalism. The basic question raised by these nationalistic movements was "What should be the cultural foundation of the Indian nation?" Indian nationalism was mainly supported by the western-educated Indian elite, who were secular and utilitarian in their approach. In the words of Heimsath, this brand of nationalism had "at its base an anti-traditional, liberal democratic, secular and politically oriented concept of the nation", so at an early stage a nationalist ideology was developed which "could properly encompass all Indian cultures and religions" (1964:39). Hindu nationalism developed as a reaction against the liberal and inclusive Indian nationalism.

Cultural Controversies in the National Congress

A second stage in the development of a modern Indian nationalism emerged in 1885 with the foundation of the National Congress by

Allan Octovian Hume. The Indian National Congress tried to define a new India in terms of borrowed ideas from the European political experience and Western social ethics. Most of the leaders of the Congress understood the need for a truly all-India nationalism which would rise above regional and communal loyalties (*see* Smith, 1963:88).

By the end of nineteenth century there was a mighty struggle for the control of the Congress. Two factions, the moderates and the extremists, held radically different views as to the proper ends and means of the nationalist movement. While the moderates in the National Congress such as Dadabhai Naoroji, Madhava Govinda Ranade and Gopal Krishna Gokhale promoted reforms in Hindu culture, extremists glorified Hindu culture and opposed any kind of reform in it. While liberals envisioned a modernization of India through the adoption of the Western parameters of justice, order, rationality and the secular state, Tilak glorified the Vedic civilization (Parvate, 1959:463). According to him Vedic religion was the religion of the Aryans from a very early time. During Vedic times, India was a self-contained country. It was a united and great nation (Varma, 1967:197). He became the proponent of the *Hindutva* ideology of his time.

Tilak's overall consideration was the promotion of solidarity among the Hindus, and so he emphasized the superiority of their religion, encouraged revivalism, politicized the Ganapati festival in 1893 and converted Shivaji into a cult figure in 1895, thus serving both religious and political objectives (Michael, 1986: 185-197). Tilak effectively invoked the spirit of resurgent Hinduism to support the nationalist cause, but at the inevitable cost of alienating the Muslims.

The leaders of the Hindu nationalist movement in favour of a revival of Hindu culture openly acknowledged their identification of nationalism with Hinduism. Tilak at one time put the matter this way: "The common factor in Indian society is the feeling of *Hindutva* (devotion to Hinduism)" (*see* Wolpert, 1962:210). The style of the revivalists was more aggressive and tended to reflect a *Kshatriya* (warrior) worldview. The partition of Bengal in 1905 created a Muslim-majority area, widened the breach between the Hindu and Muslim communities, and gave further stimulus to extremist activities.

The religious symbols that Tilak used so effectively in Maharashtra had no appeal in Bengal, but others of even greater potency were at hand. The land of Bengal, and by extension all of India became identified with the female aspect of the Hindu godhead, and the result was the concept of a divine Motherland. Bankim Chandra Chatterjee's (1838-1894) poem

Bande Mataram ("Hail to the Mother") soon became the Congress nationalist song popular throughout India. The country was the Mother, but not a defenceless female: "Thou art Durga (the Mother Goddess), Lady and Queen, with hands that strike and swords of sheen" (Smith 1963:90). According to Majumdar, Bankim's nationalism was Hindu rather than Indian. In his novel he converted "patriotism into a religion and religion into patriotism" (Majumdar, 1965:479).

Some of the most passionate statements of the extremist creed came from Aurobindo Ghose who wrote in 1907: "Liberty is the fruit we seek from the sacrifice, and the Motherland the goddess to whom we offer it". "Nationalism is not a mere political programme; nationalism is a religion that has come from God" he declared (Ghose 1965: 135).

The cult of Durga or Kali, with its tantric ritual and animal sacrifices, quickly became associated with revolutionary terrorism in Bengal. A pamphlet printed secretly called upon the sons of India to rise up, arm themselves with bombs, and invoke Mother Kali: "What does the Mother want? A coconut? No! A fowl or a sheep or a buffalo? No!... The Mother is thirsting after the blood of *Feringhis* (foreigners) who have bled her profusely" (Quoted in Griffiths 1952: 296; also in Smith, 1963:91).

The marriage of politics and religion was consummated in the formation of the Hindu Mahasabha in 1915. In 1909 the famous Arya Samajist nationalist leader Lala Lajpat Rai declared, "Hindus are a `nation' in themselves because they represent a type of civilization all their own" (Jaffrelot, 1996:19). He was echoing the use of the German word `nation', which connoted a people, implying a community possessing a certain civilization and culture. He published some articles by Lala Lalchand in the paper Punjabee on how to build a Hindu country: "This can only be achieved by asserting a purely Hindu interest, and not by an Indian propaganda. The consciousness must rise in the mind of each Hindu that he is a Hindu, and not merely an Indian, and when it does arise the newly awakened force is bound to bring its result." In another article Lala Lalchand wrote: "The point I wish to urge is that patriotism ought to be communal and not merely geographical".

Muslim Nationalism as a Response to Hindu Cultural Nationalism

The monopoly of the nationalist movement by Hindus who had a culture different from that of the Muslims, created nervousness among the Muslims as to the future of their own culture should the Hindus succeed in attaining independence. Moreover, the large-scale participation by the Hindus in the nationalist movement inevitably put a stamp of its own on the movement. The various symbols used for promoting the nationalist movement like the anthem *Bande Mataram* were suggestive of Hindu culture. A historical figure like Shivaji was a political hero to most Hindus; but to many Muslims he was an opponent of Muslim rule in India. All this drove a wedge between the Muslims and the Hindus and the division became more acute with the gradual politicization of religion. During this time a number of Hindu-Muslim riots occurred in various parts of India.

Sir Sayed Ahmed Khan, a prominent Muslim leader realized the position of the Muslims and opened a college for Muslims in Aligarh in 1877, which later developed into the Aligarh University. At first an ardent nationalist, Sir Sayed affirmed that Hindus and Muslims in India formed one nation. At the same time, however, he opposed the Congress movement from its inception, urged the Muslims to stay away from it, and set up organisations with a view to opposing it, all because he feared that the Hindus as the majority community would ride roughshod over the interests of Muslims.

Sir Syed Ahmad's advice to the Muslims not to join the Indian National Congress was based on the following considerations. He held that its aims and objectives reflected ignorance of history and the present reality, and that the Congress did not take into consideration the fact that India was inhabited by several nationalities. As India lacked homogeneity, the result of differences in educational background and political consciousness, it would not be in the interest of the Muslims to caste their lot with the Congress, which was largely dominated by the Hindus. This fear continued to dominate the minds of Muslim leaders thereafter and shape their political objectives and course of action in subsequent years. Like the parallel movements among the Hindus, the Muslims too formed their own organizations. These Islamic movements tried to assert the superiority of their religion, their culture and their past and succeeded in at least giving substance to the idea that their religion, culture and philosophy were not inferior to others (Haq, 1992). To serve them as the political platform to propagate their views of identity in India they founded the Muslim League in 1906.

Revivalist Response to Gandhi

Revivalism was a movement the object of which was to promote a renewed interest in traditional religion. The followers of Arya Samaj and the Congress faction led by Tilak wanted the revival of Hindu tradition in building modern India. After the death of Tilak in 1920, when Mohandas Gandhi publicly emerged on the Indian political scene as the Mahatma, he received widespread revivalist support. Indeed, many believed him to be one of them.

While Gandhi has much in common with revivalists, gradually many came to oppose him as they became better acquainted with his ideas. Gandhi strove unceasingly for Hindu-Muslim unity, convinced that ultimately both religions were true and valid (*see* Gandhi, 1949). His deepest conviction was that God, Truth and *Ahimsa* (non-violence) were all one and the same. *Satyagraha* (truth-force, non-violent resistance) was based on Gandhi's personal religious faith and which he successfully employed against the British who were firmly committed to the maintenance of law and order and *vis-à-vis* non violent resistance appeared ruthless and brutal.

The revivalists were disturbed by Gandhi's ascetic non-*kshatriya* style of leadership, his definition of *dharma* (right conduct) as the non-violent pursuit of "truth," and his assimilationist conception of the Indian nation, which he saw as a brotherhood or a confederation of communities.

Dr. Kurtakoti, *Sankaracharya* (religious head) of the Karvir Peeth, expressed the views of many revivalists when he wrote in the 1920's that Gandhi's use of *ahimsa* (non-violence) in the non-cooperation movement would "uproot the very principle of Hinduism and Aryan philosoply" (*Mahratta,* Pune, 20th October, 1922). He claimed that *ahimsa* as employed by Gandhi weakened the Hindus. Moreover, he maintained that "passive and non-resisting sufferance is a Christian and not Aryan principle". He implored Hindus to return to the militancy advocated by Tilak, Vivekananda, and Ghose. Many other revivalists were in agreement, and when Gandhi took control of the Congress in the 1920's the stage was set for a revivalist search for new forms of protest (Anderson and Damle, 1987:20).

As a result of the intensification of Hindu-Muslim tensions between 1921-1923, a renewed importance was attached to the dormant Hindu Mahasabha (Great Assembly), formed in 1915 as a forum for a variety of Hindu interests (e.g., cow protection, Hindi in the Devanagri script, caste reforms, etc.) (Anderson and Damle, 1987: 28).

It is in this setting of Hinduism-in-danger that a new influential Hindu militant organisation known as the Rashtriya Swayamsevak Sangh (RSS) (Association of National Volunteers) was established in 1925 by Dr. Keshab Baliram Hedgewar who was deeply influenced by Tilak. The RSS purports to defend Hinduism against its so-called antagonists. Its avowed objective is the unification of the Hindu community and the inculcation of a militant awareness of its common heritage and destiny.

One of the most influential works in the development of the Hindu nationalist ideology was the treatise on *Hindutva: Who is a Hindu?* first published in Nagpur in 1923 by a Maharashtrian Brahmin and future president of the Hindu Mahasabha (1937-42) Veer D. Savarkar (1883-1966), a close associate of Tilak. *Hindutva* refers to a people united by common country, blood, history, religion, culture and language. The concept stems from the mythical reconstruction of the Vedic Golden Age of the 'Aryan' race (Klostermaier, 1989:33). The idea of *Hindutva* became influential in all RSS's organizational activities. While rejecting politics as the means to attain its particular objectives, the RSS has nevertheless in the past supported the political work of the Hindu Mahasabha, and has been closely linked with the Jan Sangh and Bharatiya Janata Party.

The Hindutva Vision of Nationhood

According to Golwalkar, who succeeded Hedgewar, the Hindu nation has existed for 8,000 to 10,000 years, and Hindustan has been in the possession of the Hindus for at least that length of time. In fact, the Hindus are not immigrants but indigenous sons of the soil, whatever scholars may say to the contrary. At the heart of the Hindu religion are the noble ideas of the *Vedas*. Golwalkar claimed Bharatvarsha had been a *rashtra* (country) since Vedic times. He states that every race develops a language of its own. The diverse languages of India are offshoots of Sanskrit, the dialect of the gods.

Race is a population with a common origin and with one culture. Therefore, the maintenance of racial unity in a nation necessitates the assimilation, or inextricable fusion, of foreign populations in it into the mother race—in other words, they should merge fully into an original national race not only economically and politically but also religiously, culturally, and linguistically. Race is by far the most important of the five ingredients in a nation. Hindustan, suggests Golwalkar, can learn and profit from Germany, where racial pride led to the attempt to eliminate the Jews because deep-rooted differences prevented their total assimilation into the German race.

Golwalkar makes it crystal clear that India is a Hindu nation. Muslims and Christians, though born in this country, do not feel that they are the children of the land, after they have changed their faith. He goes on to suggest that such people should be placed behind bars during the time of national crisis.

Golwalkar reiterates that secularism is not his path for national integration; it should come through Hinduization. His idea of the best solution to the problems of minorities is contained in one word—assimilation. According to him they should be "wholly subordinated to the Hindu nation, claiming nothing, deserving no privileges, far less any preferential treatment—not even citizen's rights" (Golwalkar 1947:55-56). Like Savarkar's *Hindutva*, Golwalkar's definition of Hindu is political rather than religious (Heehs, 1998:117).

Linked to the RSS in India are several affiliated organizations (referred to in the RSS literature as the "family"), working in politics, in social welfare, in the media and among students, labourers and Hindu religious groups. The symbiotic links between the RSS and the "family" are strengthened by the recruitment into the affiliates of *Swayamsevaks* (members) who have already demonstrated organizational skills in the RSS (*see* Lambert, 1959; and Seunarine, 1977; Koenraad, 2001).

So the river of Hindu revivalism flows on. The origin of *Hindutva* and its promotion by Hindu nationalistic groups such as the Hindu Mahasabha, the Rashtriya Swayamsevak Sangh, the Ram Rajya Parishad, The Jan Sangh, the Vishva Hindu Parishad, the Shiv Sena, Bajrang Dal and Bharatiya Janata Party, have their roots in the traditions of late nineteenth-century Hindu nationalism (*see* Anderson and Damle, 1987; also Malik and Singh, 1995).

In an interesting speech a Hindu Mahsabha leader attempted to list the cultural changes which Indian Muslims would have to undergo in order to become acceptable nationals of the Indian (Hindu) state of the future. First, they would have to accept the *Ramayana* and *Mahabharata* as their epics and reject the Arabic and Persian classics. They would have to regard Ramachandra, Shivaji, and Hindu gods Ram and Krishna as their heroes, and condemn various Muslim historical figures as foreign invaders or traitors (Despande, 1949:10; Smith 1963:375).

The formation of Vishva Hindu Parishad (VHP) in 1964 marks a new phase in the history of *Hindutva*. The VHP was specifically set up to forge a corporate Hindu identity, to unite all Hindu sects in opposition to Islam and Christianity. The VHP uses the latest media technology to exalt Puranic heroes as the model of Hindu character. A bid is made for a Hindu state ruled by an explicitly "Hindu" political party.

Thus, Hindu nationalism in India emerged at that phase of the Nationalist Movement where religion was sought to be made the basis for the emerging identity of India. As Juergensmeyer explains, when a religious perspective is fused with the political and social destiny of a nation, it is referred to as religious nationalism. He maintains that religious nationalists were not just religious fanatics. For the most part they were political activists who were seriously attempting to create a "modern" language of politics and provide a new basis for the nation-state (1994:406).

An Alternative Cultural Vision of Indian Nationhood—The Voice of the Oppressed

The concern for social reform at the beginning of the Indian nationalist movement was given a back seat with the emergence of militant Hindu nationalism. Upper caste Hindus identified "nation" and "national culture" as basically Hindu, as deriving from Vedic times, and as fundamentally a creation of the Aryan people. And with this they tended to accept as an inherent part of their culture some form of the *varnashrama-dharma* and to relegate other Indian cultural traditions to a secondary and inferior position. As we have seen, they not only made use of high-caste religious symbols in their mass organizing; they also made use of the "Aryan theory of race" in interpreting cultural traditions. It is in this context of what constitutes Indian national culture that we should examine the alternative vision of prominent non-Aryan or non-brahmanic leaders within India.

The main figures of this larger non-Aryan and anti-Brahmin vision of Indian nationalism are Jotiba Phule, E.V. Ramasamy 'Periyar' and Babasaheb Ambedkar, with many others throughout India (Narayanswami Guru in Kerala, Acchutanand in Uttar Pradesh, Mangoo Ram in the Punjab). They attacked of exploitation at all levels, culturally, economically and politically.

The Vision of Jotirao Phule (1826-1890)

Jotirao Phule was the first Indian in modern India to proclaim the dawn of a new age for the common man, the downtrodden, the underdog and the Indian woman. It was his aim to reconstruct the social order on the basis of social equality, justice and reason.

The "Aryan theory of race" constituted the most influential intellectual guideline in discussion on caste and society in Phule's time. European Orientalists used it to establish an ethnic kinship between Europeans and the ancient Vedic peoples. The constant interest of European scholars in ancient Aryan society and their praises of this society was an important moral boost to high caste Indians. Thus, Indian civilization was seen as primarily derivative from Aryan civilization, and the caste system was lauded as a means by which people of diverse racial and cultural backgrounds were brought together and subjected to the civilizing influence of Aryans (Omvedt, 1976:103).

At one level, Phule simply reversed the perception, arguing that the low castes, whom he sometimes called "*Shudras* and *Ati-Shudras*" and sometimes simply listed as "Kumbis, Malis, Dhangars ... Bhils, Kolis, Mahars, and Mangs", were the original inhabitants of the country, enslaved and exploited by conquering Aryans who formulated a caste-based Hinduism as a means of deceiving the masses and legitimizing their power.

It was the confirmed view of Jotirao that the ancient history of India was nothing but the struggle between Brahmins and non-Brahmins (Keer, 1964:120). Hence, Phule consciously sought to bring together the major peasant castes (these were, besides the Kumbis or cultivators, the Malis or 'garden' cultivators and Dhangars or Shepherds) along with the large untouchable castes of Mahars and Mangs in a common 'front' against Brahmin domination.

Jotirao's attack on Brahminism was unmistakable. He realized that the seeds of Brahmin power, supremacy and privileges lay in their scriptures and *Puranas*; and that these works and the caste system were created to exploit the lower classes. Phule also reinterpreted sacred religious literature, for example, by reading the nine *avatars* of Vishnu as stages of the Aryan conquest. He used King Bali (a non-Aryan king) as a counter-symbol to the brahminical scriptures and *Puranas*. He revolted against priestcraft and the caste system and set afoot a social movement for the liberation of the *Shudras*, *Ati-Shudras* (untouchables) and women.

To achieve his life's ambition for a casteless society, Phule founded the *Satya Shodhak Samaj* on September 24, 1873. The *Samaj* opened the first school for girls and untouchables and organised widow remarriages, marriages without Brahmin priests, etc. Phule's view of exploitation was thus focused on cultural and ethnic factors rather than economic or political ones.

Pariyar's (1879-1973) Self-Respect Movement

E.V. Ramasamy Naicker, known as Periyar (Great Sage), was born in 1879 in Erode of a respectable middle class family of artisans. He married at the age of 13, but after six years he became a *sannyasi*, travelling as a religious mendicant over the whole of India. In his visits to pilgrim centres, he gained an intimate knowledge of the evils of popular Hinduism and also the exploitations of the masses by Brahmin priests.

Periyar was convinced that casteism and Hinduism were one and the same. He wanted Hinduism, as he saw it, to go altogether out. His movement took a turn towards racial consciousness and became a 'Dravidian' movement, seeking to defend the rights of the Dravidians against Aryan domination. The Aryans were blamed for introducing an unjust and oppressive social system in the country (*see* Hardgrave, 1965:17).

Periyar immediately realised what the new ideology of the Indian elite, the 'Aryan view of race', would imply. This view was adopted enthusiastically by the Indian elite as a new model for understanding caste. That is, Brahmins, Kshatriyas and Vaishyas were held almost as a matter of definition to be the descendants of the invading Aryans; Shudras and untouchables of the native conquered inhabitants. In the light of the new ideology to claim "Aryan" descent was equivalent to claiming "twiceborn" status; to say "Dravidian" or "non-Aryan" almost equivalent to saying "*Shudra*." The high caste elite of India began to define Aryan and Sanskritic culture as the basis of "Indian nationality", but by so doing they were in fact highlighting the culture of the north Indian upper castes and mistaking this fraction of Indian culture for the whole.

Periyar sought to defend the rights of the Dravidians against Aryan domination. He saw in the Brahmins the representatives of Hindu arrogance and a stronghold of social injustice. He left the Congress attacking it as a tool of Brahmin domination. In 1925, he organized the "Self-Respect Movement," designed as Dravidian Uplift, seeking to expose Brahmin tyranny and the deceptive methods by which they controlled all spheres of Hindu life. Periyar publicly ridiculed the *Puranas* as fairy tales, not only imaginary and irrational by grossly immoral as well. He also attacked religion as a tool of Brahmin domination.

The Hindu religion was denounced as an opiate by which the Brahmins had dulled and subdued the masses. "A Hindu according to the present concept may be a Dravidian, but a Dravidian in the real sense of the term cannot and shall not be a Hindu" (A.S. Venu cited in Harrison, 1960:127). Measures were taken to destroy the images of Hindu deities such as Rama and Ganesha. According to Periyar, "Rama and Sita are despicable characters, not worthy of imitation or admiration even by the lowest of fourth-rate humans." Ravana (a Dravidian hero represented as a demon in the north), on the other hand, is depicted as a Dravidian of "excellent character". In his preface to *The Ramayana: A True Reading*, he states that "the veneration of the story any longer in Tamil Nadu is injurious and ignominious to the self-respect of the community and of the country" (Naicker, 1959: iii-iv).

Today, several Dravidian political parties in Tamil Nadu trace back their inspiration to Periyar in their efforts to build a Dravidian civilization in the Indian subcontinent.

Ambedkar (1891-1956) — A Revolutionary

Dr. B.R. Ambedkar was very much inspired and guided by the noble example set by Mahatma Jotiba Phule. Phule was no more there to guide Ambedkar. Nevertheless, his example made an indelible impression on the mind of Ambedkar, who was determined to complete the work began by Jotiba: this became his life's ambition (Rajashekhriah, 1971:18-19; also *see* Keer, 1974: vii).

Ambedkar was a revolutionary. He led the fight against untouchability, Hinduism, and the Brahmin caste. He taught that caste was not only unjust but also immoral. He established a new dispensation, a new religion (Neo-Buddhism), whose foundation is its unequivocal rejection of Hinduism.

Ambedkar criticized the caste system vehemently. For him the fight against casteism and untouchability was central, at the heart of his agenda. Hence, he was very critical of the two prevalent approaches in his time to reform the caste system, namely, that of Dayananda

Saraswati and of Gandhi. Society should be based on the three fundamental principles of liberty, equality and fraternity.

If caste was to be destroyed, he said, then its religious foundation, the *Vedas* and *Shastras*, must also be destroyed. Faith in these scriptures was nothing more than a legalized class ethic favouring the Brahmins.

If you wish to bring about a breach in the system, then you have got to apply the dynamite to the *Vedas* and *Shastras* which deny any part to reason, to the *Vedas* and *Shastras* which deny any part to morality. You must destroy the Religion of the *Smritis* (Ambedkar, 1945:70).

Ambedkar also rejected the position of Gandhi with regard to caste and its reform. Gandhi felt that the ancient Hindus had already achieved an ideal social system with the *varnavyavastha*. So according to Gandhi, "the law of *varna* means that everyone will follow as a matter of *dharma*—duty—the hereditary calling of his forefathers . . . . he will earn his livelihood by following that calling". In contrast Ambedkar believed that an ideal society had yet to be achieved in India. For him, the priority was not making "Hinduism" or Hindu society "shine forth" but building a new, equal, free, open, non-hierarchial, modern India.

According to Ambedkar, "it is wrong to say that the problem of the untouchables is a social problem . . . . The problem of the untouchables is fundamentally a political problem (of minority *versus* majority groups)" (Ambedkar, 1945a:190). Hence, Ambedkar launched his revolutionary movement for the liberation and advancement of the *dalits*. On 20th July, 1942, he declared at Nagpur:

> With justice on our side, I do not see how we can lose our battle. The battle to me is a matter of full joy. The battle is in the fullest sense spiritual. There is nothing material or sordid in it. For our struggle is for our freedom. It is a battle for the reclamation of human responsibility which has been suppressed and mutilated by the Hindu social system and will continue to be suppressed and mutilated if in the political struggle the Hindus win and we lose. My final word of advice to you is, "educate, organise and agitate"; have faith in yourselves and never lose hope (*see* Das and Massey, 1995: viii).

Thus Ambedkar was able to put the untouchability issue at the centre stage of Indian politics.

Ambedkar painfully realised that in Hinduism the untouchables would never be able to obtain a respectable status and receive just treatment. He was also convinced that individual and group mobility was difficult for untouchables within the Hindu social system. In this context, he saw two possibilities of social emancipation: the political unity of untouchables and mass conversion. Hence, in 1936 he talked of conversion to another religion: "Though I have been born a Hindu, I shall not die as a Hindu" (1936—31st May, Bombay). He had already made a first mention of conversion in the Yeola Conference of 1935.

Hearing the conversion call of Ambedkar, Hindu leadership was very disturbed. Several leaders began to persuade him not to go ahead. Ambedkar expressed surprise that the caste Hindus who had never shown fellow-feeling for the untouchables were suddenly beseeching them to stay within Hinduism. Since untouchables have been for centuries ill-treated and humiliated by caste Hindus, why did they now suddenly take such an interest in keeping them within the Hindu fold ?

After long deliberation and a conscious choice in favour of Buddhism, on the 14th October, 1956, Ambedkar took his *diksha* (initiation) at Nagpur at 9:30 a.m. Assembled were about five lakh Mahars, who all were converted to Buddhism on that day. His embracing Buddhism was a strong protest aimed at all that the Hindus had failed to do. For him *swaraj* (freedom) did not mean anything if it did not also put an end to the slavery of the untouchables (Gore, 1993:144).

The above Phule/Periyar/Ambedkar tradition represents the effort to define an alternative identity for the people, based on non-Aryan and low caste perspectives, that was critical not only of the oppressiveness of the dominant Hindu castes, but also of the claim to antiquity and to being the major Indian tradition (*see* Michael, 1999; Oommen, 2001). The issue, however, was not basically racial but cultural, a matter of group identity.

Formation of Indian Constitution in the Context Contending Visions of India

The above survey on identity in India shows that there have been several contending visions of Indian identity. All these visions were active and influential in the formation of the modern Indian State during the freedom struggle. A continuous dialogue took place with regard to identity in free India. The failure to reach a satisfactory conclusion on the question of Indian identity resulted in the separation of Pakistan from India. Mahatma Gandhi fell a victim to excessive and narrow nationalism.

In spite of these setbacks, after almost three years of deliberation, the Constituent Assembly of India on 26th November, 1949 adopted a constitution for the world's largest liberal democracy. The debate in the Assembly reflected the paradoxes of the Indian situation, which we highlighted above as the contending visions for India. The founding fathers of the Constitution of India defended the notion of a pluralistic society and a neutral state based on equal rights and citizenship. The Constitution of India may justifiably be described as secular and multicultural. Recognition and protection was offered to religious, cultural and linguistic minorities. Equal respect, fairness and non-discrimination were to be the guiding principles of state policies towards minorities.

Differences are recognized but so are the values of equal citizenship and equal rights. After protracted discussions in the Constituent Assembly, the Constitution was passed upholding ethnic, linguistic, cultural and religious pluralism in India and promising recognition and protection for all and non-discriminatory state policies. It articulated a secular and inclusive nationalism of equal opportunities and equal liberty for all, regardless of their religious affiliations or social status. It meant that the state itself was not to become partisan to any particular group, nor does it privilege any particular religion. The equidistance to all religions became the quintessence of secularism and this is ensured in the Constitution.

Constitutional Achievements and Limitations

Prime Minister, Pandit Jawaharlal Nehru, the Deputy Prime Minister Sardar Patel, Rajendra Prasad, the President of the Constituent Assembly, K.M. Munshi and Dr. B.R. Ambedkar played an important role in the formation of the Constitution of India. They understood well the different aspirations of contending groups and the importance of recognition in the Indian nationhood. The idea that all Indian citizens should inherit as their birthright such basic civil rights as were recognized by all modern nations in the world was enshrined in the Constitution of India.

All the same, the Nehruvian and Ambedkarian vision began to breakdown by the late 1960s and several constitutional rights are being questioned today. Over the past two decades the rise of Hindu nationalism and the growing political strength of regional and low caste and tribal parties have helped expose the tears in the fabric once again. As a result of the differing ideologies between *Hindutva* and of the oppressed and marginalized forces, we observe today the emergence of two opposite socio-political and cultural movements. On the one hand, backward castes and classes are in search of a culture based on egalitarian social and economic principles with greater political participation; on the other hand, upper caste Hindus are equally strong in trying to retain control of their present position of privilege and dominance by consolidating ancient hierarchical Brahmanical Hindu values. Thus, culture in India has become polarised by the contrasting interests of the upper and the lower groups, the former vigorously clinging to their traditional status, and the latter fighting for justice, equality and human dignity.

The most vociferous and militant Hindu nationalists are now training their guns on the very basic constitutional concept of pluralism. Public opinion is being shaped to the effect that some people, i.e., the upper and middle classes/castes are patriotic whereas others are not. Tribal people are looked at with suspicion and their national loyalty is being questioned. Similarly, the aspirations of the whole *dalit* community and their movements for equality have been brushed aside as suspect. There is, in the minds of religious nationalists one supreme value—the Hindu nation—on whose altar everything including claims for equality must be sacrificed. Their policy of cultural regimentation has one aim—the consolidation of a Hindu national identity.

Today, there is an imminent danger that anti-liberal forces may set the agenda for government policies. History is now being rewritten to suit Hindu nationalism. The educational system is being redefined in order to influence young minds to believe in *Hindutva* ideology. Hate literature is being distributed to create aversion against Christians and other religious groups. Propaganda is being designed to turn Christians and Muslims into enemies of true patriotism and supporters of anti-national activities. Such a policy is highly dangerous for Indian society, which is basically multi-cultural and multi-religious. Today the terms nationalism and patriotism need clarification.

The concept of patriotism is much-debated. Sometimes, the word is given such an ethnocentric and narrow meaning that it is bound to wreak havoc among us, if applied in practice. It is a general observation that where the spirit of extreme nationalism prevails people are being taught from childhood to hate the 'enemy'. That is why Rabindra Nath Tagore wrote long before the country won independence; long before it witnessed partition, "Nationalism is a great menace. It is the particular thing which for years has been at the bottom of India's troubles" (Tagore, 1992:83 original 1917). Tagore sees in nationalism instincts of self-aggrandisement, of whole peoples organized together with all the paraphernalia of power and prosperity, of flags and hymns and patriotic bragging, nations engaged in a wrestling match; and not bound to listen to the voice of truth and goodness. His version of Indian nationalism can be discerned from the following statement:

> "Even though from childhood I had been taught that idolatry of the nation is better than reverence for God and humanity, I believe that I have outgrown that teaching, and it is my conviction that my countrymen will truly gain their Indianness by fighting against the education which teaches them that a country is greater than the ideals of humanity" (1992: 84).

Writing in a similar vein, Earl Stanley Jones, a visionary and close associate of Mahatma Gandhi wrote: "One of the greatest dangers to world peace is the rise of modern nationalism. It has taken that lovely sentiment called patriotism and has turned it into the deadliest enemy known to the modern world. It causes men to sin where they otherwise would not".

People of one nation usually have no reason to hate people of another. But narrow and exclusive nationalism takes hold of different communities and subjects them to propaganda, instills fear, inspires hate, puts bayonets into their hands and flings them against one another.

What does nationalism mean for the poor, for the oppressed and marginalized? Is it possible for them to experience a sense of common and shared humanity in the Indian nationhood? Or is nationalism the luxury of the rich and the powerful? As citizens of this country, we need to be concerned about human dignity and the integration of all Indians. In the face of economic globalization where the rich are becoming rich and the poor are becoming poorer, we need to define nationalism in such a way that the poor and the downtrodden receive their due attention and care. As concerned citizens we need to ask what nationalism means for the poor; for *dalits*, for tribals and other weaker groups. Behind the dreams and aspirations of these marginalized groups lingers the hope that a nation of fairness and justice will be realized, a nation, humane and inclusive.

Such a humanistic nationalism has to be pursued by all right thinking people not by themselves alone but in collaboration with emerging humanistic peoples' movements. Widespread support of the cause of suppressed groups and identities will take us in the direction of a more complete and integral understanding of nation. Ordinary citizens should be motivated to get involved in issues of justice, equality, fraternity and ecology. People must be active in the civil society. A healthy civil society marked by an active pluralism will ensure also an authentic and humanistic nationalism. Scholars should collaborate with secular humanist intellectuals in bringing to light the history and cultural traditions of tribals, *Dalit* and other marginalized people. This would be a constructive move in promoting a holistic and integral nationalism in India.

Conclusion

India is a multi-cultural and multi-religious country. Its unity derives from the fact that it welcomes and embraces diversity. When the issue of the nature of Indian nationhood was being discussed during the freedom struggle there were contending visions of India. A continuous dialogue was alive and the outcome was an inclusive secular Constitution. But today, there is an active and powerful move to unify India in terms of Hindu *Rashtra* (Nation). The impression has been created that upper and middle caste Hindus are the true patriots, whereas others are not. Steps have been taken to rewrite history to suit the above agenda. The education system has been revamped to influence young minds to accept the *Hindutva* ideology. To carry out the *Hindutva* agenda, devices have been envisaged to change the Constitution. We have in this chapter attempted to highlight the informal dialogue which took place during the freedom struggle for the purpose of defining an Indian nationhood. Dialogue of the past could guide us in our present situation. Indian nationalism should give dignity to all Indians and make them wanted and respected citizens. But what we see today is that *dalits*, tribals, backward castes and other marginalized and suppressed communities are in search of a nation inspired by egalitarian values, social justice, economic opportunities and participation in political decision making; the *Hindutva* ideologues, on the other hand, are equally strong in trying to retain control of their present privileges and dominance by insisting on ancient hierarchical Brahmanic Hindu cultural values. Thus, culture and nationalism in India has become polarized by the contrasting interests of the upper and lower groups, the former vigorously clinging to their traditional status, and the latter fighting for justice, equality and human dignity.

The future lies in strengthening the inclusive nationalism as visualized by the Founding Fathers of this great nation. The question the intellectuals in India need to address is how can the citizens strengthen the pluralistic characteristics of Indian society. Our attention should be also to give equal opportunities to all the citizens of India. Special attention has to be paid to the plight of tribals, *dalits* and farmers who feel the marginalization very acutely in the last 60 years of the formation of Constitution of India.

REFERENCES

Ambedkar, B.R., *Annihilation of Caste*. Bangalore: Dalit Sahitya Akademy.

Ambedkar, B.R., *What Congress and Gandhi have done to the Untouchables*. Bombay: Thacker & Co.

Anderson, W.K. and S.D. Damle, *The Brotherhood in Saffron. The Rastriya Swayamsevak Sangh and Hindu Revivalism*. New Delhi: Vistaar Publications.

Chatterjee, P., *Nationalist Thought and the Colonial World—A Derivative Discourse*. New Delhi: Oxford University Press.

Damle, Y.B. and Jacob Aikara, *Caste, Religion and Politics in India*. New Delhi: Oxford & IBH Publishing Co.

Das, Bhagwan and James Massey, *Dalit Solidarity*. Delhi: The Indian Society for Promoting Christian Knowldege (ISPCK).

Dayananda, Swami, *The Light of Truth*. Allahabad (Translated and introduced by Ganga Prasad Upadhyaya)

Deshpande, V.G., *Why Hindu Rashtra?* New Delhi: All India Hindu Mahasabha.

Devanandan, P.D., *The Dravida Kazagham: A Revolt against Brahmanism*. Bangalore: Christian Institute for the Study of Religion and Society.

Gandhi, G.K., *Communal Unity*. Ahmedabad: Navjivan.

Gellner, E., *1994, Encounters with Nationalism*. Oxford: Blackwell.

Ghose, Sri Aurobindo, *Sri Aurobindo, On Nationalism*. Pondicherry: Sri Aurobindo Ashram.

Golwalkar, M.S., *We or Our Nationhood Defined* (4th ed.). Nagpur: Bharat Prakashan.

Gore, M.S., *The Social Context of an Ideology. Ambedkar's Political and Social Thought*. New Delhi: Sage Publications.

Griffiths, Percival, *The British Impact on India*. London: McDonald and Company.

Haq, Jalaul, *Nation and Nation-Worship in India*. New Delhi: Genuine Publication.

Hardgrave, Jr. Robert L., *The Dravidian Movement*. Bombay: Popular Prakashan.

Harrison, Selig, *India: The Most Dangerous Decades*. Princeton: Princeton University Press.

Hastings, A., *The Construction of Nationhood. Ethnicity, Religion and Nationhood*. Cambridge: Cambridge University Press.

Heehs, P., *Nationalism, Terrorism, Communalism. Essays in Modern Indian History*. New Delhi: Oxford University Press.

Heimsath, Charles H., *Indian Nationalism and Hindu Social Reform*. Princeton: Princeton University Press.

Jaffrelot, C., *Hindu Nationalist Movement in India*. New York: Columbia University Press.

Jordens, J.T.F., *Dayananda Saraswati: His Life and Ideas*. Delhi: Oxford University Press.

Juergensmeyer, M., *Religious Nationalism Confronts Secular State*. New Delhi: Oxford University Press.

Keer, Dhananjay, *Mahatma Jotirao Phuley. Father of Indian Social Revolution*. Bombay: Popular Prakashan.

Klostermaier, K.K., *A Survey of Hinduism*. New York: State University of New York Press.

Koenraad, Elst, *Decolonizing the Hindu Mind: Ideological Development of Hindu Revivalism*. New Delhi: Rupa & Co.

Kohn, H., "Nationalism," *International Encyclopedia of Social Sciences*. The Macmillan Co. & The Free Press, Vol. II, pp. 63-69.

Kothari, Rajni, "Integration and Exclusion in Indian Politics," *Economic and Political Weekly*. October 22, 1988: 2223-9.

Lambert, Richard D., Hindu Communal Groups in Indian Politics," in Richard L. Park and Irene Tinker, (eds.) *Leadership and Political Institutions in India*. Princeton: Princeton University Press.

Majumdar, R.C., *The History and Culture of the Indian People. British Paramountcy and Indian Renaissance II*. Bombay: Bharatiya Vidya Bhavan.

Malik, K.Y. and V.B. Singh, *Hindu Nationalists in India*. The Rise of the Bharatiya Janata Party. New Delhi: Vistaar Publications.

Michael, S.M., (ed.), *Dalits in Modern India: Vision and Values*. New Delhi: Vistaar Publications.

Michael, S.M., "Politicization of Ganapati Festival," in *Social Compass*. XXXIII/2-3: 185-197.

Naicker, Ramasamy, E.V., *The Ramayana: A True Reading*. Madras: Rationalist Publications.

Omvedt, Gail, *Dalit and Democratic Revolution*. New Delhi: Sage Publications.

Oommen, T.K., *Citizenship, Nationality and Ethnicity: Reconciling Competing Identities*. Cambridge: Polity Press. *Understanding Indian Society: The Relevance of Perspective from Below*. Occasional Paper Series: 4. Pune: Department of Sociology.

Pannikar, K.N., *Culture, Ideology and Hegemony. Intellectuals & Social Consciousness in Colonial India*. New Delhi: Tulika.

Parvate, T.V., *Gopal Krishna Gokhale*. Ahmedabad: Navjivan Publishing House.

Rajasekhariah, A.M., *B.R. Ambedkar: The Politics of Emancipation*. Bombay: Sindhu Publications.

Sarda, Harbilas, *Hindu Superiority—An Attempt to Determine the Position of the Hindu Race in the Scale of Nations*. New Delhi.

Seunarine, J.F., *Reconversion to Hinduism through Shuddhi*. Madras: Christian Literature Society.

Singh, Yogendra, "Social Processess and Dimensions of Indian Nationalism" in *Social Transformation in India*. (ed. By) Ghanshyam Shah, Jaipur: Rawat Publications.

Smith, Donald Eugene, *India as a Secular State*. London: Princeton University Press.

Smith, W.C. *Modern Islam in India*. London: Princeton University Press.

Smith, William Roy, *Nationalism and Reform in India*. London: Yale University Press.

Tagore, Rabindranath 1992 (original 1917) *Nationalism*. Calcutta: Rupa & Co.

Varma, V.P., *Modern Indian Political Thought*. Agra: Lakshmi Narain Agarwal.

Vivekananda, Swami, *The Complete Works of Swami Vivekananda*. Calcutta: Advaita Ashrama.

Wolpert, Stanley A., *Tilak and Gokhale*. Berkeley: Berkeley University Press.

10

Role of Panchayats in Establishing Communal Harmony through the Process of Governance and Development

G. Palanithurai

Introduction

The increasing tendency of conflicts in India[1] based on larger and narrower identities both at the national and regional levels brings an argument that the whole of the conflict dynamics is being managed politically through governance and administration and thus the role of state is more critical in maintaining secular credentials and establishing communal harmony and peace. In Indian context there are six sources of conflicts namely patriarchy, inequality, sectorality, peripherality, externality and hierarchy[2]. The conflicts generated based on cultural, lingual, regional, ethnic and religious identities at the regional and national levels are being managed by the state by evolving conflict management formula[3]. But the conflicts at the grassroots are being managed mostly by organizations evolved over a period of time. While the intensity of conflict increases beyond the capacity of the community organizations, state institutions involve themselves in managing the conflict. As state has management formula communities have their own management formula. Justice is done both by the state institutions and community organizations. Injustice is also done by both. The cost of conflict management is also a factor. Many of the occasions people have invested heavily to get justice from the state and finally they got justice lost even their livelihood. Many have got relative justice through the community structure even without investing much[4]. But after the establishment of the grassroots governing institutions based on 73rd Amendment to the Constitution of India, the scholars have raised questions as to what extent these identity based conflicts are being tackled at the local level as conflict arises on sharing public resources for development based on the local identities namely the caste and religion[5]. Further conflict arises on making use of development opportunities provided by the Central and Sate governments through schemes and programmes. While claiming entitlements as rights normally in a hierarchical society tend to create conflict. The western model of representative democracy with added strength of creating opportunity to people to participate in governance and development has started with interacting with community structures and norms at the grassroots. The whole process is being looked both as opportunities and threats. In this process those who find opportunities in the new governance arrangements tend to step into the governance system through a process of struggle. Those who are losing power in the new process of governance arrangement tend to redesign the strategy of keeping power with them. In the same way the caste groups are competing with each other utilizing the natural resources which are under the control of the community based organizations. Thus at the grassroots two governance models are at work. State initiated democratic structure and community evolved governance practices are constantly interacting with each other both in harmony and conflict. In order to make governance and development inclusive, reservation of seats has been done to both women and *dalits*. Though reservation of seats has been made for *dalits* and *dalit* women, there is no reservation for Muslims and Muslim women and in the same way there is no reservation for Christians and Christian women. Yet they come to power at the grassroots and perform their duties and responsibilities. While performing their development functions, they have to address the issue of various communities and tackle the problems arise out of the communal identities based on caste and religion. Because major source of conflict is in sharing development resource by the communities. India has got rich social capital and the social capital are active[6]. Hence, they are to be used effectively for the benefits out of the social capital only through the effective handling of the same by the Panchayats[7]. The quantum of benefits vary from region to region and it depends on the intensity of relationship between social capital and Panchayats. In order to find out the reality of the conflict dynamics based on identity, some of the Gram Panchayats have been studied and they are being analysed and explained in this article. In this article we focus primarily on democracy is plasticized and development is used as strategy to establish peace and harmony.

Theoretical Consideration

The very basic objectives of the new dispensation—decentralization of powers are: (a) deepening of democracy, (b) democratization of society, (c) making the people to participate in the power of governance and development, (d) evolving micro plan for development, and (e) achieving economic development and social justice. By doing so, democracy and development should be made inclusive. The objectives are lofty and objective conditions at the ground are challenging. The Panchayats have to perform the tough tasks. Even, after the experience of sixty years of representative democracy in India, still communities are in the clutches of informal traditional institutions. Hence, our representative democracy could not be practiced as a culture; and hence still they are in institutional form alone. Procedures and practices are not in tune with the representative democracy. In this context, the elected representatives at the grassroots are drawn from the marginalized. Primarily, the elected leaders have to equip themselves to respond to the social and political challenges in the governance domain as they are in a hierarchical social system, particularly, feudal agricultural background, and dominant bureaucratic system. Add to the above background the governance and administrative processes are highly complex. To overcome all the barriers and to respond to all the challenges the elected representatives of the local bodies have to develop their skill and capacity. Moreover, the leaders have to develop a perspective. Effective functioning result of adequate devolution of powers, functionaries and finance, building the capacity and skill of the leaders and support structure provided by the civil society and the state. Apart from the above factors leadership plays a vital role. Leadership adopts difficult strategy to change the social environment. How the grassroots leaders are able to manage the communities, Panchayats and achieve development and social justice? is the question to be answered in this article.

Methodology

The case study method has been adopted to study the initiatives taken by the elected Panchayat representatives to achieve development and communal harmony. Along with case study method, focused group discussions were also held in the respective case studies area. Along with the above a very intensive participant observation method is also used to get many insights into the issues of the rural communities and the role performed by the Gram Panchayats. Thus, combination of methods are adopted. They are being presented as case analysis and finally an integrated analysis is made to draw conclusion.

Case Study I

Personal Background

Ms. Jamrud Beevi (50) is the President of Devipattinam Village Panchayat[8]. She is a graduate and her husband is also a graduate. Her husband was in Saudi Arabia for some time. But, after a bypass heart surgery, now he is in Devipattinam, working as a bank manager. They have two daughters, of whom one is married and the other is studying in an engineering college. From her college days, she has been inclined towards public service. She was a sportsperson in school and in college, spending considerable time on games. She gained openness, risk-taking ability, responding to challenges through her sports activities. She has overcome her shyness and inhibitions only through sports. This has added to her personality.

Her father is the Chairperson of the local Jamaat, the Committee for Muslims. He was the most respected person in the village for his honesty and social service. She said that she imbibed many of her father's qualities, which prompted her to move towards the public space. Even after her marriage, the freedom she enjoyed was never curtailed by her husband. He is a very mature person. When the Devipattinam Village Panchayat Presidentship was earmarked for women in 1996, Muslim women as well as caste Hindu women suggested that Jamrud Beevi should contest. The Jamat of the Muslims tried to avoid any contest but the political parties did not accept the view of the Jamat leaders. So there were four candidates who opposed Jamrud Beevi. Of the four three belonged to the Muslim community and one was a Hindu woman. She won by 800 votes margin. She contested in the second election in 2001 also. She won the second election by 1200 votes. Her performance was evaluated and, based on her commendable performance, she was re-elected. Her father's service and her education and her own service were the major factors that contributed to her success in the elections.

Social Backdrop

Devipattinam is a Hindu pilgrim centre but dominated by Muslim families in terms of numerical strength. Both Hindus and Muslims live together without any difference and lead a peaceful life in this village. Even among the Hindus there are many caste divisions like Nadar, Mutharaiyar, Brahmin, Vellalar, Fisherman, Carpenter and Dhobi and they lead a peaceful life without difference and conflict. Her concern is that, in the days of communal and caste rivalry in the whole of the country, this village has to be protected from this menace and peace has to be preserved. She gives utmost importance to communal harmony. She wanted to maintain the leadership provided by her father to this village. Further, she recollected the advice given by her husband and brother that the prestige of the family has to be protected at any cost and hence she wants to be objective and do justice.

According to her, the Panchayat should work on the issues of the people and, accordingly, the Panchayat should be made their institutions. Sometimes it should function as a community organization. The demands of the people have to be respected and then only people will feel that they have somebody to respond from the Panchayat. Sometimes the demand of the people may be unjust or obsolete. The leader should not regard it negatively. Either they have to be convinced that their demands are not just or the demands have to be met. The Panchayat is the people's institution. It should be a responsive institution attending to the basic needs of the community. If people come to the Panchayat, first they have to be respected and their demands have to be responded to. The Panchayat should not behave like the government. It should not be a mini kingdom. It should be a mini republic. The Panchayat should function with the participation of the people from all social and economic segments of the society. Panchayat leaders should stand by the people. We have seen the autocratic and authoritarian attitude of officials. The Panchayat leaders should not behave like the officials. They should behave like humble servants, she observed. There is yet another perception that Panchayat leaders need. The Panchayat should not be considered a space for politics. It should be perceived as a space for development. If politics enters, competition will crop up. If it is development oriented, nobody will compete.

Toilets and Bathrooms for Pilgrims

She promoted the clean village concept and yet she finds it difficult to maintain it as thousands of pilgrims visit her Panchayat everyday. She collects the waste from all the streets and classifies the same and puts it in a yard for compost. For this exercise she has entered into an agreement with an NGO called NACCS. Every month the Panchayat pays Rs. 19,500 to the NACCS to manage the waste. Of the Rs. 19,500, Rs. 12,000 is given as salary. She has purchased vehicles to transport the waste to the yard.

Bridge Surrounding the Shrine

Being a Muslim woman, she felt that she should evolve herself as a model among Panchayats in the days of communal conflict. In her Panchayat area there is a pilgrimage centre which attracts thousands of devotees of the Hindu religion everyday. All pilgrims visiting Rameswaram use to visit this place. There are nine deities inside the sea. The place is known as "Navabashanam". The story is that Lord Rama worshipped the "Navabashanam" to expiate the sin of killing Ravana. People who feel that they have committed sins use to go over to this place and perform *puja* in the shrine to expiate for the sin. But all the deities are in the sea. People have to cross the water either by boat or on foot, walking in the water. To reduce the inconvenience of the pilgrims, she thought of constructing a small bridge for about 90 feet, for which she approached the District Collector. The District Collector promised her that he would give sanction from the Pilgrim Centre Development Scheme Fund, which is obtained from the Government of Tamil Nadu. She obtained a grant of Rs. 13 lakh from the district administration to develop the pilgrim centre. She constructed a bridge around the deities, a small room to change clothes after the holy dip in the sea by the devotees, a toilet and a bathroom complex. Now, without the help of a boat, one can reach that place and worship the deities. None attempted to do this work before. This enhanced her image among the people in her village. She not only constructed this bridge, but also made the entire area neat and clean by removing encroachments. She provided a sodium vapour light to the Agraharam as the Brahmins use to come to the sea to perform *puja* at all hours. Further, the temple tank has been desilted and a boundary wall has been constructed. She provided a mercury light near the tank. She prepared a proposal to make this pilgrim centre more attractive and she has sent the proposal to the government. She said that she will get the sanction at any moment. If it comes, it will bring revenue to the Panchayat. Local people will get some gainful employment also.

Next to the temple her concern was to provide drinking water to everyone in the village. Her target is to provide water to the unreached. But there is no adequate water source in her Panchayat area. Geologists indicated a land with potential for water in the adjacent village which was owned by a private owner. She approached the person. The owner of the land was a Muslim woman. She was very rich and hence there was no necessity for her to sell the land. The Panchayat President pleaded that she has promised the people that she would give water if she comes to the Panchayat as President. After hearing the plea of the President the lady agreed to give the land for digging a borewell to take water. Jamrud Beevi got Rs. 10.5 lakhs from the Government and spent an additional Rs. 1 lakh to complete the project. By completing this work she has provided drinking water to all. She has not given water to individual houses. She has provided water through public taps. She has developed a perception that providing water through public taps will rationalise water distribution to meet the requirements. She has rejected the idea of earning money for the Panchayat by giving pipe connection to individual houses as water is precious and it is to be conserved and preserved.

According to her perception, by giving water through public taps, equality can be maintained and water could be saved. In all the houses rain water harvesting structures have been created. Yet another major work done by her in her Panchayat is a very big water reservoir. She got information about this Poovodai from the elders of this Panchayat. She interacted with the elders on the reasons for the watertable going down to 90 feet. When there was a water conservation structure water was available at 5 feet depth. She asked what was the water conservation structure. The elders informed her that the Poovodai was the water structure. In 1955 there was heavy rain and, as a result, the Poovodai developed a breach and subsequently there was no repairing of the reservoir. All the years water came to this reservoir and moved away through the breach to the sea.

Water Harvesting Structure

She started thinking about the Poovodai. When she visited the Poovodai, she found a lot of encroachments. The coverage of the area is seven kilometres in length and 100 metres in breadth. When she invited a Minister to her Panchayat, she made a presentation about the condition of the Poovodai and sought assistance. But the Minister, instead of responding to her request, craked a joke and left the place. The Minister said that the Panchayat has to think of what is possible and feasible. The Poovadai is a troublesome project which cannot be done by the Panchayat. This speech irritated her. She felt very much and made a declaration that the Poovodai will be made a reservoir to save water for the Panchayat. She approached the Collector and explained to him about the Poovadai and got sanction for Rs. 25 lakhs under the SGRY scheme. She collected money from the local Jamat and the Saudhi Association for this work. They contributed Rs. 75,000 for this work. She removed all the encroachments with the help of the people and the district administration. The Poovodai has now been desilted, deepened and seven small inner tanks have been created. She considers it a major and memorable work done for the community. She commented that it was possible only because of the District Collector who is sincere and sensible on the issues of the rustic folk.

Yet another major work is graveyard reconstruction. She fenced the entire area. For each and every caste a place has been earmarked for which a committee has been constituted. A small *oorani* has been created and a small well has been dug. Burial and burning can be undertaken in two different places. A road has been laid to the graveyard. A solar light has been provided. Observing the activities of the Panchayat President, the Kanchi Shankaracharya has invited her to his place and offered his blessings, saying that a Muslim woman has done yeoman service to the Hindu religion. This was appreciated by all Muslims.

She participated in an International Conference held at Dakka from 11th to 13th June, 2004. She was sponsored by the Institute of Social Sciences, New Delhi. The broad theme of the Conference was Women's Position in Local Governance, under which two main issues were taken up namely, Capacity Building and Policy Advocacy, for deliberation.

Social Mobility

Jamrud Beevi said that there is a good trend emerging in the villages, namely, that SC and other poor communities are giving encouragement to their children to continue their studies after primary and secondary levels. A competitive spirit is developing in this regard. The Muslim community, after obtaining education and exposure by getting employment abroad, have changed their traditional mindset. The SC people are acquiring new skills, particularly in the construction industry and trades like carpentry to improve their life. The consumption of alcohol or Indian made foreign liquor has also increased among the SC, Nadar and Fishermen communities. Hence, their economic standard is still stunted. For steady upward progress all liquor shops should be closed. Even licensed liquor shops should be removed. If the Panchayat is empowered in this regard, this menace can be stopped.

Linkage with Higher Level Representatives

The MLA, after visiting the Panchayat school, sanctioned a computer centre at a cost of Rs. 8. lakhs. The MP sanctioned an additional school building. The District Councillor helped to avail of funds for providing cement concrete roads and extension of street lights. The Union Councillor brought funds for school building, cement road, noon meal centre and ring wells. The works were carried out by local contractors who are very much conscious about maintaining quality. She never expects any commission or any other favour from them and so she asks them to maintain quality. She claims that she has availed of the discretionary funds from the Block Panchayat Councillor, the District Ward Members, the MLA and the MP belonging to different political parties. Since, she is a non-party person, she has no hesitation to approach anybody. Further, she has community support which is linked to the political prospects of the party candidates. The Panchayat President has to maintain political neutrality to attract all political parties towards Panchayat work.

Struggle with Samasthanam

The Sivagangai Samasthanam administration employed their staff and collected a toll from the vehicle owners at Navapashanam, a famous pilgrimage centre. It is not their right as the temple does not come under their jurisdiction. But the Vishnu temple in Devipattinam is under their jurisdiction. In the name of Perumal temple, they issued tickets and collected toll at Navapashanam. After she became the

President, she objected to this and a case was registered with the police and the revenue officials. After verifying the tickets issued by the Samasthanam, the authorities warned them and permitted the Panchayat to collect the toll. There are shops around the temple. Earlier tax was not collected from them. But, after she became the President, a tax was fixed for them and the same was collected. The building tax is not yet fixed for the shops as the Devasthanam demanded that the tax has to be levied in its name. The dispute is not yet settled. There are 15 houses located around Chathiram for which house tax is not yet fixed. The problem is in whose name the tax has to be levied. So it is delayed. Irrespective of the reputation of the Samasthanam, the Panchayat is trying to assert its rights and authority to levy taxes and collect toll.

Summary

Mrs Beevi was able to maintain her secular credentials by working with the Hindu women for Hindu temples. She carried out series of temple activities and by which she maintained her support base. It is a Hindu pilgrim centre known for the whole country. She was able to win the election only with the support of the Hindu votes despite a Hindu women contested in the election. Her activities in the Hindu temples raised her name among the Hindus. Equally, the Muslims have also appreciated her as she maintained communal harmony and peace in the village which ultimately kept the Hindu fundamentalist out of the village politics. By carrying out all the activities in the temple premises she had reduced the burden of district administration in law and order maintenance. Hence, the District Administration helped her in all possible ways. Likewise the MP and MLA extended support to her. She had increased the income for the Panchayats. Muslims never gave any trouble to them as she concentrated much on Hindu temples. Her educational background helped to understand the problem from the perspective of communal harmony. Her honesty added strength to all her activities.

Case Study II

Mr. Noor Mohammad (57), President of Sakkarakpotai Gram Panchayat of Ramnad district[9], educated upto SSLC, a trader by occupation, moved over to the Panchayat setting to work for the people in order to transform the village by providing people with all basic facilities. He has five children (four boys and one girl). Of them two are doing business in Kuala Lumpur, Malaysia. He owns agricultural land and cultivates rice and coconut. His economic background is very sound. Having assessed the poor performance of officials in rural development activities for the past several years, he took a decision that this was a fine opportunity to contest and set right the maladies in rural development activities. He said that the government spends every year several lakhs in each and every village through several programmes implemented for the benefit of the people. But their demands are unmet and are constantly growing. Government spending is increasing every year but it is not solving the demands of the people. Moreover, people do not have representatives at their place of residence to redress their grievances. But the New Panchayati Raj System provides this new opportunity for the local populace to take up the responsibility to decide their destiny. Hence, he decided to contest in the election for the post of Gram Panchayat President of Sakkarakottai.

His predecessors had not done anything for the villagers. Yet he did not use this factor for the poor performance of his predecessors—in the election campaign. He projected only his promises. He put forth his election promises as provision of water supply, road for smooth transportation, street light for brighter evenings and temples for worship. Of all the demands people projected only the temple and the water as major and basic needs in all the hamlets. The temple was projected as a basic demand even in the SC colony. It is a wonder that while the living conditions are extremely poor in the SC colony they also projected the temple as a basic need. Noor Mohammad understood the reality that people could be mobilized either on the issues of water or temple. They are the bases of Indian society. There were other basic demands which were not emphasized so much. He further noticed that the demand was not the demand of the uneducated, but the demand of all. Hence, he decided to give utmost importance to these issues. Instead of raising a hue and cry why not take the responsibility in the Panchayat and show the way to others? This was the thinking which prompted him to contest in the local body elections.

It is the popular perception in India that coming to public office is to earn money. But, fortunately, he said that he has enough money. He can contribute money to public activities. Being a minority person by religion, he was able to occupy the post of Panchayat President with the help of the majority, the Hindus. Eventhough the Hindus were the majority, only the people of his religion contested in the Village Panchayat President's election the first time but he was able to secure more votes with the help of the Hindus and the Jamaat also helped him to realize his dream of becoming President. In the second election three others contested and of these one lost his deposit. Two belonged to the Hindu religion and yet they could not get the votes of the Hindus. In the first election he won the election by a difference of 511 votes and in the second election by a difference of 476 votes. Though he belongs to a political party, he didn't show his identity as a party member to secure votes. His idea of contesting elections is to serve the community. To serve the community he need not seek the support of the party. It is not an MLA or MP election. If people have faith and confidence in him, they will cast their votes; otherwise they won't. Against this background he contested.

All the segments helped him to get elected. As soon as he decided to contest in the election, he approached the Hindu leaders seeking their support and promised to fulfil all their basic needs. Construction of Hindu temple was their primary requirement and Mr. Noor Mohammed promised to do it. Basically, Mr. Noor Mohammad's family is known for its philanthropy and they have assets devoted to charity. Following his ancestors, he also concentrated on temple and water. A major share of his property has been spent for the temple work and for providing water supply. His primary concern was to preserve communal harmony and, at the same time, attend to the felt needs. Invariably people demanded a place for worship and regular water supply. They were the two vital demands projected by the people when he met them while doing his election campaign. Knowing fully well that the Panchayat has no money to construct temples, he promised that he would fulfil their demands. Hence, temple works were carried out from trust money and only water works were carried out from Panchayat money. He firmly believes that people's genuine demands could be met by the Panchayats provided Panchayat leaders have commitment. He further feels that by providing water for their need and constructing small temples one can earn the support of the people. In his Panchayat area there are about seventeen small community temples which are being supported by the community, and incidentally, the Panchayat President is also helping.

Works around Water

After he got elected as a Prèsident, he started working towards fulfilling his promises by focusing on the water. Water being a primary requirement of the people drew his attention and Ramnad District being drought hit area further motivated him to the fullest extent to solve the problem quickly. He desilted tanks, dug wells and provided the people with individual house tap connection and also common tap in each street of the village. There was a small tank adjacent to the main road leading to Rameswaram a leading pilgrimage centre in South India which attracts thousands of devotees all over India. Wherever, the devotees go over to Rameswaram, they use to take bath in this tank since it keeps water throughout the year. He felt that this tank has to be desilted and expanded. He deepened that tank and three sides of tank retaining walls have constructed with bathing facilities. Further, he has constructed a small dressing room for women to change their dress after their bath. No Panchayat has taken such an initiative. Apart from these things a major work done by him worth mentioning here was the desilting of oorani carried out by him in Vani hamlet, where the oorani stretches out for 22 acres. This was a major task carried out by the President. He informed that by providing water, many problems in the village could be solved. Scarcity of water for bathing, drinking and even for agriculture would create a number of social problems which disturb the harmony of the community. People should have a feeling that they can get enough water for drinking, bathing and agriculture purposes. He feels that solving the water crisis in a Panchayat many of the problems are solved. He has constructed road with the desilted sand making comfortable for the womenfolk to fetch the water from the tank. Sometimes he merges government scheme with his own money and with the help of the TWAD Board he has placed several syntax tanks near the well, so that people need not draw the water from the well instead they can get water from the tap which saves their energy. The people get adequate water for both bathing and drinking purposes.

Works around Temples

He took earnest efforts to construct temples and took responsibility to mobilize resources for the construction. He involved himself in the temple activities either for construction or for renovation or for organizing festivals. His main role is to contribute and collect. In all the Hindu temples his name has been written very prominently as the prime contributor. His involvement in the following temples is immense.

Works around Temple

Sl.No.	Name of the Temple		Contribution
1.	Muthu Mariamman (Kavalar Kudiyiruppu)	Rs.	80,000.00
2.	Mahasakthi Mariamman (Sivaganapuram)	Rs.	45,000.00
3.	Murugan (Kuyavankudi)	Rs.	15,000.00
4.	Mariamman (Pasumpon Nagar)	Rs.	30,000.00
5.	Vinayagar (Prison Ramanathapuram)	Rs.	30,000.00
6.	Santhana Mariamman (Sethunagar)	Rs.	80,000.00
7.	Muthu Mariamman (VOC Nagar)	Rs.	50,000.00
8.	Mahamariamman (Kelachothurani)	Rs.	60,000.00
9.	Sidhivinayagar (Vaani)	Rs.	20,000.00
10.	Vinayagar (Nehru Nagar)	Rs.	20,000.00
11.	Kannel (Yadavar Kudiyiruppu)	Rs.	25,000.00
12.	Sonai Kovil (MGR Nagar)	Rs.	10,000.00
13.	Manchana Mariamman (Kovil Theru)	Rs.	20,000.00
14.	Kali Kovil (Arunthadiyar Colony)	Rs.	40,000.00
	Total	**Rs.**	**5,25,000.00**

Note: Information provided in parenthesis is the location of the temple.

He not only contributes money for construction of temple or renovation of temple or organizing festivals of temples but also participates in the functions like a Hindu. He performs all rituals in the temples and Hindus allow him to do the same: He invites Hindus to his house during the festivals of the Muslims.

Another striking feature is both a Hindu temple and a mosque in the same location and people of both the religions praying peacefully in the same area. The importance which he gives to religious sentiments is high and it reflects in all his works. This kind of activity leads to the peaceful coexistence of people belonging to both the religions. Politicians in modern India play with the religious sentiments of the people by arousing communal conflict to gain political upliftment. But man like Noor Mohammad, who is much dignified, spend their own money to secure the unity of the people of various religions. He maintains that a leader can survive only if he pays heed to the necessity of the community and interests of the people. From his experience we can conclude that it is not the community which is communal in nature. Politicians are communal. At this juncture it is necessary for India to nurture leaders like Mr. Noor Mohammad. He initiated temple activities in fourteen places. He has mobilized the needed resources and added his contribution and completed the task. It is strange to note that in all the temples people belonging to Hindu religion inscribed his name either inside or outside the temple, which is unique in the Panchayat. He made the people to maintain the temples neat and clean. He feels that he is doing a community work not Panchayat work.

Concentration on SC Colony

He has provided all the facilities to the SC colony named after Gandhi. Group houses have been constructed and proper roads laid. Adequate water supply is also provided to the people in that colony. At his own cost, a temple was also constructed for the *dalits* for their worship in that area. He often visits the SC colony and enquires about their requirements. He also advises the people to take care of their health and hygiene and insists on their using the toilet properly. He has installed solar lamps in this colony and totally 17 solar lamps have been installed in his Panchayat.

Mr. Noor Mohammad, by religion a Muslim, respects all religions and the secret of his success lies in the secular principle followed by him. His philanthropic character moulds him as a good leader of the people. He has made his Panchayat a model for communal harmony. He knew the sentimental needs of the Hindus. He has invested huge money for constructing temples. His support base from the Hindus has increased. His participation in Hindu temple festivals have got recognition from the Hindus. In all temples his name was inscribed. His second activity is the provision of water, which is the primary requirement of the people. This has made him popular among the people. His concern for the SCs is yet another feather in his cap and his interest in cleanliness earns income to his Panchayat, keeps the village clean and provides jobs to poor people. Finally, all this put together, Mr. Noor Mohammad has emerged as a good leader serving the needs of the people at their door steps from maintaining communal harmony to providing infrastructure facilities.

Summary

Noor Mohammad clearly perceived the needs of the community and worked on the demands. Being a Muslim he gave utmost importance to communal harmony. He has to rely on the support of the Hindus. In the two elections he was elected as President. Community also demonstrated its secular credentials by electing a Muslim as President. Hindus can easily manipulate voters to defeat him. But they did not do. Further his performance were evaluated. Further his honesty also worked in his electoral victory.

Case Study III

Ms. M. Kala, President of Noothulapuram Gram Panchayat, Dindigul district[10] is a daughter of an inter-caste married couple. Though she was educated up to the Tenth standard, she worked as a coolie. With the help of an NGO, namely ASSEFA, she received training in health education and served in villages in and around Nilakottai. She also served as a sales promotion agent for the small savings scheme. Her husband runs a travel agency by getting a bank loan. When the Panchayat elections were declared in the year 1996, Noothulapuram Village Panchayat President's position was reserved for *dalit* women. The villagers of Noothulapuram encouraged Kala to contest and her husband also did so. Hence, she contested and won in the election.

Communal Dispute and Intervention of the President

Goddess Chelliamman shrine is the village temple and both *dalits* and Thevars jointly celebrate the 3 days festival. The Thevar community enjoys the right to the sanctum sanctorum. This is the traditional practice. During the recent festival the *dalit* youth got into the sanctum sanctorum. It became a communal dispute. Government officials intervened and it was settled peacefully through negotiation. The *dalits* and the Thevars were to celebrate the festival separately. The first day was reserved meant for the Thevar and the second day for the *dalit* community.

Recently, in the year 2001, when the celebration was declared, anticipating communal clash police officials did not permit the celebration. Kala met the Police officials and explained the practice earlier adhered to. The representatives of the non-*dalits* who were present during this meeting appreciated Kala's the leadership as she took a neutral position and explained the truth. She assured the police that no dispute would arise during the celebration. The Police as well as the leaders of the non-*dalits* accepted this assurance and permission was granted for the celebration and it was completed without any dispute.

The youth of the *dalits* felt very much about the unfolding of the truth in the Police Station. Kala as she referred to the earlier practice of privilege to the Thevar community. But President Kala convinced the youth that during the celebration this practice could be removed in the presence of the police and the *dalits* can also enjoy the privilege of going into the shrine. Since any further difference created would disturb the communal harmony most of the youth agreed to Kala's advice but a few radical youngsters did not agree. Yet Kala conducted the celebration successfully.

When Kala contested for a second term, she felt that the *dalit* youth particularly men, entertaining enmity for caste Hindus, would work against her. But the village women has got socialized through SHGs. Women of the *dalit* and the non-*dalit* communities joined together through SHG activities and eliminated the differences between these two communities. The power pump of the drinking water system is being operated by women of both the communities through an SHG. There is no dispute between these groups on any aspects. Wherever necessary, the women of both the communities work jointly for the common cause. Being a woman hailing from the *dalit* community occupying the post of Gram Panchayat, Kala encourages understanding among the womenfolk in Noothulapuram.

Kala contested in the election again as the Government of Tamil Nadu ordered that the reservation of seats for women continue for a second tenure also. Though huge amounts of money were spent by the other candidates in the election, Kala projected the activities carried out by her, cutting across castes and won the election by a margin of 380 votes. Kala said that she served fairly, treating all communities alike, and so she won in the election.

Panchayat Activities

The scheme fund earmarked for the welfare of *dalits* is more than the fund earmarked for the non-*dalits* and so a large number of terms of work have been carried out in the hamlets of the *dalits*. During the Gram Sabha meeting she explained the fact that since more *dalits* live in the Panchayat, the Panchayat gets more for the *dalit* community. To provide necessary basic facilities for the habitations of the non-Dalits, Kala mobilized funds from other sources like the MLA fund, the District Councillor's fund, the MP fund and the Union fund. In this way she is able to retain the support of all the communities.

People's Expectations

Irrespective of caste, lower middle class and poor families demand loan facilities for economic activities, *patta* for house sites, group houses and improvement of facilities in their streets. In the Gram Sabha there is good participation by the non-*dalit* community. Available funds position and priorities of work are properly deliberated upon the Gram Sabha meeting. It is only through the Gram Sabha she has proved herself a genuine and sincere President.

Reservation of Seats for Dalits

According to Kala, reservation of seats for *dalits* and women is the right approach to empower them. Through the position of elected representatives, individuals belonging to the so called marginalized sectors have got exposure and established contacts with officials by which they have enhanced their leadership qualities.

Only those women Presidents who are able to get the support of their own families and womenfolk in general could sustain their leadership. The socio-economic conditions of *dalits* could be improved only if they are oriented in many activities other than farm sector activities, as the scope for employment in agriculture is shrinking nowadays. Economic background, group support, caste association support, encouragement given by family, educational background and patronage from the general public are the enabling factors determining the upward mobility of *dalit* leadership emerging through reservation. The NGOs are not fully involved in the election campaign even though they support their own SHG members. Political parties in general do not work seriously in Village Panchayat elections whereas in the case of the other two positions, namely Union Councillor and District Ward Member the candidates depend mostly on the political parties. When the Presidents of Village Panchayats gain popularity political parties try to draw them into their party and encourage them to contest for higher positions. Through the Panchayats, *dalits* have come to understand the system of governance and avail of their entitlements and now psychologically they feel better. The community will be benefited by interlinking panchayat with the sectoral department particularly the *dalit* community for whom plenty of schemes and programmes are available.

Her Outstanding Leadership

Mrs. Kala, a decade ago was an ordinary housewife of a *dalit* family. Reservation in PRIs brought a new change in her life. Constant support of her husband and cooperation from her son and daughters are the main factors which contributed for her onward march in the public life. During her first tenure she faced opposition from four candidates and won in a small difference of 22 votes. Her hard works to improve the socio-economic welfare of the villagers and her contribution in bringing peace and harmony between the members of *dalit* and Other Backward Communities spoke her talents and leadership qualities. She was encouraged to contest again when the Panchayat election was held in the year 2001. Kala remarked that in the earlier election, votes of backward community were distributed to all candidates. But during the second tenure, the village community who witnessed her performance, defeated the four candidates who opposed Kala. Kala won with a difference of 389 votes. It is possible as the majority of the members belonging to backward community cast their votes in her favour, Kala pointed out.

Leadership Process of Kala

Kala's background was a simple one. Her association with the NGO namely, ASSEFA after her marriage changed her lifestyle. Earlier she even has been engaged in manual labour. But orientation given by NGO improved her understanding on her own-self as well as about the society. She served as a health educator in the NGO activities. She used this opportunity to move freely with the villagers. Her husband being a member in the Indian National Congress Party, had a perspective with regard to women empowerment. He at his capacity used to serve villagers in availing credit assistance from THADCO and from other line departments of the State Government. From these interventions also Kala learned issues in public life.

The reservation of seats for women in Panchayati Raj Institutions (PRIs) was a boon to her. Kala's husband though disappointed on the declaration that the President position in Noothulapuram Village Panchayat was reserved to Schedule Caste (women), he quickly decided to field his wife and encouraged her to independently function.

The occurrence of communal dispute in Noothulapuram Village Panchayat was successfully managed by Kala. Without any prejudice she involved in the negotiation process for mutual understanding cutting across caste, and people understood her leadership potential. She duly got the recognition and right to serve to the *dalit* community with regard to temple celebration. Her close interaction with youth helped her to analyse the mindset of *dalit* youth. She was able to pacify them to sit across for negotiation. She has developed a conflict resolution methodology in her village. The process can be studied.

Her association with women self-help group cutting across castes won recognition to her. She had used this opportunity to assist women belonging to Backward Caste (BC) community wherever possible using her good office. Further to improve the basic amenities in the habitations of BC, she contacted MLA and MP and representatives of higher tiers of Panchayat Raj System. She made use of the Village Panchayat source for the welfare of *dalit* habitation. She realized the importance of fair deal though she belonged to SC community.

Her close association with the Congress Party helped her to understand the major dimensions of politics and governance. She had opportunity to accompany the local MLA Mrs. Ponnammal and participated in the party meetings. Steadily she gained insights and equipped her leadership through better relationship with the supportive institutions like Rajiv Gandhi Chair for Panchayati Raj Studies, Human Right Foundation and State Institute of Rural Development. She never missed any events of training or other programmes meant for Village Presidents. Her public speech in stages was focused on reality rather than creating pipe dream.

Kala gained knowledge and understanding of the functioning of government machinery. She never hesitated to make visits to various departments and availed the details of schemes and assistances executed by those line departments, and made use the same for the development of her villagers. She moved steadily from the activities of providing basic amenities to the economic assistance to eligible poor.

She enhanced her capacity in the system of Panchayat administration. She herself used to verify the entries in the records made by the Panchayat clerk. She used to line out the ways of sending communications to querries made by the officials. If necessary she used to avail the support of Rajiv Gandhi Chair for Panchayati Raj

Studies. Her interest to learn the system pushed her to the position. Her ambition raised to a height, she started realizing the scope of a potential SC women leader in politics due to emerging trend of accommodation of women leaders by the political parties. She made use of all the opportunities to associate with the activities of the Congress Party. She wished to contest in the MLA election as the constituency is reserved to Scheduled Caste. A consecutive period of 10 years equipped her leadership through the process of Village Panchayat administration, SHG activities and political activities. The capacity building improved her vision. Her perspectives, understanding, approach, commitment towards delivery of services, access to people, interface with officials developed his capability, skill and capacity. Without antagonizing the caste Hindus, she delivered all services to the *dalit* hamlets. She is a role model for women leaders in Panchayats. She fought with officials to maintain her dignity. She is sensitive towards the issues of *dalit* and women. Her interest is to move further in the ladder of power from Panchayats to Parliament or State Legislative Assembly.

Summary

Though her educational economic background were weak, her passion for public service through occupying public space took her to the zenith. Being a *dalit* she has crossed several barriers and to face her own community men. She is extraordinarily courageous and committed leader and hence she evolved a conflict management formula to settle the disputes between the *dalits* and caste Hindus. She had not only settled the disputes but to make them to work together. Her poverty or backwardness never tempted her to be corrupt. Her strength was honesty and hence she was elected again.

Case Study IV

Mrs. Pappa aged 33 is a science graduate. She hails from the *dalit* community. Her college education helped her to understand the sufferings of the *dalit* community. Being a cadet in the NCC unit in her college, Pappa had the opportunity to live in villages other than her own. Pappa informed that the plight of *dalit* in the villages around Palani was agonising. They lived in sub-human living conditions.

Moreover, they lived in abject poverty, completely depending on the caste Hindus. Pappa expressed her concern for that status of the *dalits.* She was longing for an opportunity to help dalits.

Pappa as a Social Worker

Pappa did not want to sit idle in the house. She is a highly motivated, committed and educated woman among the members of the *dalit* community. She used to render assistance to her neighbours by offering guidance and counselling in their family affairs. In the meantime she came to know the activities of Dr. Ambedkar Development Society functioning in Perungudi near Madurai, which called for the service of young and dedicated, men and women to contribute for the advancement of education of the *dalit* students. She applied and got the post and served as animator. She conducted coaching classes for school students in her house. Further, she used to mobilize adults and elderly women, shared their concern and created awareness among them about the conditions of the poor and especially women. She helped them to acquire literacy which considered as a main factor for empowerment. Realizing the potential of Pappa, many women used to visit her and get her guidance for many matters relating to their family. She was paid for these activities also by Dr. Ambedkar Development Society. Her in-laws expressed happiness over the development. They even appreciated her for her approach and method of doing services. Her husband also encouraged her activities. Being a politically oriented person of the Congress Party, her husband used to involve her in the public welfare activities also. Thus, Pappa slowly prepared herself to shoulder higher responsibility in the public in the ensuing days. Her family stood as support structure for her public activities.

In the service of our animator, Pappa had a good company of students and youths. She spent from her pocket to meet the educational needs of poor dalit students. She organized excursions and picnics to the students to the nearby mountains, religious places, and dam sites. Parents of these children witnessed the attitudinal and behavioural changes among the school students and used to frequently visit Pappa and express their gratitude. Pappa became a significant woman in the village of Athankaraipatti. She has come to the public space already on her own.

Panchayati Raj Election in 2001

When the election to Panchayati Raj Institutions was held in 2001 villagers, suggested to Pappa to file her nomination. Though Pappa had the mind to serve community, with regard to contesting in election she had some reservation. The villagers influenced the in-laws of Pappa. The family members of Pappa finally agreed to the suggestion of the villagers. There were four candidates in the fray who were not at all oriented in social activities. Moreover, they were less educated than Pappa. The villagers suffered a lot during the first tenure in the hands of ill-equipped leadership. So they were determined to elect a potential woman this time. Pappa and her team of women and young men projected the necessity of better qualified, independent and easily accessible leader in the Village Panchayat. The propaganda worked successfully. Pappa won the election in the four-cornered contest. Pappa told that she was able to get more votes from the backward community also.

Her Struggle for Entitlement

Athipatti is the nearby Village Panchayat of Athankaraipatti. There is an irrigation kanmoi, benefiting the ayacatdhars of these two Village Panchayats located in that area. When they experienced severe drought during 2003-04 the government decided to undertake maintenance work in that kanmoi. Accordingly, at a total estimate of Rs. 2.60 lakhs the work was given to Athankaraipatti Village Panchayat by an administrative sanction earmarked to that Panchayat. But in the meantime, the work of desilting and strengthening of bunds have been executed by a contractor without the knowledge of the Athankaraipatti Village Panchayat. Hence, Pappa raised her objection against the contractors work. Moreover, the work was very unsatisfactory as the desilting was done only to a limited extent. It was easy to observe for any ordinary person that a cost of Rs. 2.60 lakhs work was not really carried out when compared to the quantum of work and removal of earth which existed there. The issue was brought to the notice of the union as well as the district officials. But it was unnecessarily dragged to find out the truth, she complained. In the meantime, due to poor and sub-standard work, there was a breach in the bank and the rainwater flooded into the field causing a heavy damage, Pappa added. When the issue of damage was highlighted the union administration just engaged the contractor who did a surface work instead of strengthening the bank. Till today the administration played the hide and seek in the issue of giving the work to a contractor by the union administration despite of administrative sanction to the Village Panchayat, Pappa remarked. The bureaucracy used to play second fiddle to the ruling party men, Pappa commented.

Issue in Selecting the Beneficiary of Indira Awaas Yojana (IAY)

Pappa used to show real concern in selecting the eligible poor families under IAY. The allocation and the details of norms, procedure and rules and regulation were properly explained to the villagers in the Gram Sabha meeting with regard to all schemes and programmes assigned to the Village Panchayat, she informed. So far about 40 poor families (34 SC and 6 BC) have been provided with the IAY house. There was no procedural lapse in this regard and the work was completed successfully, Pappa shared. But during the year 2005-2006 it was told that 10 houses have been allotted. But a list of beneficiaries was sent by the union administration instead of the written rule that the selection had to be in the Gram Sabha meeting. Hence, Pappa did not yield to the pressure made on her to pass resolution in this regard.

In the meantime, the Gram Sabha was convened at the marriage hall owned by the backward community and Pappa sought police protection. Pappa had the practice of availing police protection whenever she convenes Gram Sabha meetings as there would be anti-social elements or drunkards who tried to disturb the proceedings. On that day of Gram Sabha where the issue of list of beneficiaries sent from the union administration, was taken for discussion, Pappa availed police protection.

Pappa maintained the procedure with regard to the seating arrangements during the Gram Sabha meeting, and thereby avoided any special importance to anybody. But the officials resorted into breach of the customary practice. When the Union Chairman came to attend the meeting (he is a local resident) the officials arranged seating especially to him and his companies. Pappa refused to have a break in the system and the proceedings of that Gram Sabha was disturbed. She was instructed to convene another Gram Sabha. In the meantime Pappa discussed the issue of denying the legal right entrusted with Village Panchayats and Gram Sabha in respect of selection of IAY beneficiaries, with institutions like Rajiv Gandhi

Chair for Panchayati Raj Studies, and at last she decided herself to seek the direction of the court in this regard. She moved the petition in the Madurai bench of High Court of Tamil Nadu and the court ordered the stoppage of activities in this regard, Pappa informed. Realizing the consequences of legal action, the union administration and the Union Chairperson agreed to adhere to the list of beneficiaries selected by the Gram Sabha. Among the ten beneficiaries proposed by the union administration six of them were found ineligible and they have been replaced with six eligible families identified by the Gram Sabha, Pappa told.

Her Contribution to the Welfare of Women

Pappa explained that she was constantly working to create a social climate in which her village women would be in a better position. She told that she could observe a change in the mindset of her village women. They never used to come in front of unknown male visitors and always shown inhibition in conversation. They won't come to undertake journey independently even to nearby cities and towns. They never individually visited government offices and other public institutions like banks, etc., Pappa pointed out. The Self-Help Group (SHG) activities and personal encouragement given by her brought a new life to the majority of womenfolk in her village, Pappa claimed.

The number of girl students who continued their studies after primary school increased, the practice of early marriage has decreased, the participation of women in SHG activities is enhanced, girls are permitted to undergo professional courses like nursing and computer study, and the women in general courageously express their opinion in families as well as in public forum; Pappa listed out the attitudinal and behavioural changes occurred among women of her village within a short span of five years, thanks to the reservation to women especially Scheduled Caste women in Panchayati Raj Institutions, she reiterated. She herself is a role model and she constantly interacts and facilitates women to move further in the public space.

Promoting Social Harmony

Athankaraipatti is a multi-caste Village Panchayat. The relationship among the various communities of Athankaraipatti Village Panchayat is a cordial one. It is told that there is no communal clash in this area.

Pappa shared that there is a village temple Samathi Pattaiya situated in a site belonged to SC community, but the temple affairs are managed by Naicker and Vellalar community. There are common temples, Mariamman Temple and Vinayakar temple where all the communities participate in the celebration. Moreover, each member of SC community contributes to the *pooja* activities during the annual celebration where meals prepared from the contribution of paddy by each SC member and all communities irrespective of castes partake in the food commonly. It is a grand celebration of two days. Villagers from 18 villages located around the area used to participate in the celebration. The temple *poojari* belongs to Naicker community. Inspite of a huge congregation of people from different castes, the celebration adhered peacefully, Pappa explained. Pappa told that as the President of Village Panchayat she was very much serious in promoting the communal harmony in her Panchayat area as many villages are witness of communal conflict among the castes.

She used her good office and position when dealing with issues which involve more than one community to ease the tension by her personal visit to the houses of both community members, freely shared with men and women and assessed their feelings and emotions related to issues and instead of projecting the negative feelings if any shared, Pappa used to project positive feelings of the opponents. Hence, she acted wisely to reduce tension and contributed for the promotion of communal harmony. Pappa opined that it was all possible because, being a woman President it is easy to get into touch with the female and youth members among the disputed families, she pointed out.

Her Contribution to Social Reform Activities

Pappa has another dimension as an agent of Life Insurance Corporation of India. In connection with enrolling policyholders she maintains a wide contact with a large number of families in many Village Panchayats of Sedapatti Union. Pappa shared that it was a great opportunity to mingle with family members and able to lend her ears to their emotional sharing especially of women members, she added. She facilitated for successful widow remarriages. In one incident it was a widow member in her group with one child, got married. It took about two years to pacify the parents of the bridegroom. Now that women is pregnant and Pappa and her group members participated in the celebration. Another marriage was for a widow of backward community with two children. Both couples are living happily, Pappa remarked. Being a woman she was able to realize emotional problems of women, Pappa pointed out.

Pappa as a Winner of the Heart

It is a well-known fact that female infanticide is in practice in the area of Sedapatti Union of Madurai District. Government of Tamil Nadu has taken series of steps in preventing the inhuman cruelty of female infanticide. Law is also enacted to give punishment apart from programmes like creation of awareness, cradle scheme of adoption of unwanted female are implemented by the government. Pappa being an educated woman as well as in the capacity of woman President took much efforts in this regard. She used to associate with the village health nurse in meeting mothers who delivered female children and offered guidance and counselling to rear the female children. Pappa narrated her experience in this respect. In a family there is a delivery of one female child. The abovesaid mother already has two female children. Having a third female child, the grandma of the child advised her daughter to desist herself from feeding the child and let it die itself naturally avoiding the accusation of female infanticide. Pappa having known that informed the village health nurse and accompanied her to that house with an intention of getting the female child admission under cradle scheme for adoption. But the family members refused to give the baby and even resorted to react angrily towards Pappa and the nurse. The grandma of the baby threw away the loincloth on the nurse. But nurse showed patience and both advised all the members of the family to immediately save the baby otherwise they had to face legal action. Further, Pappa family persuaded the mother to feed the baby. At last she won the heart of mother. The mother fed the baby and as the baby eagerly waited for the mother's love and care enjoyed her feeding. A lamp is protected to burn, Pappa quoted.

Activities in the Federation of Women Panchayat Presidents

Pappa is serving as the President of Madurai District unit of the Association of Elected Women Representatives of Panchayati Raj Institutions. She is the treasurer in the union level committee of Village Panchayat Presidents of Sedapatti Union where both men and women

Presidents were members. She is the Secretary of the Dalit women Presidents District Unit, Madurai District.

Pappa informed that though education is very much essential to the empowerment of women, it was her active involvement in public affairs brought her to limelight. Her struggles and achievements have been featured in many newspapers and electronic media. She opined that even less educated women could perform well provided they got needed orientation and guidance whenever they demanded. It is by performance only the women Presidents could get recognition in the community and the society. In this regard she acknowledged the services of supportive institutions functioning in the State of Tamil Nadu.

Summary

Primarily she is an educated and motivated individual who has a passion for public service. Even before contesting in the election, she has come out for public service with the support of the family. Moreover, the family has got political connections. Her husband is also supportive. One important factor which helped her to assert herself as leader is that she has gone to police station, she has gone to court and she went to different offices. Finally, she won in all her ventures and that provided confidence. She got strength from her family external agencies like Rajiv Gandhi Chair to overcome the barriers created by a political class and bureaucracy. But she was always on the right path. Her moral strength and community support made her to face all ordeals. Many popular articles have been written about her struggle and success and some of the articles got awards also. Her story is both a struggle and success. The moment she got success, she begins another struggle. In the whole process, she has built up her capacity. She is conscious of *dalit* problems and her commitment towards the issues of *dalit* is visible and yet her approach is that *dalit* problems could be solved with the support of the Caste Hindus. She said that it is possible and it is happening in her Panchayat.

She has moved further frontiers in socio-political transformations of the villages. She has not confined her activities only in her Panchayat areas. She has expanded her activities in and around the Sedapatti Block Panchayat areas. She is not looking into the powers assigned to Panchayats. She has a tendency to respond to the demands and calls of the people. As her administration is transparent, non-corrupt, she has been fighting against injustice. She is being supported by the community. Her movement with higher officials and support agencies helped a lot to strengthen her position in Panchayats. She is a role model for other *dalit* women leaders. She is the head of many associations including *dalit*. Her multifaceted role enhanced her capacity and capability.

It is to be noted here that the institutional mechanism that was created for a society, which did not have deep diversities and divisions socially and economically, had been operationalised in a social setting which is highly fragmented and hierarchical because of the social and economic inequality in Indian society[11]. Theoretically speaking democracy has potential to resolve conflict provided the requisite leadership is available in the help of affairs[12]. Further it is to be understood that the power transfer will happen at the grassroots only through struggle. Hence, panchayats will witness conflicts. The whole process will happen through a struggle and conflict[13]. How these struggles and conflicts are managed at the community level depend on the quality of leadership and the strategies adopted by the leaders. Theoretically speaking, democracy has to orient the people and made them as citizens. The explicit objective of democracy is to achieve maturity. Democracy is an instrument for perfecting individuals and groups is resolving their own affairs through an institutional process is a mentally acceptable way from the lowest level to the highest. The assumption is that this kind of practice will enhance the maturity of the people by which the quality of the democratic practice will also be enhanced[14].

Integrated Analysis

Of the four case studies, two are from Muslim community and two are from *dalit* community. Of the four, three are women leaders. All are from Gram Panchayats. Our representative democracy first time entered into villages to achieve economic development and social justice as governance and administration units. All the four Gram Panchayat leaders have adopted different strategies to keep the communities together. The two Muslim leaders are from affluent families. The two Muslim leaders have adopted a strategy of keeping communal harmony by getting the support of the Hindu families in this Panchayat area. Both of them have worked in Hindu temples with the sense of commitment. Communities also cooperated with the Panchayat leaders. Since both leaders have maintained communal harmony the District Administration has cooperated with the Panchayats for all development activities. Since all development activities were carried out continuously in the Panchayats, people have extended their support to these leaders. These leaders have got elected to Panchayat by defeating the opponents belonging to Hindu community. Thus, these two leaders have proved that communities are not communal but they are development oriented.

Of the two *dalit* women leaders, Ms. Kala adopted a dialogue approach and her conviction is that by antagonizing caste Hindu one cannot bring development to the *dalit* in a village where caste Hindus are majority and predominant. Though she was vehemently opposed by the *dalit* youth in the beginning, she was supported by all at the end after seeing the development activities carried out by her for the *dalits* with the approval of the caste Hindus. She always maintained her equipoise and by appeal she convinced the caste Hindus. By achieving development for *dalits*, she convinced the *dalit* youth. Her performance especially in social justice has improved her image to get victory in the second election.

Ms. Pappa is another *dalit* women representative chosen her path of struggle. Working with marginalized and mobilized the people to agitate against the injustice is not so easy. She relentlessly worked for the *dalits*. But she opposed only the strategy of the caste Hindus. In all her struggles she got recognition. She finally took responsibility in organizing the *dalit* women representatives. Both *dalit* women representatives maintained their rectitude which made the high image about their leaders. Of the two Mrs. Kala is economically poor. Yet she maintained honesty. Mrs. Pappa not only worked for her Panchayat but also worked for other *dalit* representatives.

Conclusion

Social and political conflicts based on different identities both broader and narrower are being managed by the government through different conflict management formulae developed. Many of the conflicts emerge in the society at present on sharing the public resources. In this context governance mechanism is created at the grassroots. While creating space for women and *dalits* in governance and administration communities are in conflict. At the grassroots community practices have developed conflict with constitutional practices. The new exercise of deepening democracy at grassroots created more of conflicts as society has not reached the level of maturity required to adopt particularly democracy. But proper leadership development and capacity building, the elected leaders can achieve development at the grassroots and by which communal harmony could also be maintained. Social justice was achieved through development for all sections of the rural community by these leaders. Honesty and creative leadership established secularism and communal harmony through development initiatives. By doing so it is demonstrated that community is not communal. Two Muslim leaders contributed immensely for the Hindu temples and communal harmony is achieved. *Dalit* leaders have managed the conflict between the *dalits* and the caste Hindus. Very effectively and established harmony between the two communities. By doing so they proved that leadership matters much at the grassroots. Leaders at the grassroots are the real models for our higher level representatives.

NOTES

1. Amartya Sen in his book brought an argument about the relative justice and how it is being delivered. Amartya Sen, *The Idea of Justice*, New York: Allen Lane an imprint of Penguin Books, 2009.
2. Amrita Basu and Atul Kohli "Introduction" in Amrita Basu and Atul Kohli (eds) *Community Conflicts and the State in India*, New Delhi: Oxford University Press, 1998, pp. 2.3.
3. Anirudh Krishna, *Active Social Capital: Tracing the Roots of Development and Democracy*, New York: Columbia University Press, 2002.
4. Atul Kohli, *Democracy and Discontent: India's Growing Crisis of Governability*, Cambridge: Cambridge University Press, 1990.
5. Dwaipayan Bhattacharyya, Niraja Gopal Jayal, Bishnu N. Mohapatra and Sudhapati (eds) *Interrogating Social Capital: The Indian Experience*, New Delhi: Sage Publications, 2004.
6. G. Palanithurai, M.A. Thirunavukkarasu and G. Uma, *Change Makers at Grassroots*, New Delhi: Concept Publishing Company, 2008.
7. G. Palanithurai, "Democracy, Development and Conflict at Grassroots" *Local Government Quarterly* (July—September 2009), Vol. LXXIX: No. 3.
8. G. Palanithurai, *Management of Ethnic Conflict in India and Canada: A Comparative Analysis*, New Delhi: Kaniska Publishers and Distributors, 1993.

9. G. Palanithurai, *Leadership Matters in Grassroots Governance* (Path Finder Series 2) Gandhigram: Rajiv Gandhi Chair for Panchayati Raj Studies, 2005.
10. G. Palanithurai, *Leadership Matters in Grassroots Governance* (Path Finder Series 3) Gandhigram: Rajiv Gandhi Chair for Panchayati Raj Studies, 2005.
11. G. Palanithurai, *Leadership Matters in Grassroots Governance* (Path Finder Series 22) Gandhigram: Rajiv Gandhi Chair for Panchayati Raj Studies, 2006.
12. G. Palanithurai, G. Uma and J. Vanishree, *Networking of Elected Women Representatives at Grassroots*, New Delhi: Concept Publishing Company, 2008.
13. J.S. Mill, *Considerations on Representative Government*, London: Frontana, 1976.
14. M.N. Srinivas, *Village, Caste, Gender and Method*, New Delhi: Oxford University Press, 1996.

11

Engendering Democracy at the Grassroots : Challenges and Opportunities

V. Ragupathy

Introduction

In the constitutional history of Republic of India, the 73rd Constitutional Amendment Act is a major initiative towards inclusive democracy. Women, *dalits* and tribals have got opportunities to participate in governance of three lakh village local self-governments in India. This was the great dream of Mahatma Gandhi. Gandhi wanted a *dalit* woman to become the first President of the republic of India. For him democracy means devolution power to Village Panchayats and power to people at the bottom.

The 73rd Constitutional Amendment Act is a historical step in the process of empowerment of women *dalits* and *tribals.* It is a challenge to the social structure at the bottom. But, in a feudal rural society where inequality is institutionalized, democratic decentralization and devolution of powers to rural local governments have been considered a threat to marginalized sections of the village society. More power to Panchayats[1] means more power to high caste, majority community and dominant groups in villages and it may result in more exploitation of the poor and other socially deprived sections. Against this background, the 73rd Constitutional Amendment Act has included social justice as one of the major objectives of the new system of rural local governance. The amendment has provided reservation of not less than one-third of the elected offices in Panchayats for women. Based on this policy, the State governments have provided reservation for women from one-third to 50 per cent. Reservation for women in elected offices at the grassroots level has opened up opportunities for bringing about fundamental changes in the existing rural power structure and the right to participate in governance.

In the new system, every village local government has a village assembly to generate people's participation. The Constitution has allocated 29 functions, mostly related to social development, gender, land, water and welfare programmes to village local governments.

One Million Women in Local Governance

More than one million women elected representatives have been involved in rural local governance in India since 1994 as a result of the policy of reservation for women. But legislation alone cannot bring about social transformation. In India, many laws enacted for social transformation have not been able to bring about social changes to the desired level. According to Upendra Bakshi, the renowned Indian legal sociologist, there are two sets of laws: social and constitutional. Sometimes social laws are more powerful than the laws of the state in rural society.

The Amendment has created an ambivalent situation in the rural society. Even though feudal and traditional, the Indian society has a great capacity for adaptability and remarkable resilience. India is a subcontinent and reactions to such changes are varied and different. In the rural society empowerment of women is a long process of struggle. When the reservation policy was first introduced, violent resistance was reported in a few pockets of India. The stringent caste system, feudal values, gender inequality and inhuman poverty are some of the challenges to be faced. In States like Madhya Pradesh, elected women representatives were attacked, stripped naked, gang raped and tortured, particularly the *dalit*[2] women. Elected leaders were harassed (Buch, 1999). The north eastern States of India, with a very huge tribal population, enthusiastically adopted the process of women empowerment. In States like Kerala it is reported that the State Government took initiatives to make women empowerment in Panchayats successful. The process of political empowerment is gaining momentum; but, when one looks at the overall status of women, the situation is not quite impressive.

Gender and Development in India—Ambivalent Situation

In rural India, the human development indicators of women are simply poor. In the global gender gap index 2007, (WEFORM, 2007), India is ranked at 114 out of 128 countries. India has a sex ratio of 933 females to 1000 males. Maternal mortality is high at 301 per 1,00,000 live births. Anemia among women is 56 per cent. 41 per cent of women and 18 per cent of men (15-49 age groups) have never attended school. Only 43 per cent of married women are able to get income from any form of employment. Most of the women are engaged in informal, unorganized and non-remunerative economic activities.

There is a sharp contrast in the status of Indian women in political empowerment. India is ranked 21 out of 128 countries in political empowerment of women. The number of women elected to political offices is higher in India than in many western countries. Four major political parties of India are headed by women. There are significant numbers of independent and powerful women leaders. India had a strong and independent woman Prime Minister for seventeen years. At present, the most powerful person in Indian politics is a woman. India has a woman President and the Speaker of the Lok Sabha (the Lower House of the Parliament) is also a woman. 10 per cent of the members of Lok Sabha are women. A very powerful movement for reservation for women in Parliament and legislatures is active in India. In spite of all these positive factors, India ranks 114 at the bottom of the list in gender development.

Prior to the 73rd Amendment, women formed a marginalized and disempowered group. Before the Constitutional amendment, women did not have any significant role in public affairs and governance at the grassroots level and they mostly accepted their marginalized status. Following the 73rd Amendment, women have a very strong representation in the councils of the Panchayats at the grassroots. More than one million women, constituting about 37 per cent of the elected representatives are involved in governance in the Panchayats at the grassroots. This is a landmark achievement in the history of Indian democracy.

"When a group remains a distinct minority within a larger society, its members will seek to adapt to their surroundings, conforming to the predominant rules of the game . . . . but once the group reaches a certain size, the critical mass theory suggests that there will be a qualitative change in the nature of group interactions, as the minority starts to assert itself and thereby transform the institutional culture, norms and values" (Norris and Lovenduski, 2001).

It appears that in grassroots governance, women representatives have the required critical mass to influence politics and governance.

But a decade of women representation has produced only a mixed picture. Changes are found in the status of women. But they are not uniform all over the country and not substantial. It appears that, as many feminist thinkers believe, reservation for women alone cannot help in changing the nature of the existing political system and empower women.

Dahlerup maintains that the critical mass has to be followed by critical action to bring about desired changes in favour of women (Dahlerup, 1998). It means building the ability of women to mobilize political resources for Empowerment. Studies on Indian experiments in Women Empowerment tend to suggest that the presence of women in governance and the critical mass are not sufficient.

The desired outcome is not forthcoming. It appears that there are many strong obstacles in the process. Agency and opportunity structures are hypothesized by some scholars to be associated with the process of empowerment. Agency is defined as an actor's ability to make choices and opportunity structure is defined as the formal and informal contexts within which the actor operates (Alsop and Nina, 2002 and Alsop *et al.*, 2006). A woman Panchayat President may like to submit a representation to the district authorities on the creation of a childcare centre, but she may not have the ability to formulate an acceptable proposal. She may have the ability to prepare a proposal for a woman literacy centre but the local community leaders may prevent her from realizing her choice. In India, substantial changes in agency and opportunity structures have to take place.

The critical mass of women may not be able to change the context automatically. Here, critical action, such as mobilization of political resources and other such means are considered significant. It is true that women representatives can be trusted to a greater extent to promote women's interests than men. Women have different priorities and concerns. But it is not enough if women are in large numbers; it is important who they are. Women empowerment needs descriptive representation (Gargarella, 1998); a situation whereby women are able to represent the women constituency. A critical mass of women is significant for change but it cannot determine the change. Women have to be organized ideologically into a political constituency. Women empowerment in local government does not include building an organization of women. There are fragmented groups of women leaders but, in no State of India, have cohesive organizations or movements of elected women leaders emerged.

Some argue that mainstream politics are designed to disempower and marginalize women and that mainstream politics is indeed *male stream politics*. The elements of patriarchy are very strong in the mainstream political system. So the present institutional context will not allow empowerment of women beyond a level (HDRC, 2001). It will allow them to participate but it will not allow them to govern. Some scholars have found that the Panchayati Raj system is designed to allow women leaders to deal with certain specific issues affecting women but does not allow them to bring about any fundamental changes in the gender relations at the grassroots. The term *Panchayat* means 'Council of Five'. Panchayats were traditionally strong patriarchal village councils with the primary purpose of establishing a patriarchal system of governance. So Indian social revolutionaries like Dr. B.R. Ambedkar were not in favour of strong Village Panchayats.[3] The discriminatory social structure has to be dismantled to give women their due.

In India, the reservation of seats has enabled one million women to get elected. But the critical mass has not been followed by critical action. Legislation has created opportunity for empowerment. But the space needed for women to enter into politics and empower themselves cannot be created by legislation. It requires many other changes at several levels. There is a need to change the ideological system, and the political structures at different levels in the larger community. Quotas have not created space for women empowerment but have created only a political vacuum, which men can manipulate to their purposes. Some of the studies tend to confirm this argument (Palanithurai, G., 2005). Fundamental changes in the society require broad based mass movements of all marginalized groups, including men also.

India's freedom struggle was a landmark in bringing women to the public space. Mahatma Gandhi, the leader of the Indian freedom movement, insisted that Women, *dalits*, Muslims and other minorities must play a significant role in the anti-imperialistic struggle. About one lakh women participated in the non-violent freedom struggle and were imprisoned.

In independent India, no such powerful movement of women could emerge for the empowerment of the marginalized. In the semi-feudal discriminatory society in India, it is not possible to bring about changes without a powerful movement and struggles at various levels. But the affirmative action of reservation of seats for women initiated through the Constitutional Amendment Act has brought them into the political sphere. They have managed to occupy positions in governance but whether they are able to govern is an important question to be answered.

Inter-Sectionality and Multiple Subjection of Women Representatives at the Grassroots

Women representatives in the rural local governments are subjected to multiple forms of discrimination. Women experience various forms of oppressions in varying configurations and various degrees of intensity (Ritzer, G., 2007). They face an interlocking system of oppression which limits their ability to participate in governance at the grassroots. India has a caste system, a peculiar form of discrimination. Within a single race, caste divides people into different layers.

Caste status is gained by birth and cannot be changed forever. About 20 per cent of the people are considered untouchables and pushed out of the village society. Even though the practice of untouchability is illegal, it is still practiced in most parts of India. Among women representatives about 25 per cent belong to the *dalit* (untouchable) community. It is extremely difficult for the *dalit* women to use their legal right to participate in governance at the grassroots. Most *dalit* women are the poorest among the poor and they do not have any assets. In Indian villages women generally do not own property and the properties of the families are mostly owned by the males. Women do not enjoy economic freedom and they depend on men. The religious practices in rural India are also discriminatory. Particularly Hinduism and Islam do not permit women to enjoy equality. Religious practices are very oppressive and exploitative. They restrict the rights of women to take decisions in their personal and social life. Women representatives at the grassroots are subjected to all forms of discrimination common to rural women in India. In States like Kerala women enjoy better conditions in many areas of life. But even in Kerala political parties, particularly communist parties, have not facilitated women's participation in politics. The masculine nature of political parties discourages women's participation in governance. Discrimination is not restricted to gender and women at the grassroots are challenged by multiple forms of discrimination. The status of elected women representatives and their capacity to govern is determined by their location within multiple axes of oppression.

Status of Women Representatives in Governance

Based on the field study conducted by the Rajiv Gandhi Chair for Panchayati Raj Studies, Gandhigram Rural Institute Deemed University, among the women Panchayat Presidents in Tamil Nadu, it is found that women in the decision-making position at the grassroots level are at different stages in the process of empowerment (Ragupathy, 2007). They are explained hereunder.

Fake—Fake women leaders are not uncommon in Panchayats. In most of the States of India, powerful social groups are not ready to allow women to occupy the reserved positions in Panchayats. Particularly, the positions reserved for women dalit candidates are commonly operated through the proxy system. A study in Tamil Nadu shows that about eight per cent of the women leaders are affected by the system (Ragupathy, 2007). Women leaders are in position, but they are not allowed to function. They are not allowed to sit in the office, attend meetings, participate in training programmes and meet officials. Their functions are discharged by someone who has brought them to the position. Even the women leaders' signatures are forged in official correspondence, documents and cheque books. The elected leaders do not know anything about the functioning of the Panchayats. In their names someone attend to official duties. It is an illegal method just to satisfy the requirements of law.

Dummying—Here the reservation policy is followed systematically and without any violation of law. It appears that women have access but no control over governance; they have assumed power but not to exercise it. Dummying is more dangerous than proxying. Here one can find a woman President in the Panchayat office. She presides over meetings, affixes her signature, sits for photos and appears in public, but the decisions are taken by someone else. Women leaders have only symbolic power but not the real power. In such cases mostly family members of elected leaders or the community leaders or party leaders enjoy real power.

Compromise—When women leaders want to assert their legitimate power to govern, powerful groups in the villages do not allow them to act independently. The family members of the women leaders themselves are not ready to accept their right to take decisions. For varied reasons women are not able to resist male domination. They depend on the other males of the Panchayat Council, village assemblies and committees for effective governance. A majority of the women leaders are not economically independent and they are also governed by the social norms. Because of the system of election they have to keep up good relationship with different social groups. They may not have the required capability and support to govern independently. So women leaders are forced to compromise with powerful groups of men. It is the only pragmatic and practical way available for most of the women leaders to function. They do not try to bring about any fundamental changes in the existing social structure.

Struggle—Struggle is the most significant stage in the process of empowerment. When women elected leaders have the capacity and confidence, they tend to assert their legitimate rights to govern and discharge their responsibilities. Sometimes they attempt to challenge the social discriminations, wrong policies of the state and demand social justice. In such situations struggle becomes inevitable. In many cases women are not able to go beyond the stage of compromise. They are not permitted to discharge even very simple responsibilities in their Panchayats and can do so only through a process of struggle even in their day to day functioning. In rare cases women Panchayat leaders struggle for the empowerment of women and are able to bring about changes in the social structure.

Empowerment—Empowerment is the ideal stage where women are able to make decisions and execute them on their own. They are able to work towards social justice and to bring about significant improvement in the status of women and other marginalized groups. They work for the overall development of the entire community. In the Indian context it is extremely difficult for women elected leaders to attain this stage in Panchayats. In spite of difficulties there are a few women leaders who are able to reach the final stage of empowerment.

Process of Empowerment in Two Different States

The process and the nature of empowerment may differ from State to State. There are many case studies available on empowered women Panchayat leaders in India (Palanithurai, G., 2005). Due to the complex nature of the process and the vast size of the country, the impact of the policy has not been fully understood. The process of empowerment is affected by varied factors like policies of provincial governments, conditions of the political culture, status of women, role of political parties and the political will of the provincial governments. The reservation system is similar in all the States, but the level of empowerment differs from State to State. This chapter intends to discuss the status of empowerment in two of the southern States of India, viz., Tamil Nadu and Kerala. In these two neighbouring States, the reservation policy was implemented in 1994. These two States have many similarities in social and human development. In gender development, Kerala stands first, and Tamil Nadu stands second among the major States of India. Kerala is projected as a model for development among Indian States. The process of empowerment and the status of women in local governance and empowerment in the two States are compared here.

Empowerment in Kerala

Kerala tops the list in gender development among the States of India. Many indicators suggest that women enjoy better social status in Kerala than in many other States. The sex ratio is in favour of women in Kerala. Under the matrilineal system practiced till recently, women traditionally enjoyed the right to inherit family property. Social movements and movements by leftist parties helped to remove caste based discrimination and the practice of untouchability in Kerala. Kerala was the first State where the Communist Party could win elections and form a government in 1957. The Communist government effectively implemented land reforms in Kerala, resulting in the dismantling of feudal social structures in the village society. Village politics in Kerala is relatively free from caste and feudal forces unlike in most of the other States. Political parties play a determining role in village politics and Panchayat elections. While the political parties are well organized in Kerala, the left parties, particularly, are professionally organized and known for party discipline. Political parties in Kerala are patriarchal in nature and there are very few women leaders within the political parties (Chathukulum, 2000). Women do not have much Space in state politics and only a few women are elected to the Parliament and the State Assembly in Kerala. In 1994, the Left Front Government introduced the Kerala Panchayat Act and provided one-third reservation for women in elected offices of Panchayats and fulfilled the constitutional minimum requirement. Political parties play a determining role in the Panchayat elections. The law enables party based elections for Village Panchayats, intermediate Panchayats and District Panchayats. In Kerala, reservation is rotated among constituencies once in five years. In some other States like Tamil Nadu reservation for women in a particular constituency continues to remain for a second term.

Affiliation/Support from Political Parties

(*Percentage*)

	President-Female		*Ward Member-Female*	
	Yes	No	Yes	No
All India	38.7	907	27.1	3973
Tamil Nadu	28.1	32	15.3	144
Kerala	96.0	32	97.9	143

Source: Ministry of Panchayati Raj (2008), *Study on Elected Women Representatives in Panchayati Raj Institutions.*

Some of the policies of the Government of Kerala like promotion of micro-finance, allocation of ten per cent of the Plan funds for women-related projects, intensive training to women leaders and participatory village development plans have contributed significantly to the empowerment of women. Varied factors influence the process and status of women empowerment in Panchayats and a mixed picture has emerged.

Proportion of Presidents who have received Training in Tamil Nadu and Kerala

(*Percentage*)

	Presidents—Female	
	Yes	*No*
All India	81.8	18.2
Tamil Nadu	90.6	9.4
Kerala	100.0	100.0

Source: Ministry of Panchayati Raj (2008), *Study on Elected Women Representatives in Panchayati Raj Institutions.*

In Kerala, the policy of reservation has brought large number of women into grassroots governance. But it is not significantly more than the minimum constitutional requirement. In some States like Karnataka women have occupied about 45 per cent of the positions. There are only a few women who could win elections from general constituencies in Kerala. Very few women seek reelection. In spite of high level of gender status, women have not gained much political space in Kerala. But the practice of proxy rule, which is a very big problem in most of the States, is not found in Kerala. In Kerala, feudal rural structures have been eliminated and women Panchayat leaders are free from the control of caste based organizations. In most of the other States of India, it is common to see women leaders enjoying only symbolic power and tokenism being practiced. In Kerala it is very difficult to find such cases.

It is not caste but political parties that play a determining role in the affairs of Panchayats. Because of the patriarchal nature of parties very few women are able to gain power within the party structures. Political parties scout for women candidates to contest on behalf of their parties in Panchayat elections and parties select women amenable to their control. Mostly family members of faithful party workers and sympathizers are selected to contest. Parties normally avoid women engaged in non-party women movements. Women with independent views are also avoided. In short, very rarely does the male dominant party leadership favour the emergence of independent women who reveal a degree of feminist consciousness. It is striking that 97 per cent of women Panchayat Presidents have been nominated by the political parties in Kerala (Ministry of Panchayati Raj, 2008). Even though, 97 per cent of the women Presidents have party affiliation, they are not politically rooted. These women Panchayat Presidents are vulnerable to party control. Local party units have control over the day to day functioning of the elected leaders belonging to their parties. The outcome of the meetings of Panchayat Councils and committees in Panchayats are mostly decided by the local party units. Selection of development schemes, budget allocation and selection of beneficiaries for various welfare schemes and other important decisions are influenced or dictated by the party units. Particularly Leftist parties maintain strict party discipline. Any violation of party direction may attract disciplinary action.

One strange feature of the Kerala Panchayati Raj Act is the right of the political parties to issue whip to their elected representatives in the Panchayats. Party affiliated representatives must obey the whip of their parties. Otherwise they will be disqualified and removed from office. Even though party control is common to both men and women leaders, women leaders are more vulnerable to such control. Most of them do not have political roots and political experience. Normally women leaders are elected only for one term because of the system of rotation.

The nature and the intensity of party control over men and women elected leaders significantly differ. Women are not able to resist or assert their rights. In many places they have to face harassment to various degrees. In spite of these problems, parties act as support structures for women Panchayat leaders. They are confident and have a feeling of security because of the party support. Experienced party members educate, guide and advice women Presidents. When women Panchayat Presidents face difficulties the party extends a helping hand. The party helps Panchayat Presidents in their dealings with higher level government agencies and officials. Parties other than the Left parties are not professionally organized and women representatives from these parties enjoy more freedom than the members of the Left parties. Because of their education and social background, the women leaders are more qualified to address women's issues than their counterparts in other States.

Educational Attainment of Female Presidents

(*Percentage*)

	Illiterate	*Up to primary school*	*Up to middle school*	*Middle school and above*
All India	11.40	19.80	16.40	52.40
Tamil Nadu	3.10	9.40	12.50	75.00
Kerala	Nil	Nil	6.30	93.80

Source: Ministry of Panchayati Raj, 2008, *Study of Elected Women Representatives in Panchayati Raj Institutions.*

They are able to mobilize women for development. It is found that women's participation in Village Assembly meetings is very high in Panchayats headed by women. Performance indicators show that women leaders are in no way inferior to men. Women leaders pay more attention to primary education, primary health care, women and child care, drinking water and sanitation (Ministry of Panchayati Raj, 2008).

Distribution of Data on Primary Occupation on the basis of Time Spent by Female Presidents

(*Percentage*)

	Farming	*Labourer*	*Panchayat works*	*Small business*	*House wife*	*Others*
All India	8.20	2.30	26.50	0.40	58.00	4.60
Tamil Nadu	18.80	Nil	12.50	Nil	65.60	3.10
Kerala	Nil	Nil	90.60	Nil	6.30	3.10

Source: Ministry of Panchayati Raj, 2008, *Study on Elected Women Representatives in Panchayati Raj Institutions.*

Women Usually Attending Gram Sabha[4] Meetings in Women Headed Panchayats Headed by Women

(*Percentage*)

	Less than 10%	*10-15%*	*25-50%*	*More than 50%*
All India	24.80	33.20	26.60	13.90
Tamil Nadu	6.30	15.60	46.90	31.30
Kerala	Nil	Nil	12.50	87.50

Source: Ministry of Panchayati Raj (2008), *Study on Elected Women Representatives in Panchayati Raj Institutions.*

Few women leaders in Kerala are able to go beyond basic issues and take up issues like women empowerment, gender justice, environment protection and globalization. Based on fifteen years of performance it is possible to conclude that women elected representatives in Kerala are relatively at a higher stage of empowerment than those in many other States of India. A study conducted by the Government of India on women Panchayat leaders ranks Kerala as the first State in India based on their performance.

Initiatives taken by Female Presidents to Increase Enrolment in Schools

(*Percentage*)

	Yes	*No*
All India	80.80	20.00
Tamil Nadu	90.60	9.40
Kerala	100.00	Nil

Source: Ministry of Panchayati Raj (2008), *Study on Elected Women Representatives in Panchayati Raj Institutions.*

But in Kerala women Panchayat leaders are trapped in the powerful party system and they are caged birds with a lot of potential. In spite of their political resources and numerical strength, women are not able to emerge as a critical mass in Kerala and generate significant changes in the status of women. They are not able to create a political space for women in Kerala. Organizing women Panchayat leaders as a single group in Kerala is impossible because of the very strong party system. Organizing women within a party is also not possible because of the patriarchal nature of the political parties. Women do not have a critical mass within the parties. Yet women Panchayat leaders enjoy a better status than women Panchayat leaders of other States of India. They have not been empowered in the true sense. In spite of their great potential, they face the problem of glass ceiling.

Case Study

Scheduled Caste Woman Village Panchayat Presidents in Kerala

This is a case of a Village Panchayat woman President of Vaikom Block of Kottayam District in Kerala. The Village Panchayat President was a woman belonging to the Scheduled Caste (SC). She was elected from the constituency reserved for SC women. Untouchability is not practiced in Kerala. But SC people are economically poor and without much assets. The father of the Panchayat President was a Communist Party worker and the President was a member of the youth wing of the Party. She was used by the Party for canvassing during general elections. The secretary of the local Party helped her to get Party nomination to contest in the Panchayat election and, with the support of the Party, she won the election. After the election, the local Party secretary helped her in the Panchayat administration. Everyday he visited the Panchayat office and guided her in the day-to-day functioning. The local Party unit advised her on selection and implementation of development projects. It also tried to select beneficiaries for various government schemes to be implemented by the Village Panchayat and the Party gave priority only to its members. The executive officer of the Village Panchayat was also a Communist Party sympathizer. With his help the local Communist party unit tried to bring the entire Panchayat administration under its control.

When the woman Panchayat President tried to consult members of other parties on issues related to the development of the village she was abused by her own Party people. She was always forced to take directions from her Party. She was considered an inexperienced child needing training. She was not ready to contest in the election for another term.

Empowerment in Tamil Nadu

Tamil Nadu stands second in Gender Development among the States of India, next only to Kerala. Women enjoy better social status in Tamil Nadu compared to other States of India (Ministry of Panchayati Raj, 2008). Tamil Nadu has had many progressive social movements. But they could not remove social discriminations based on caste. There were no honest efforts at land reforms in Tamil Nadu. The State is not able to remove the practice of untouchability in rural areas. Political parties with an ideology of social justice are ruling the State for more than forty years. But they are not able to change the discriminatory social structure.

Village politics in Tamil Nadu is still controlled by the caste-based social institutions. Untouchability is practiced in almost all the parts of the State. In most of the villages of Tamil Nadu certain caste groups are socially excluded and they live in separate colonies. Women in villages of Tamil Nadu do not enjoy equal rights. Female infanticide is practiced in some parts of Tamil Nadu. By tradition women do not inherit family property, but they get dowry at the time of marriage. Villages have caste organizations and they are involved in the decision-making process. State level federations of castes operate and they influence State politics and general elections too. In villages caste assemblies and caste Panchayats are also functioning. They interfere in the day-to-day activities of Village Panchayats.

In 1994, the Government headed by Jayalalitha, a strong woman Chief Minister, enacted the Tamil Nadu Panchayat Act. It provided one-third reservation for women in Panchayats as prescribed in the Constitution. The Tamil Nadu Panchayat Act has not provided any role for political parties at the level of the Village Panchayat. At the intermediate level and the district level parties can participate in the affairs of Panchayats but at the village level they do not have any direct role in governance. In Tamil Nadu reservation of a constituency for women continues for ten years. It helps women leaders to contest in elections for two tenures.

Number of Elections Won by Women Leaders

(*Percentage*)

	Third-timer
All India	3.30
Tamil Nadu	6.70
Kerala	1.70

Source: Ministry of Panchayati Raj (2008), *Study on Elected Women Representatives in Panchayati Raj Institutions.*

In Tamil Nadu there is a very effective women's movement of micro-finance. It is promoted by the State and the NGO sectors. Almost forty per cent of the village women are involved in the movement. It helps women's participation in Panchayats. Three Panchayat elections have been conducted based on the principle of reservation in Tamil Nadu and women participation in elections is significantly increasing. In Tamil Nadu factors like government policies, feudal structures like caste, attitude of political parties, nature of bureaucracy and capability of leaders are the significant factors affecting the process and status of women's empowerment. At the village level family and caste are the biggest challenges to women's empowerment. Fake Panchayat leaders are very common in Tamil Nadu. Powerful caste groups are not able to accept the policy of reservation for women. Caste and customary rules are more powerful in villages than the laws of the State. Caste groups do not accept empowerment of lower caste people and women. It is a threat to the traditional power structure. They want to sabotage the policy of reservation in Panchayats. Particularly *dalit* women are prevented by force from contesting elections. Even if they are elected, often they are forced to resign. A woman candidate amenable to the majority community is elected from the reserved constituency and the legal requirement is fulfilled. After the election, the woman is not allowed to attend to any official duties. She even cannot come to the Panchayat office and attend meetings. Someone will attend to all work on her behalf. Even her signature will be forged by someone else. A study in Tamil Nadu shows that about eight per cent of the Village Panchayats come under this category (Sivakumar, S., 2008). In most cases women's empowerment is at the stage of dummying. Women leaders are sponsored by powerful social groups. They are permitted to enjoy only symbolic powers. Women Presidents can come to the office, attend meetings, affix signatures on official papers and appear in public. But they cannot take decisions.

Sometimes independent women are able to win elections in alliance with powerful caste groups and to get elected, they have to come to an understanding with these groups. Political parties may also play a role in such cases. After elections such women have to compromise with the caste leaders, party leaders and family members for their smooth functioning in Panchayats. In recent years, a majority of the women elected as Panchayat Presidents are able to reach the stage of compromise. In Tamil Nadu women Panchayat leaders do not have any support structure for their independent functioning. They have to depend only on the support of their family members, local community leaders and political parties. They try to attend to basic functions and provide basic facilities to the people by getting support from different sections of the society. In Tamil Nadu women leaders have to struggle to come out of the boundaries laid by the traditional and caste based the rural social power structures of the village society. If they want to bring about any fundamental changes in the existing social structure in favour of women a struggle becomes inevitable.

In Kerala, political parties are more progressive in their outlook towards women than the political parties in Tamil Nadu. Women leaders in Tamil Nadu do not get political support in their efforts for social transformation. Instead such attempts are discouraged. In most cases such women leaders are harassed by political parties, local communities and government officials. Some of the leaders have been attacked and even imprisoned. In Tamil Nadu, there are only a few empowered women leaders. Mostly they are in the stage of compromise or struggle. At the Village Panchayat level women Panchayat leaders do not get much support from political parties. About 72 per cent of the women leaders do not get support from political parties (Ministry of Panchayati Raj, 2008). More than 92 per cent of them are not part of any women organization (Ministry of Panchayati Raj, 2008).

Some Non-Government Organizations (NGOs) try to create networks or federations of elected women leaders. Because of various reasons they are not able to succeed in their efforts. Even though there are a large number of women elected representatives they are not able to organize themselves into cohesive groups. They do not have the required capacity and resources to build such organizations. State agencies have created networks of Self-Help Groups (SHFs)[5] of women engaged in micro-finance. But no such efforts from the State have come to create networks of women elected leaders in Panchayats. Leftist parties have created networks of members of their parties. The major political parties have not made any significant efforts to create such networks for their own party members. Unlike in Kerala women elected leaders of Panchayats have to function on their own in Tamil Nadu. They are not controlled by political parties. They do not have much affiliation with any political organizations and they do not get any significant level of support from any political organization. They are fragmented individuals. They are vulnerable and soft targets for attacks. They have to walk a long way to reach the stage of empowerment. In spite of their difficult situation, some women leaders are able to perform their functions effectively. The performance index of the Government of India gives seventh rank to Tamil Nadu women Panchayat leaders among the States of India.

Case Study from Tamil Nadu

Ms. Magudeshwari was the President of Peraiyur Panchayat in Dindigul District, which was reserved for SC women. When the elders in her Panchayat came to know that the post of the Village Panchayat President was reserved for SC women, they commanded Magudeshwari, a coolie and a domestic servant, to contest in the election. She functioned as per the direction of the caste Hindus and elders in the Panchayat. She said that she could not do anything against their wishes because of being a woman and that too an SC woman. Her destiny was to follow the command of the people who put her in the position as the Panchayat President.

She also said that her presence in the Village Panchayat Council meeting was ignored and she could not speak anything during discussions and the resolutions were passed without her consent. The activities of the Panchayat were carried out without her knowledge and sometimes she was forced to sign cheques. Many times she signed the cheques without knowing for what the amount was being utilized. She did not know about accounting and auditing procedure carried out in the Panchayat and she simply affixed her signature wherever she was asked to do so. Only the caste leaders and the Vice-President, a man from the upper caste, decided everything. Information from the government officers were communicated only to them. She felt that she was left out of the Panchayat and accepted her status because she was a woman from a low caste. The high caste men were not allowing her to act on her own as they considered her a person without any knowledge and ability. SC women from rural areas have triple handicaps of being a woman, belonging to SC and poor (Narashimhan, 1999).

Conclusion

Women can Participate but Cannot Govern

The study concludes with a few assumptions. Women at the grassroots have attained numbers in local governments but not gained the power to govern. Political parties in Kerala have played a significant role in determining the status and performance of elected women. These women enjoy a higher status within the Panchayat than their counterparts in Tamil Nadu. In Tamil Nadu due to the prevalence of a feudalistic patriarchal structure, caste plays a significant role and the supremacy of patriarchy makes women Presidents proxies and dummies. Women can be easily enslaved by men, by the caste group and by the traditional Panchayat. This becomes easier if a woman from the SC becomes President. In Kerala this kind of enslavement is not possible as women are assertive in exercising their rights. The deep rooted Marxist ideology has a profound impact on the elimination of feudalism and caste based discrimination. The party supports them in contesting and winning elections. No other social institution can influence them other than their party. They can exercise a certain degree of power within their Panchayats. They are able to use their power to contribute to women's development to a significant extent. But they have to limit their functions within the purview of the political party. The political party plays a dominant role in determining the functioning of the Women Panchayat Presidents. They are kept under the control of the party. Indeed they represent the party and not the women. The party allows elected women leaders to work for women's development. But hardly has it permitted women leaders to engage in any significant women empowerment activities. They are not even allowed to organize themselves into a cohesive group. This shows that the political system in Kerala is highly patriarchal and does not encourage elected women leaders to determine their own course of action and to involve in women political movement.

The experience from both Kerala and Tamil Nadu shows that women have attained the critical mass by numbers in local governance. According to the critical mass theory women are expected to perform for the development and empowerment of women. But in reality this is not so. In Scandinavian countries the critical mass of women are able to perform the critical action. They are able to initiate policies for the empowerment of women. But, in India, which has diverse social institutions and a feudalistic and hierarchical nature, the critical mass of women are not able to do the critical function. Tamil Nadu is dominated by a feudalistic society and in Kerala the political party dominates the women even though they are allowed to perform women development activities. The patriarchal nature of the society and multiple forms of oppression challenge the notion of the critical mass. Fifteen years back in rural Indian society there was absolutely no space for women in governance and women were nowhere near the rural power structure. Reservation has certainly brought more than a million women into the process of governance. But there is no women empowerment and equity as expected. The process can be only slow and painful. The success will be mixed and not without backlash. Reservation policy alone cannot dismantle and reconstruct a new social order and change does not happen. The review of the process of empowerment in two southern States of India gives us many insights. Indian society has adopted the process of democracy with greater efficiency than many other developing countries. Now a silent social revolution is taking place in Indian villages in favour of women. Sometimes, changes are not visible. Millions and millions of rural women are drawn into Self-Help Groups of micro-finance. Gradually, these women are able to understand their rights in the political space. In the recent general election women groups were able to negotiate with political parties and parties which promoted women friendly policies only could win elections. It appears that silently women in India are emerging as an invisible political class. Women may be able to cross the feudal and party structure on their way to empowerment.

Acknowledgements: I wish to acknowledge the help extended by Dr. G. Palanithurai, Dr. J. Vanishree, P. Selvamani, Department of Political

Science and Development Administration, Gandhigram Rural University, Dr. Jos Chathukulum, Centre for Rural Management, Kottayam and Ms. R. Abarajitha, SRM University, Chennai in preparation of this paper.

NOTES

1. Panchayat means rural Local Self-Government in India.
2. Socially excluded class.
3. Village Panchayat means Village Level Local Government.
4. Gram Sabha means Village Assembly of voters created by the Constitution.
5. Self-Help Group means small groups promoted primarily for micro-finance.

REFERENCES

Alsop, Ruth, Bertelsen, M. and Holland, J. *Empowerment in Practice from Analysis to Implementation*, Washington DC (2006), World Bank.

Alsop, Ruth, and Nina Heinsohn. *Measuring Empowerment in Practice: Structuring Analysis and Framing Indicators,* Washington DC (2002), World Bank.

Buch, Nirmala. *From Oppression to Assertion: A Study of Panchayats and Women in Madhya Pradesh, Rajasthan and Uttar Pradesh (Mimeo)* New Delhi (1999), CWDS.

Chathukulum, Jos; M.S. John, "Empowerment of Women Panchayat members: Learning from Kerala" (India) in *Asian Journal of Women Studies,* Vol. 6., No. 4, 2000.

Dahlerup, Drude. "From A Small to Large Minority: Women in Scandinavian Politics", *Scandinavian Political Studies*, 1998, Vol. 14.

Dahlerup, Drude."Using quotas to increase Women's Political Representation" in Karam, Azza (Ed.), *Women in Parliament: Beyond Numbers,* Stockholm (1998), The International Institute for Democracy and Electoral Assistance.

Gargarella, R. "Full representation, deliberation and Impartiality" in J. Elster (Ed.), *Deliberative Democracy,* Cambridge: Cambridge University Press.

Government of India, Ministry of Panchayati Raj. *Study on Elected Women Representatives in Panchayati Raj Institutions,* New Delhi (2008).

HDRC, *Decentralization in India: Challenges and Opportunities*, New Delhi, (2001), HDRC, UNDP.

Narashimhan, Sakuntala. *Empowering Women: An Alternative Strategy from Rural India*, New Delhi (1999), Sage Publications.

Norris, Pippa and Joni Lovenduski. *Blair's Babes: Critical Mass Theory, Gender, and Legislative Life,* John F. Kennedy School of Government, Harvard University, Faculty Research Working Paper Series (2001).

Palanithurai, G. *Process and Performance of Gram Panchayat Women and Dalit Presidents,* New Delhi: Concept Publishing Company, (2005).

Ragupathy, V. *Report on Empowerment of Women, Process and Status in Tamil Nadu, Gandhigram* (2007), Rajiv Gandhi Chair for Panchayat Raj Studies, Gandhigram Rural University.

Ritzer, G. Contemporary, Sociological Theory and its Classical Roots: The Basics. Boston (2007), McGraw Hill.

Sivakumar, S. Empowerment of Women Village Panchayat Presidents in Rural Local Governance in Theni District, Tamil Nadu, Gandhigram: Unpublished Ph.D. Thesis (2008), Gandhigram Rural University.

12

Secularism in India

Vasundara Mohan

Introduction

The Preamble of the Constitution adopted by independent India on 26th November, 1949 (effective from 26th January, 1950) declared India as a "Sovereign Democratic Republic". Till the 42nd Amendment in 1976, the Constitution did not contain the word 'secular", although the spirit of secularism is evident in the various Articles of the Constitution. There were, however, efforts in the Constituent Assembly to make a specific mention of the principle of secularism in the Constitution. During discussions on the Draft Constitution, Prof. K.T. Shah and H.V. Kamath tried to get the following provisions included in the Constitution.

> "The State in India being secular shall have no concern with any religion, creed or profession of faith; and shall observe an attitude of absolute neutrality in all matters relating to the religion of any class of its citizens or other persons in the Union."[1]
>
> "The State shall not establish, endow, or patronize any particular religion. Nothing shall however prevent the State from imparting spiritual training or instruction to the citizens of the Union."[2]

However, all such amendments were summarily rejected.[3] The reason as to why the word "secular" was not in the Constitution adopted in 1950, is attributed to the fact that "so ingrained is the Indian concept of the secularism in our national culture that it did not even occur to the architects of the Constitution that they should specially mention it as one of its preambulatory principles."[4]

Secularism as a political concept gained prominence in the 1940s, after the Muslim League demanded a separate homeland for the Muslims on religious and cultural grounds. The Congress party objected to the demand by pointing out the syncretic religious traditions of India. Affirming its faith in secularism, Congress said that it did not contemplate misusing religion for accomplishing its political objectives, but believed in confining religion to the private sphere. It assured that the post-colonial state would not discriminate on the basis of religion. Thus, the Congress invoked secularism "to distinguish its politics from the communalism" of the Muslim League.[5]

But prior to and even during the independence movement, Indian national leaders like Bal Gangadhar Tilak and even Mahatma Gandhi used religion and religious symbols to unite Indian masses against British Colonialism, by, for example, providing a nationalistic interpretation of the *Bhagavad Gita,* holding up *Ram Rajya* as the post-independence scenario, and popularising the celebration of the birthday of Shivaji and *Ganesh Chaturthi* festival to promote communitarian solidarity among the Hindus. Further, even during the British period, the government was drawn to interfere in religious affairs of both Hinduism and Islam, which is continued in independent India in the form of establishing Departments of Religious Endowments, Wakf Boards, appointing Trustees of Temples and Wakfs, subsiding Hajj pilgrimage, etc., and to deal with issues concerning its reforms. Under the circumstances, it was difficult for the Indian State to divorce itself from religion.

The words "Socialist" and "Secular" were added to the Preamble of the Constitution by the 42nd Constitutional Amendment Act of 1976. The word "Secular" was meant to imply equality of all religions and religious tolerance. However, H.M. Seervai, an authority on Constitution, opines that the words 'Socialist' and 'Secular' are ambiguous and should not have been inserted in the Preamble without a reason.[6] In view of the 42nd Amendment, secularism has become an integral part of the basic structure of the Constitution and the Supreme Court has also decreed as such in the case of *S.R. Bommai* vs. *Union of India.*[7]

Definition of Secularism

A perusal of the Constituent Assembly debates reveals that several Members were clearly at sea about the meaning of the word "secularism." So, what exactly is "Secularism"? Miriam-Webster's Online dictionary (1851) defines secularism as "*indifference to or rejection or exclusion of religion and religious considerations*".[8] The Free Dictionary[9] defines secularism as:

The term secularism was coined in 1846 by George Jacob Holyoake, a leader of the English Secularist and Free Thought Movement, to describe "a form of opinion which concerns itself only with questions, the issues of which can be tested by the experience of this life." His early usage of the term "secularism" did not explicitly portray the concept as opposed to religion; rather, it only referred, in passing, to the idea of focusing upon *this life* rather than speculation about *any other life*.[10]

Despite its importance, there is no agreement on what secularism really is. For, the concept secular can be used in a couple of ways which, while closely related, are nevertheless different enough to make it difficult to know for sure what people might mean. The word secular means "*of this world*" in Latin and is the opposite of religious. As a doctrine, secularism is usually used to describe any philosophy which forms its ethics without reference to religious dogmas and which promotes the development of human art and science.[11] There is no specific statement that secularism involves the *absence* of religion. Secularism was designed as a materialistic philosophy, both in terms of the means by which human life was to be improved and in its understanding of the nature of the universe.

Perhaps the most common understanding of the word "secular" today stands in opposition to "religious". According to this usage, something is secular when it is not worshipped, when it is not venerated, and when it is open for critique, judgment, and replacement.[12] Donald Eugene Smith defined a secular state as one "which guarantees individual and corporate freedom of religion, deals with the individual as a citizen irrespective of religion, is not constitutionally connected to a particular religion nor does it seek either to promote or interfere with religion."[14] As a modern political and constitutional principle, Secularism involves two basic propositions:[14]

- People belonging to different faiths and sections of society are equal before the law, the Constitution, and government policy; and
- There can be no mixing up of religion and politics.

In essence, a "secular state" is not one where religion is abolished but the state distances itself away from religion and there can be no discrimination against anyone on the basis of religion or faith nor could there be room for the hegemony of one religion or majoritarian religious sentiments and aspirations. It is from this understanding that our Constitution safeguards secularism, however, imperfectly. Doubts were expressed even during the debates in the Constituent Assembly whether India could really practice secularism, when religion is an indispensable part of the Indian society and culture.[15]

Lok Nath Mishra (Member, Orissa) wondered in the Constituent Assembly: "Do we really believe that religion can be divorced from life, or is it our belief that in the midst of many religions we cannot decide which one to accept? If religion is beyond the ken of our state, let us clearly say so and delete all reference to rights relating to religion. If we find it necessary, let us be brave enough and say what it should be".[16]

Mahatma Gandhi on Secularism

Writing in *Harijan*, Gandhi categorically said: "the state should undoubtedly be secular. Everyone living in it should be entitled to profess his religion without hindrance *so long as the citizen obeys the common law of the land*". He also said: "Religion is a personal matter and if we succeeded in confining it to the personal plane, all would be well in our political life. If officers of the Government as well as members of the public undertook the responsibility and worked wholeheartedly for the creation of a secular state, we could build a new India that would be the glory of the world".[17]

Nehru's Concept of Secularism

Jawaharlal Nehru believed that religion itself was irrelevant, backward and superstitious. He looked at secularism from a humanist and scientific point of view. Highlighting the importance of secularism in Modern India, Nehru said: "We have to function in life with the humanist ideals of the age we live, these ideals may be classed under two heads; Humanism and scientific spirit". As regards the concept of secularism, Nehru explained:

> "We call our state a secular one. The word 'secular' is not a very happy one. And yet for want of better word, we have used it. What exactly does it mean? It does not obviously mean a state where religion is discouraged. It means freedom of religion and conscience including freedom for those who have no religion, subject only to their not interfering with each other or with the basic conceptions of our state . . . . The word secular, however, conveys something much more to me, although that might not be its dictionary meaning. It conveys the idea of social and political equality. Thus, a caste-ridden society is not properly secular. I have no desire to interfere with any persons' belief but when those beliefs become petrified in caste divisions, undoubtedly they affect the social structure of the state. They, prevent us from realising the idea of equality which we claim to place before ourselves". (Jawaharlal Nehru, 1963: 327)

As Prof. Ninan Koshy asserts, "The stance of the minorities was acknowledged by the leaders of the nation, as a significant contribution to secularism. This had a positive influence on the law-makers and was reflected in the constitutional provisions on religious freedom and on minority rights in education. The minorities took that position on the basis of the conviction that being a minority in a secular state gave them full and equal rights with all and that there was constitutional guarantee that there would be no discrimination on the basis of religion. Historically it can thus be shown that minority rights were a response to the secular commitment of the minority communities".[18]

Nehru's concept of secularism had its critics too. For instance, Subramanian Swamy rejects Nehru's brand of secularism which does not allow public functions of cultural symbolism such as lighting a lamp to inaugurate a conference or breaking a coconut to launch a project. "This orthodoxy induced a reaction in the Indian masses for whom religion was a way of life. Nehru had also failed to define what historical roots ought to be a part of the modem Indian, and what was to be rejected. Instead in the name of `scientific temper', he rejected most of our past as 'obscurantism'. . . . His orthodox secularism sought to alienate the Indian from his hoary past".[19] J.N. Dixit, a former Foreign Secretary, also observes that Nehru did not underline the fact that the secular ethos of Indian society was rooted in two factors. That Hindus constituted the majority of the people of the country and that Hindu ethos at the profoundest intellectual and spiritual levels believed deeply in religious tolerance and respect for other religions".[20] But, "Nehru put the Hindu majority somewhat on the defensive, predicating Indian secularism on certification by the minorities, that the majority is secular. This resulted in a certain defensiveness and self-conscious denial of their religious and cultural identity by the Hindu community, which has perhaps made secularism a surface phenomenon in India's socio-political processes".[21]

Nehru's belief that "if we lay stress on it (the economic factor) and divert public attention to it we shall find automatically that religious differences recede into the background and a common bond unites different groups. The economic bond is stronger than the national one." This was not to happen. On the other hand, religiousness among all the Indian masses has started increasing and remains to be so even in the twenty-century.

Constitutional Provisions

When the Muslim League insisted on Pakistan as a nation of Muslims, what would have happened if the Hindu leaders of the period had said that what remains will be a Hindu state? But, fortunately India did not become a religious or a theocratic state because of the generally non-communal character of the Congress party and the wise leadership that guided Indian polity at the initial stages. The debates in the Constituent assembly show that there was unanimity on the point that there would be no discrimination based on religion, though there was no common understanding what secularism meant".[22]

Till the sixties there was no serious discussion on "secularism" in the public and there was no judgment either of a High Court or of the Supreme Court dealing with the subject to provide an opportunity for such debate even in the academic circles.

Indian Constitution lays down that the state shall not deny to any person equality before the law or equal protection of the laws [Article 14]; shall not discriminate against any citizen on grounds of religion, race, caste, sex, place of birth, or any of them [Article 15 (1)];

and no citizen shall, on grounds of only religion, race, caste, sex, place of birth or any of them, be subject to any disability, liability, restriction or condition with regard to (a) access to shops, public restaurants, hotels and places of public entertainment; or (b) the use of wells, tanks, bathing *ghats,* roads and places of public resort maintained wholly or partly out of state funds or dedicated to the use of the general public [Article 15 (2)].

Similarly, Article 25 of the Constitution declares that "all persons are equally entitled to freedom of conscience and the right to freely profess, practice and propagate religion" and Article 26 grants every religious denomination or any section thereof, to manage its own affairs in matters of religion, and to administer such property in accordance with the law and Article 26 grants every religious denomination or any section thereof, to manage its own affairs in matters of religion, and to administer such property in accordance with the law.

The Constitution also prohibits religious instruction in educational institutions wholly maintained out of State funds (Article 28) and no person shall be required to take part in any religious instructions that may be imparted in any educational institutions recognized by the State or receiving aid out of State funds or be required to attend any religious worship in such institutions or in any premises attached thereto, unless such person (or his guardian in the case of minors) gives his consent for such participation.

The above constitutional provisions make it clear that *the State has no religion and limits the validity of religion in the public arena and society*. While individuals in society may base their values on particular religious tenets, where such questions impinge on society as a whole, the basis of discussion and social consensus cannot be religion; much less one particular religion.

Despite the weaknesses in actual practice, elements of this understanding of secularism have been an essential part of the accepted political values of modern Indian society, leading, for instance, to the rejection of untouchability and *sati*, to the formal rejection of caste, and to the institution of affirmative action as a means of redressing socio-economic inequalities.

However, while the Constitution is based on secularism or *dharma nirapekshata,* our society is steeped in religion. Observance of religious festivals and rituals is part of our day-to-day life. Religious feelings govern our mode of thinking. Thus there is a clear contradiction between the basic tenets of the Constitution and the character of our society. For secularism to survive, it is not enough if the state declares itself to be secular, but the society should also be secular. If not, the society's religiousness gets reflected in politics and public administration, which often work in a manner contrary to what is envisaged in the Constitution.

Sangh Parivar and Secularism

Late M.S. Golwalkar, the former RSS *Sarsanghchalak*, is quoted as having written in his book "*We or Our Nationhood Defined*":

> "In Hindustan, Religion is an all absorbing entity. . . . it has become eternally woven into the life of the Race, and forms, as it were, its soul. With us, every action in life, individual, social or political, is a command of religion. Naturally, therefore, we are what our great religion has made us . . . . all those not belonging to the national, that is Hindu race, Religion, Culture, and language, naturally fall out of the pale of real 'National' life".

However, it is denied that the book was Golwalkar's original work but an English translation of a Marathi book *Rashtra Mimansa* (Discourse on Nation) by G.D. Savarkar and that Golwalkar later distanced himself from this radical work. Balbir Punj, BJP, MP contends that Golwalkar had actually said: "Indeed, our concept of 'state' has always been 'secular' and emphasising the secular nature of the state by the adjective 'secular' is redundant in our country."[23] Secularism is a "positive approach," he says, in that "the king became the symbol of support and protection to all faiths and creeds and never negation of religion. The "king" in our case represents the "state" or its sovereign function. Golwalkar emphasises that "the wide and all comprehensive view of life ingrained in the Hindu ruler made him to respect and even encourage every single religious thought . . . . to grow according to its own genius".[24]

"Secularists" contend that Indian secularism has suffered damage following the rise of Hindu Nationalism. The Hindu nationalists who remained dormant for a long time surfaced with Janata Party coming to power in a coalition following the 1977 post-emergency elections. Long-term RSS members and founders of *Jan Sangh* like L.K. Advani and A.B. Vajpayee were partners in the coalition. Having come to power for the first time since independence, the Hindu nationalists were convinced that a Hindu nationalist party could become a viable political force in India. The coalition was, however, short-lived. Coming under criticism for their association with the RSS and Hindu Communal interests, prominent members of the Jan Sangh and those formerly associated with the RSS formed a new party, the Bharatiya Janata Party in 1980.

Vajpayee stated that the BJP's ideology was based on Gandhian Socialism, and presented the Party as a modernizing and scientifically-oriented political party. The BJP adopted what it called *positive secularism*, an ambiguous concept ultimately based on the *Hindutva* view that Hinduism was not a religion and could not be other than secular. However, in 1993 Vajpayee said that *dharma nirapekshata,* the indifference of state to religion, was neither secularism nor a reflection of the dominant (*Hindutva*) ethos of India. Hence, positive secularism could seemingly incorporate both the existing conception of *sarva dharma sambhava* (the view that the orientation of the state should conceive of all India's religions as equal) and the view that treating minority religions differently through what were conceived as 'special privileges' or 'concessions' would advantage them in comparison with Hindus."[25]

Dedicated to transforming India on the ideals of *Hindutva*, the BJP and the Sangh Parivar could mobilize support for its activities by presenting itself as a disciplined party, in which members were subject to the aims and values of *Hindutva*. This position became increasingly stronger, as Congress continued to fragment because of its inability to define what it stood for. The BJP exploited the Hindu sentiments by creating a master narrative of Indian history in which the idea of an Indian Nation was equated with that of a Hindu Nation, and in which Muslims, in particular, were presented as the "other." The BJP provided a clear, unproblematic, and distinctive cultural identity especially to the trading community and middle classes, who believed that the Nehruvian secular model had failed. Controlled by the upper castes, the BJP, through its comprehensive ties with the RSS and VHP, skilfully mobilized mass support among certain castes and tribes by utilizing communication and information networks, through which it could construct a new form of Hindu identity.[26]

One of the arguments in the political discourse in India is that India is secular because Hinduism is tolerant and non-violent; that such tolerance nurtured a diversity of faiths, religions, and cultures in India. Hindu nationalists claim that secularism, understood as equal respect for all religions, is a natural corollary of the Hindu tradition of tolerance. Hence, they reiterate that their struggle is to uphold "positive" secularism—meaning equal treatment of all and appeasement of none; and not for establishing a theocratic Hindu state. Such "liberal" statements masks the main political agenda that derives its strength from Hinduism. In plain terms, the message that is sought to be concretized is that India can afford to be secular only because of Hinduism. If a sophisticated version of this argument emphasizes the "long history of tolerance and eclecticism" in Hinduism, a less sophisticated one points out at the "innate intolerance of Semitic religions like Islam and Christianity". They cite the treatment meted out to Salman Rushdie and Taslima Nasreen by Islamic clerics in support of their argument.

Islam and Secularism

Does Islam believe in secularism? The answer from one quarter is a categorical "no" which asserts that "secularism contradicts Islam in every aspect. They are two different paths that never meet; choosing one means rejecting the other. Hence, whoever chooses Islam has to reject secularism".[27] The proponents of this philosophy affirm that secularism makes lawful what Allah has made unlawful and that the Rule of Allah (Shariah) is compulsory and cannot be changed. They also argue that "secularism is based on separating religion from all the affairs of this life and hence, it rules by law and regulations other than Allah's laws. Hence, secularism rejects Allah's rules with no exception and prefers regulations other than Allah's and His Messenger's. In fact, many secularists claim that Allah's laws might have been suitable for the time they were revealed but are now outdated. As a result, most of the laws governing the daily affairs of life in the countries ruled by secular systems contradict Islam".[28] The Islamic antagonists of secularism also criticise the secularists' view that there should be "no religion in politics and no politics in religion". Such sayings portray the view of Islam as a religion is to be practiced in the mosque only, and that it should not be allowed to rule life outside the mosque. They also hold that democratic slogans like "personal freedom" and "people governing people" mean that people come first and no place is made for the ruling of Allah. "This is why secularism is clear *Kufr*, this is why secular systems have no legality and authority and should be rejected by Muslims".[29]

If the above are the views are one end of the spectrum, "there is an important body of evidence showing that Islam also believes in a total divorce between faith and reason. For example, according to French Islamist Roger Arnaldez, the eleventh century Muslim philosopher Ibn Hazn thought "that God is not bound even by his own word, and that nothing would oblige him to reveal the truth to us".[30] Abu Hamid al-Ghazali (eleventh century) considered as the most important Muslim authority after Mohammed, argued (*The Incoherence of the Philosophers)* that God is not bound by reason, thus denying the very possibility of scientific investigation. Al-Ghazali also thought that reason was darkened by passions and, hence, could not be trusted. Thus, morality could be known solely through Revelation. "No obligations flow from reason but from the Shariah".

Asghar Ali Engineer disagrees that Islam is not compatible with secularism and writes:

> "Both non-Muslims and orthodox Muslims feel that Islam is not compatible with secularism. Fundamentalist Muslims totally reject secularism as anti-Islamic and *haram*. Maulana Maududi, founder of *Jamaat-e-Islami-e-Hind* had said while leaving for Pakistan in 1948, that those who participated in secular politics were raising flag of revolt against Allah and his Messenger. The Saudi Ulema too denounce secularism as strictly prohibited in Islamic tradition. The fundamental Hindus, on the other hand, say that Muslims support secularism while in minority in any nation and oppose it while in majority. But this is not wholly true. Some Muslim countries like Saudi Arabia and others do reject secularism but all Muslim majority countries do not".[31]

By and large, many Muslim majority countries opt for Islamic state or at least make Islam as state religion. In an *Islamic State* all laws must strictly conform to the Shariah but if a country declares "*Islam as its religion*", it means that *Islam is preferred* to all other religions and it enjoys a privileged position than other religions in the country. Islam is declared to be incompatible with secularism because in a secular state there is no place for divine laws, and secular laws are unacceptable to Islam. Also it is believed that in Islam religion and politics cannot be separated. On these grounds secularism is totally rejected by orthodox Muslims. They also think that secularism is atheistic, and atheism has no place whatsoever in Islam. Asghar Ali Engineer also argues that the notion that religion and politics cannot be separated is more historical than *theological*. Indonesia, for instance, does not reject secularism though its 85 per cent population comprises of Muslims. Even Rafiq Zakaria attributes the anti-secular tendency in the Muslim community "to the fear that secularism is anti-God and pro-man and encourages materialism at the cost of spiritualism".[32]

The Muslim notion that embracing secularism or agreeing with the philosophy of secularism will make them anti-Islamic, makes Muslims, at least a section of them, shun un-Islamic ideas, secular education, even employment in secular companies having links with the west and if in the process they remain uneducated (in the contemporary sense), unemployed and poor, so be it. It is for this reason that the conservative Muslims do not want the government to impose any restrictions on the marriage of Muslim girls, do not want registration of marriages, oppose modernisation of *Madrasa* education, reject the jurisdiction of secular courts and demand the establishment of Shariah courts, and generally keep the flock together through periodical *fatwas*. Such denial of opportunities for improvement of their economic status and modernisation is, perhaps, born out of the suspicion in the Indian Muslim mind that the right-wing Hindu forces (the *Sangh Parivar*, mainly) are out to assimilate them in the Hindu society.

Secularism in Contemporary India

In spite of the fact that Secularism is one of the essential elements in the basic structure of our Constitution, Indian society is steeped in religion. Observance of religious festivals and rituals is part of our day-to-day life. Religious feelings govern our mode of thinking, which gets reflected in our politics and public administration. Breach of constitutional provisions by politicians and government functionaries is a regular phenomenon and is reflected in their participation in functions where religious rituals are observed or asking for votes in the name of religion. All political parties use religion to come to power, right from the stage of selection of the candidates, keeping in view the communal character of the constituencies. While professing secularism, vote banks are systematically built on the basis of religion and caste. Muslim elite are entertained through *Iftar* parties by political leaders, including those from the BJP, during Ramzan. If such *Iftar* parties have come to be considered as sacrilege by a section of the Muslim community, non-Muslims ask why not Diwali parties and Christmas parties?

Mixing religion with politics and public administration results in *sants* and *mahants, imams* and priests acquiring importance in public life, enabling them to play an active role in decision making. In spite of there being no constitutional provision for religion-based reservations, the Andhra Pradesh Government passed an order reserving seats for Muslims in education and employment, which was struck down by the High Court. The high point of "appeasement" as BJP describes it was Rajiv Gandhi Government's enactment of the Muslim Women Marriage and Divorce Act to placate the Muslim community which was agitated by the Court verdict in Shah Bano case. The "secular" government tried to protect the Muslim Personal Law from being interfered with by the secular courts, even if it meant sacrificing the Muslim women. The BJP accuses Congress party of promoting "votebank politics" by giving the minorities "illegitimate concessions" and alleges that such practices perpetuates servile, patron-client relations, creates a minority complex and thereby encourages fundamentalist and intolerant tendencies among Muslims.

Compared to the politicians of the past, we have today politicians of all hues who do not hesitate to foment communal violence if it serves their purpose. The communal riots in Gujarat, Haryana, Orissa, Maharashtra and some other States in the recent years, with the blessing, if not direct involvement, of political parties and/or political leaders, have tarnished the image of Indian secularism and the reputation of Hinduism as a tolerant faith.

There is a wide perception that the concept of secularism, borrowed from the West is flawed and irrelevant in Indian conditions, since it is not rooted in Indian social, cultural or political experience and hence needs to be re-conceptualised. When we talk about secularism, we take into account the relationship between state and religion. The focus, therefore, is on the secularisation of polity and the society.

A secular state in India as conceived by the Constitution was not an exclusively political-intellectual construct, but it reflected the social and cultural reality of Indian society. The choice of secularism as one of the guiding principles of Indian nation, despite the communal conflagration during the Partition, is influenced by the historical experience of Indian society. As Panikkar observes, "both Mahatma Gandhi and Jawaharlal Nehru were alive to the social reality. That is the reason why they attached great importance to communal harmony, if secularism was to survive in India".[33] Panikkar blames the *Sangh Parivar*, which, he says, "is now trying to set aside the social relations and political structure which history has bequeathed to the nation. Their success is not because a void existed in socio-political consciousness, but because they created a new one by obfuscating religious identity as national identity and by organising politics around emotionally charged religious issues".[34]

But, the recent instances of violence against Muslims and Christians do not subscribe to this belief. On the other hand, it should also be noted that a sense of superiority and intolerance is equally exhibited by the Muslims, who wish to be treated different, who wish to have their own Shariah courts and refuse to be adjudicated by secular courts. It seems that for secularism to survive there must be a common principle of tolerance, which has enabled the different traditions to live together for centuries. This call for a condition where politics are wholly secular, i.e., non-religious by nature.

Politics means solving people's problems through a government. If a government functions properly, people can have their problems of food, comfort or security solved easily. A government would discharge its duties well if it remains secular. But the interference of religious belief and spiritual considerations with the functions of a government foils the purpose. However, today's politicians need the thrust of religious sentiment to fool people, and use it as a weapon to silence ignorant people. Power-hungry politicians use the vote of the ignorant masses, and try to garner such votes by any means. The demand of certain political parties that a separate reservation should be craved out for Muslim women in the Women's Reservation Bill is a case in point. Special preferences in the name of religion do not exist as per the Constitution.

Similarly, every time a demand is made that the system of personal laws based on religious injunctions should be done away with and India should adopt a Uniform Civil Code, it is alleged that it is an assault on the identity of minority communities. Those opposed to a Uniform Civil Code seem to say that the state should not interfere with personal laws even if they are retrograde and discriminate on grounds of gender. A reform of the Muslim personal law is demanded even by a majority of the Muslim women, who are the main sufferers. But, the Personal law remains unaltered and the *Ulema* are not prepared to give up their hold. Similarly, conservative Muslims assert that the Secular courts do not have the authority to either interpret or apply Shariah, holding that such right belongs to 'Shariah courts' alone. The All-India Muslim Personal Law Board has been encouraging Muslims to take their differences to 'Shariah courts.' Although the Union Law Minister assures that such courts will have no legal validity, no effort has been made by the government to stop the movement.

As long as their religious identity is not affected, Muslim community has to agree to be governed by the secular Constitution of India. Similarly, the Hindu zealots must realise that it is not the sign of wisdom to open the wounds of the past and take revenge for what are perceived as historical injustices.

By the time India achieved Independence, the necessary pre-conditions for a secular society and polity had already evolved through a process of secularisation in the social, cultural, administrative and intellectual domains. The common participation of people, regardless of their denominational differences, marked the engagements in all these fields. The state institutions, from the medieval times itself, had officials, generals and soldiers drawn from all religions and care was taken to ensure that the officials conducted themselves in discharging public duties with a non-religious outlook. "Even the movements in the intellectual-cultural field also prepared the ground for the emergence of secular ethos in the society. The *bhakti* and *sufi* traditions enabled Hindus and Muslims to understand one another's religious and philosophical systems and thus to bridge their social differences".[35]

Secularism is not just a word; it is *an idea*. As an idea it refers to a number of norms and values regarding the way a plural Society and its state should be organised. The basic idea is that the state and its laws ought not to mingle with the realm of religion. The state should be secular, that is, its laws cannot be based in one or another religion. Secularism, for India, is not simply a point of view, it is a question of survival; a safeguard of peace, order and sanity in the society. Hindus, Muslims, Christians and several other groups were quite successful at living together in relative peace for a long period of time in India. This plural society did not fall apart. Yet, it had never even heard of "secularism" or "toleration." Therefore, the task ahead is to examine the ways of living together as they have emerged in various regions of India.

Internal pluralism exists even within Hindu traditions. Although there were clashes among these traditions, these never developed into the systematic persecution of some particular tradition or the other; rather each of these traditions absorbed or adopted elements from the other traditions. Similarly, interaction among Hindu, Muslim and Christian religions reveals similar pattern. Although there were violent clashes, Muslims and Christians were not persecuted because of their religious beliefs or their form of worship. On the contrary, even today Hindus join Muslims in showing reverence at the *dargahs* of the Sufi *pirs*, or in the celebration of *Muharram*. Hindus join Christians in the celebration of Christmas. Indian Muslims and Christians too participate in Hindu festivals and even revere some of the Hindu gods.

What is needed is a common framework—a shared set of values—which allow the diverse groups to live together. For this one would have to identify this constitutive set of values shared by the different communities. It cannot be denied that Hindu tolerance, and the belief in the *equality of all religions* has allowed all kinds of religious traditions to co-exist peacefully in the past. But, the problem arises when such belief is not shared and accepted by other religions. Nevertheless, in the past centuries, Hindu, Muslim and Christian communities were part of the relatively peaceful and harmonious co-existence of Indian society. Political analysts attribute the *Sangh Parivar's* demand for *Hindu Rashtra* to a sense of insecurity and the feeling that even though Hindus are in majority, a policy of appeasement was being followed towards the minorities, especially the Muslim minority. The *Sangh Parivar* and others also feel that the Christians are resorting to forced conversions of Hindus, which had prompted Vajpayee to call for a national debate on religious conversions. In October 2002, the AIADMK Government in Tamil Nadu enacted the Tamil Nadu Prohibition of Forcible Conversion of Religion Ordinance 2002, making religious conversions a serious offence.

If India should remain secular and peace should prevail, we should not see India as a land of Hindus alone, just because Hindus form 85 per cent of the population. It is unreasonable to expect the minorities to lose their religious identities and consider themselves as Hindus or *hinduise* their way of life. It is the responsibility of an elected government to do "justice for all." However, if there are minorities who differ from the mainstream in terms of religion and culture it becomes the responsibility of the government to protect their reasonable interests and aspirations within the limitations and provisions of the Constitution. We have a clear example in Sri Lanka where the majority Sinhalese promulgated a new Constitution giving pride of place to Buddhism, made Sinhalese the only official language and denied Tamils, the largest minority, their minimum aspirations as citizens of the country. However, there is no need for "appeasement' of the minorities but unfortunately, vote bank politics has been making the governments, especially the non-BJP ones, to cross the thin line between concessions and appeasement.

To prevent further damage to its secular credentials, the nation must withdraw its steps from the path it has been led to under the influence of misguided elements. What is needed is a deep national introspection and a sense of balance and direction. It is the responsibility of those who are at the helm of affairs in government and in political and social life to provide these. It is true that the state cannot be held responsible for irresponsible statements by political or religious organisations that would upset the delicate secular equilibrium in the country. The statement made by the RSS in Bangalore sometime back that the security of the minority community depends on the goodwill of the majority is a case in point. The statement was ominous. Security being the fundamental right of every citizen, it is the responsibility of the State to protect its citizens and no section of the population need depend upon the goodwill of any other section's goodwill.

During the early days of independent India, Donald Smith, American political analyst, had observed :

> "It is far too early to dismiss the possibility of a future Hindu state in India. However, the possibility does not appear a strong one. The secular state has far more than an even chance of survival in India."

If the conservatives in all the religious communities are reigned in and people realize that their welfare and prosperity depends on the success of secularism in India, Donald Smith's prophecy will hold good for generations to come.

NOTES

1. Quoted by Justice Jahagirdar, in his article *Secularism in India: The Inconclusive Debate*, International Humanist and Ethical Union, Available at http://www.iheu.org/node/298)

2. Constituent Assembly of India, Vol. VII, (Available at http://parliamentofindia.nic.in/ls/debates/vol7p20a.htm)
3. Lavkare, Arvind, quoting Dr Subhash Kashyap, in *The Counterfeits and Their Contentious Issues*, May 11, 1999. (Available at http://www.rediff.com/news/1999/may/11arvind.htm)
4. Advani L.K., (Available at http://www.rediff.com/news/1998/may/27cons.htm)
5. Rao, Badrinath. The variant meanings of secularism in India: notes toward conceptual clarifications, *Journal of Church and State*, winter, 2006. Badrinath Rao is an Assistant Professor of Sociology and Asian Studies, Department of Social Science, Kettering University, Flint, Michigan, USA) (Available at http://findarticles.com/p/articles/mi_hb3244/is_1_48/ai_n29260505/pg_1)
6. Available at http://www.legalserviceindia.com/article/l40-42nd-Constitutional-Amendment.html.
7. A view that religion and religious considerations should be ignored or excluded from social and political matters; and An ethical system asserting that moral judgments should be made without reference to religious doctrine, as reward or punishment in an afterlife.
8. In the said case, Justice Sawant said: "These provisions (in the Constitution) by implication prohibit establishment of a Theocratic State and prevent the State either identifying itself with or favouring any particular religion or religious sect or denomination. The State is enjoined to accord equal treatment to all religions and religious sects and denominations". (Quoted by Justice Jahagirdar, *Secularism in India: The Inconclusive Debate*, International Humanist and Ethical Union (Available at http://www.iheu.org/node/298). Available at http://www.merriam-webster.com/dictionary/secularism.
9. *Free Dictionary* (Available at http://www.thefreedictionary.com/secularism)
10. Austin Cline, *Defining Secularism: George Jacob Holyoake Coined the Term Secularism, Origins of Secularism as a Non-Religious, Humanistic, Atheistic Philosophy*. (Available at http://atheism.about.com/od/secularismseparation/a/HolyoakeSecular.htm)
11. n. 1.
12. Austin Cline, *op cit.*
13. *Ibid.*
14. Donald Eugene Smith, *India as a Secular State*, Princeton, New Jersey (1963).
15. Jayaraman, T. 'Secularism Defined' in *Frontline,* March 17, 1997 (Available at http://www.imsc.res.in/~jayaram/Articles/lfrontline/node1.html)
16. *Constituent Assembly of India* (Vol. VII) Debates, 6th December, 1949. (Available at http://parliamentofindia.nic.in/ls/debates/vol7p20a.htm)

17. *Harijan*, August 31, 1947, as reproduced in *Collected Works of Mahatma Gandhi*, Vol. 89. Quoted by La. Su. Rengarajan in Letters to the Editor, in *The Hindu*, June 15, 2005.
18. Koshy, Professor Ninan, *Minorities and Higher Education, Rights, Access and Social Justice,* in National Seminar Papers, The Kerala State Higher Education Council (Available at http://kshec.kerala.gov.in/seminar/nkoshy.htm.)
19. Swamy, Subramanian, Redefining Secularism, in *The Hindu*, March 18, 2004. Nehru's belief in secularism was so strong that he even chided K.M. Munshi for heading the Committee for reconstructing the Somnath temple in Gujarat after independence. The project was financed by public subscription and not by government funds. Jawaharlal Nehru is reported to have told Munshi: "I don't like your trying to restore the Somnath. It is Hindu revivalism." (Quoted in Jahagirdar, *op cit.*)
20. Dixit, J.N., 'The Ultimate Idealist: Jawaharlal Nehru' in *100 People Who Shaped India*, (Available at http://www.india-today.com/itoday/millennium/100people/nehru.html)
21. *Ibid.*
22. Justice Jahagirdar quotes the statement of Pandit Laxmi Kanth Maitra, (Member, Constituent Assembly, West Bengal) on 6th December, 1948: "By (a) secular State, as I understand it, is meant that the State is not going to make any discrimination whatsoever on the ground of religion or community against any person professing any particular form of religious faith. *This means in essence that no particular religion in the State will receive any State patronage whatsoever.* The State is not going to establish, patronise or endow any particular religion to the exclusion of or in preference to others and that no citizen in the State will have any preferential treatment or will be discriminated against simply on the ground that he professed a particular form of religion. In other words in the affairs of the State the professing of any particular religion will not be taken into consideration at all". (*Constituent Assembly of India*, Vol. VII, 6th December, 1948 (Available at http://parliamentofindia.nic.in/ls/debates/vol7p20a.htm)
23. Punj, Balbir. K., 'Bunch of Secular Thoughts' in *the Indian Express*, December 9, 2002. (Available at http://www.geocities.com/bharatvarsha1947/January_2003/advanihindurashtra.htm)
24. *Ibid.*
25. Bhatt, Chetan. *Hindu Nationalism: Origins, Ideologies and Modern Myths,* Berg Publishers, Oxford (2001), Pp. 168-169.
26. Mazzoleni, Gianpietro., Julianne Stewart, Bruce Horsfield (Eds.), *The Media and Neo-populism: A Contemporary Comparative Analysis,* Praeger, Westport, Connecticut, London (2003), p. 97.

27. Islam *VS.* Secularism, in *Al Jumuah*, Thc Friday Report, Vol. III, No. 10, (Available at http://www.islaam.com/Article.aspx?id=116)
28. *Ibid.*
29. *Ibid.*
30. Richard Bastien, *Are Secularism and Islam Cousins?* 26th March, 2008. Bastien is a freelance journalist based in Ottawa, Canada. Available at http://www.mercatornet.com/articles/view/are_secularism_and_islam_cousins/)
31. Engineer, Asghar Ali, *Islam and Secularism (*Available at http://www.ourkarnataka.com/religion/islam/islam9.htm)
32. Zakaria, Rafiq. *Indian Muslims: Where have they gone wrong?* Bombay (2004), Popular Prakasan and Bharatiya Vidya Bhavan, p. 250.
33. Pankkar, K.N., *The Ideas of Sovereignty and State in Indian Political Thought*, Bombay (1963), Bharatiya Vidya Bhavan.
34. *Ibid.*
35. *Ibid.*

13

Caste and Gender in a Secular, Democratic Society : A Position Note

Kalapana Satish

History of India is very amply gives evidence for the constant ideological struggle between the motives of building a secular, democratic society through the Constitution and the motive of ruling elite to keep the unequal, undemocratic power structure in tack. Dominant political structures and institutions have defeated the very intent of our Constitution, which is guaranteeing equality, democracy, secularism and plurality for the vast majority of historically marginalized. Those dominant social strata of the country have all access to resources, power and unlimited authority, while the marginalized sections of the society like the *dalits*, Scheduled Tribes, Backward Classes, cultural, linguistic, sexual minorities and women are subjected to the extreme forms of discrimination and deprivation and are excluded from the process of this so-called 'development'.

Further, the historical evolution of Indian Communities has been so overtly placed Hindu-Muslims. The vertical divide created determining the religions in this country as Hindu-Muslim—Christianity as major religions, while the actual religious life of the communities is multicultural in nature. This vertical religious division and its rule through personal laws have been allowed through the interpretation of Constitution till today. Hence, this has become basic foundational realm of nationalism. To succumb the marginalized towards the age old structures of exploitation, discrimination and exclusion, the Hindu religious discourse also goes to the extent of claiming that *Varnashrama* in itself as multiculturalism.

As Romila Thapar in her book *History of Early India — From the Origins to AD 1300* states that "Hindu and Sanskritic elements were highlighted as the contribution of India to world history and the presence of other religious and linguistic cultures were barely recognized in terms of constructing Indian civilization".

> "The source of information about Indian Culture for the British, who codified the basics of Indian legal and administrative system, was largely Brahmins, who maintained that ancient tradition was preserved in Sanskrit works about which they alone were knowledgeable. Many of these works were texts on religion or manuals or ritual, which coloured the interpretation of early Indian Culture."

Brahmanical notion of Indian culture is obviously caste based patriarchy, hierarchial in terms of ownership, family relations, customs and traditions. Though the Caste System is regional specific, its hierarchial and patriarchal form has taken root in all over through the evolution of Indian Society with the active collaboration of colonialism and Brahmanism. The mainstream political and historical process of market based development has made this unequal system of Indian life much more concrete and firm. While the institutions of modernity like education, media, and political institutions develop, the tradition of hierarchial and caste based patriarchy also further getting strengthened. The discussions and deliberations held around the 33 per cent reservation for women in the legislative bodies is an ideal example to such situation.

Another example of personal laws in which women not being natural guardians, talaq, polygamy, absence of coparcenary rights for women under Hindu undivided family, etc., should all have been declared as void by now as they all discriminate against women. But, till today those discriminatory laws continue to exist and according to the judicial interpretations it has been practiced for or against the rights of women.

Secularism in Indian Sense !

Secularism ideally demands separation of religion from state. No Public sphere shall be allowed to run or influenced by any religious group. Here in India, the mainstream political discourse perceived that the definition of secularism by the state is "as all religions have respect and majority religion will have 'majority' respect and power".

And it is celebrated as 'this is our form of secularism'. Further, this cultural homogenization through religion further enforces and reinforces the caste system and caste based patriarchy through the institutions of state. Even, the so called minority religion and its institutions continue to follow the hierarchial power structures divided between upper *vs* lower, men *vs* women. While the state maintain distance itself from the unequal social and economic life situation of its citizens in the name of secularism, the governing principle of equality and democracy has no meaning to the marginalized, who are historically deprived and continued to be deprived.

The rule of law in the country celebrated as a foundation for enforcing secularism. But the rule of public domain is under the control of religious divides. Minority *vs* Majority always kept as in-between line for any discourse. The political equality of one person, one vote has no meaning in the majority, minority number game of electoral politics under the rule of law, while the social, economic situation is under the control of powerful caste based minority. Here the actual majority, which is comprised of women, *dalits*, *adivasis*, cultural, linquistic minorities, OBCs are struggling to get Reservation, which is actually meant to include minority groups.

Interface by Caste Based Patriarchy with the Notion of Secularism

Caste system basically plays both in economic and cultural spheres of Indian society. While in economic sphere the lower caste is exploited by the landholders from the upper castes, but in cultural terms each caste group would both experience discrimination from, and practice discrimination against, other caste groups depending upon where they are placed in the hierarchy of the caste system. In both the operations the women are subservient and made to produce and reproduce the same old cultural values and maintenance of power over by men. The dominant castes enjoy social power along with control over land, including patriarchal power over women and define the culture of exploitation and have linkages with the state. World over, the religion is used as an effective tool for taking control over the state. In India too, though the multicultural nature of the different social, regional groups exist along with the constitutional values of secularism, equality and democracy, the predominant force which has control over the resources are the caste based ones. In simple term, Nation means pooling of resources together and redistribute according to principles. This caste based patriarchal forces, which have control over these resources represent the state to interpret religion to their convenience to rule the masses.

Hereby Caste as a Religious entity is negotiated with Secularism and Pluralism.

What we practice is a descriptive notion of secularism and not the prescriptive notion of secularism. But ideally, secularism means that separation of particularistic cultures and religions from the public domain or public functions of state operation.

In any cultural context, the spectrum of secular domains would operate as under :

- Personal domain,
- Inter-personal domain,
- Social domain,
- Public domain, and
- Political domain.

These domains operate independently and in its own unique form like the personal domain it can operate with utmost strong beliefs of liberty and independence.

Likewise the intra-personal domain will be restricted substantially to respect the liberty of the other person—be it a child, friend, family member, colleague or member of the same institution or anyone to be engaged apart from the personal-individual domain.

Similarly, the social domain will be destined with additional restrictions for the individual or inter-personal domain to demand or control. The social domain demands the collective community liberty and equality from every member related, whereas the public and the political domain imposes absolute restrictions to individuals to consider it as their extended personal domain. Hence, the public and political domain will have to ensure absolute equality, liberty to all irrespective of their socio-cultural, economic religious backgrounds. Secularism is having a linkage with rationalism. What is common among all the people should be the basis for organizing political and public life.

But in case of women, particularly those from marginalized sections, both their private and public domain is considered as extension of private domain of the upper caste men (there are ample case stories exist on the atrocities and oppression practiced by caste

Hindus in the rural parts of the country). For the women who are in the upper caste groups, family becomes their individual domain and their public domain is restricted through tradition, custom and in legal arena it is the personal laws respective to their religion. Hence, level of oppression varies based on the caste in which the women belong to.

Secularism in India was more a Political than Philosophical Phenomenon[3]

Secularism in India meant equal respect for all religions and cultures and non-interference of religion in the Public Domain-State affairs. Also, according to the Constitution of India, no discrimination will be made on the basis of caste, creed, gender and class. Similarly, all citizens of India irrespective of ones religion, caste or gender have right to vote. According to Articles 14 to 21 all will enjoy same rights without any discrimination on any ground.

According to Article 25 all those who reside in India are free to confess, practice and propagate religion of one's choice subject of course to social health and law and order. Thus, even conversion to any religion of one's choice is a fundamental right. But the BJP (Bhartiya Janta Party) and RSS are opposed to all this. According to them there should be Hindu Rashtra (Hindu Nation) in India and Muslims and Sikhs should be secondary citizens without any political right.

The medieval society in India was thus more religiously tolerant as it was not politically competitive. The modern Indian society on the other hand has proved to be more divisive as the Religious Identity has a strong linkage with Political identity. This competition becomes more acute while development becoming more uneven and unjust.

Thus, in case of India one can say by and large that it is secular in as much as it is religiously plural and tolerant but there are politically divisive forces quite active and create communal pressure and widen the gap between religious community thus bringing Indian secularism under great threat.

Politics of Exclusion

The three features—patriarchy, hierarchy and externalization,—are the ones which render Indian society oppressive. Patriarchy, which more basic and foundation to the formation of the society. In this all women, irrespective of their class, caste positions are made as subordinates to men. There are different cultural justifications given for the existence of patriarchy based on the values and practices of different religion and caste groups, but subordination and secondary citizenship of women as the universal principle followed in all religious societies, whether it accepts secularism or pluralism.

The second element, which contributes to totalitarianism of Indian society, is hierarchy, the product of caste system, which is unique to India, leading to the abominable practice of untouchability. The 'ex-untouchables' of India now constitute 18 per cent, which is 180 million, of the Indian population. Caste system not only institutionalized inequality but also sanctified it through the Hindu doctrines of creation, of *varnashrama dharma*, of *karma* and rebirth and the like. Although some would argue that there is no organic relationship between Hinduism and the caste system, in reality they are inextricably intertwined. All available evidence suggests that caste system is antithetical to the ethos of democracy.

The third element, Externalization is the process through which fellow citizens are defined and treated as cultural outsiders. There are two types of externalizations in India which block the flowering of democracy. One is the product of turbulence created by migration from one cultural region to another within the country, articulated through nativism. This undermines the principle of single citizenship mandated in the Constitution. The other variety of externalization is qualitatively different in that a set of co-citizens are perceived and defined as outsiders to the entire society, which becomes the bases of discrimination and exclusion. Thus, in India, followers of some religious faiths, notably Muslims and Christians, who together account for 16 per cent of India's population, that is 160 million, are viewed as cultural outsiders by some elements in civil society. This erodes deeply the democratic ethos of Indian polity as it alienates a substantial segment of Indian population from Indian society and polity.

The above all three totalitarian elements of Indian society conjointly erode individual freedom, a prerequisite for authentic democracy. When groups and communities are perceived as cultural outsiders they tend to insulate themselves socially in spite of internal differentiation among them. Similarly, when a group is eternally condemned to be inferiors, they remain in a psychological cage of their own and can rarely participate as equals in economy, polity and society.

The above all three categories, women, religious minorities and *dalit-untouchables*, the victims of patriarchy, externalization and hierarchy respectively, account for more than two-third of Indian citizens. Without their fully-fledged participation in all walks of life, one cannot think of a flourishing democracy in India. The task of democratization of Indian society is incomplete, that caste and gender discrimination continue to cause grave harm, and *adivasis* and *dalits* still face all manner of trials and tribulations, India's social evils cannot be analyzed or eliminated in isolation of other necessary changes. As Prof. Aloysius says in his book on *Nationalism without a Nation in India*, "The mixture of religion and philosophy, history and tradition, custom and social structure which in its wide fold included almost ever aspect of the life of Indian and which might be called *Brahminism* or Hinduism became the symbol of nationalism".[2]

All through human history, propertyless castes/classes have suffered social discrimination of one kind or another while private property is largely uphold by the dominant caste/class groups. Economic disparities remain a serious contributor to social inequities today. Any social system that is based on unequal access to economic assets (whether they are land, raw materials, industrial or commercial resources) will inevitably lead to severe form of social discrimination and inequity. Victims of older forms of discrimination will either continue to be victimized, or simply become victims of new forms of discrimination.

While the economic inequality is sanctified through the passion of private property in modern independent India, with the active legal back up provided by the British, the foundation rules of the ideological game plan are already set with regard to the mainstream notion of culture, tradition and modernity. It is pertinent to understand the underlying social ideology even to understand the basic forms and politics of Social Exclusion. The Indian medievalism or the caste based tradition is being projected as modernity without any change in the content. The projects of Capitalism, Secularism and Democracy are comfortably reincarnated with the same old ideology—caste based culture—reinterpreted to serve the same purpose of arresting modernity of its original sense.

Conclusion

Today, we need a more holistic conceptual discourse—praxis that can emerge as a potential alternative ideology and to consolidate that emanating from the grassroots experiences/struggles of the oppressed communities to confront and subvert the present brahmanical ideologies that are all pervading and influencing the Indian mindset. What needs to be placed here is that 'Inclusive policy is not response/ solution to social exclusion'. Exclusion is a conscious, constant, political construct and there is an agency to enforce. The need is to identify the excluding practices and bans those through state policies. There needs to be a conscious debate and discourse initiated on the definition of secularism in Indian context and its actual practice in the real life situation of the masses.

REFERENCES

Chakravarthi, Uma, *Gendering Caste—Through a Feminist Lens.*

G. Aloysius, *Nationalism Without a Nation in India.*

Geetha, V., *Theorising Feminism—Patriarchy.*

Mihir Desai, *Combat Law*, Vol. 3, Issue 4 November-December 2004.

Position paper of NAFRE—*People's Movement* presented during *All India Consultation* on Social Exclusion, Religious Marginalization and Communal Fascism in India adopted on 13th to 15th October, 2008, Bangalore.

Bibliography

Ahmad Aijaz, Radicalism of the Right and Logics of Secularism in Praful Bidwai, Harbans Mukhia and Achin Vanaik (Eds.), *Religion, Religiosity and Communalism,* New Delhi: Manohar, 1996.

Ahmad, Aijaz, The Making of India, *Social Scientist,* Vol. 33, Nos. 11-12, Nov-Dec., 2005.

Ahmad, Imtiaz *et al.* (eds), *Pluralism and Equality – Values in Indian Society and Politics,* New Delhi: SAGE, 2000.

Aiyar, Mani Shankar, *Confessions of a Secular Fundamentalist*, Penguin, 2004.

Alsop, Ruth, and Nina Heinsohn, *Measuring Empowerment in Practice: Structuring Analysis and Framing Indicators,* Washington DC: World Bank , 2002.

Alsop, Ruth, Bertelsen, M. and Holland, J. *Empowerment in Practice from Analysis to Implementation,* Washington DC: World Bank, 2006.

Ambedkar, B.R. *Annihilation of Caste,* Bangalore: Dalit Sahitya Academy.

Ambedkar, B.R. *What Congress and Gandhi have done to the Untouchables*, Bombay: Thacker & Co., 1945.

An Anti-Secularist Manifesto, *Seminar,* 1985.

Anderson, W.K. and S.D. Damle, *The Brotherhood in Saffron. The Rashtriya Swayamsevak Sangh and Hindu Revivalism,* New Delhi: Vistaar Publications.

Anirudh Krishna, *Active Social Capital: Tracing the Roots of Development and Democracy*, New York: Columbia University Press, 2002.

Ansari, M.T. (ed). *Secularism, Islam and Modernity – Selected Essays of Alam Khundmiri,* New Delhi: SAGE, 2007.

Asad, Talal, Trying to Understand French Secularism, Henry de Vries and Laurence V. Sullivan (eds), *Political Theologies – Public Religions in a Post-Secular World,* Social Science Press and Orient Longman, 2007.

Atul Kohli, *Democracy and Discontent: India's Growing Crisis of Governability*, Cambridge: Cambridge University Press, 1990.

Bajpai, Rochana. The Conceptual Vocabularies of Secularism and Minority Rights in India, *Journal of Political Ideologies*, 2002.

Basu, Amrita and Atul Kohli "Introduction" in Amrita Basu and Atul Kohli (eds.) *Community Conflicts and the State in India*, New Delhi: Oxford University Press, 1998.

Basu, Kaushik and Sanjay Subramanyam (eds.). *Unravelling the Nation: Sectarian Conflict and India's Secular Identity*, Delhi: Penguin Books, 1996.

Bayly, Susan. *Caste, Society and Politics in India – From the Eighteenth Century to the Modern Age,* Cambridge, 1999.

Berger, Peter (ed.). *The Desecularization of the World: Resurgent Religion and World Politics*, Washington, DC: Ethics and Public Policy Centre, 1999.

Beteille, Andre. Secularism and Intellectuals, *EPW,* 1994.

Bhargava, Rajeev *India's Majority-Minority Syndrome;* Meera Nanda, in Himal, Vol. 23, March, 2010.

Bhargava, Rajeev. *The Promise of India's Secular Democracy,* OUP, 2010.

Bharucha, Rustom (ed.). *In the Name of the Secular: Contemporary Cultural Activism in India,* Delhi: OUP, 1998.

Bhatt, Chetan. *Hindu Nationalism: Origins, Ideologies and Modern Myths,* Oxford: Berg Publishers, 2001.

Bjorkman, J.W. (Ed.), *Fundamentalism, Revivalists and Violence in south Asia, Monohar, New Delhi, 1988.*

Brass, Paul R. Secularism out of its Place, in Veena Das *et al.* (eds.), *Tradition, Pluralism and Identity,* New Delhi: SAGE, 1999.

Buch, Nirmala. *From Oppression to Assertion: A Study of Panchayats and Women in Madhya Pradesh, Rajasthan and Uttar Pradesh (Mimeo)*, CWDS: New Delhi, 1999.

Casanova, Jose. 1994. *Public Religions in the Modern World.* Chicago:

Cf. Harvey Cox, Religion in the Socular City, New York, A Touchstone Book, 1984.

Cf. Harvey Cox, *Fire from Heaven: The Rise of Pentecostal Spirituality and the Reshaping of Religion in the Twenty-first Century,* Reading: Addison-Wesley Publishing Company, 1994.

Cf. Hent de Vries and Lawrence E. Sullivan (ed.), *Political Theologies – Public Religions in a Post-secular World,* Social Science Press and Orient Longman Pvt. Ltd., 2007.

Cf. Patrick G., "Knowledge as Negotiation – A Critique of the Subaltern Studies Project", in Felix Wilfred (ed.), *Knowledge-Ethics for Our Times,* (*Jeevadhara*, Vol. XXXIX, No. 229, January, 2009, pp. 60-73.

Chadwick, Owen. 1975. *The Secularization of the European Mind in the Nineteenth Century.* Cambridge: Cambridge University Press.

Chakrabarty, Bidyut (ed.). 1990. *Secularism and Indian Polity.* New Delhi: Segment Book Distributors.

Chandhoke, Neera, *Beyond Secularism: The Rights of Religious Minorities,* New Delhi: OUP. 1999.

Chathukulum, Jos, M.S.John, Empowerment of Women Panchayat members: Learning from Kerala (India) in *Asian Journal of Women Studies,* Vol. 6, No. 4.

Chatterjee, P. *Nationalist Thought and the Colonial World: A Derivative Discourse.* New Delhi: Oxford University Press.

Chatterjee, Partha. Secularism and Toleration, *EPW,* 1986.

Chatterji, P.C. *Secular Values for Secular India.* New Delhi: Lola Chatterji. 1984.

Closing the Debate on Secularism: A Personal Statement, in A. Dingwaney Needham and R. Sunder Rajan (ed.). *The Crisis of Secularism in India. Durham,* NC: Duke University Press. 1983.

Communal Challenge and Secular Response. Delhi: Shipra. 2003.

Connolly, William, *Why I Am Not a Secularist.* Minneapolis, MN: University of Minnesota Press. 1999.

Contrasting Legal Approaches in England and France, Volume 17, Number 1, Spring 1997.

Cox, Harvey, *Religion in the Secular City – Toward a Postmodern Theology,* New York: A Touchstone Book, 1984.

Crimmins, J. (ed.). *Religion, Secularization and Political Thought: Thomas Hobbes to J.S. Mill,* London: Routledge, 1989.

Dahlerup, Drude. From A Small to Large Minority: Women in Scandinavian Politics, *Scandinavian Political Studies, 1998.*

Dahlerup, Drude. Using quotas to increase Women's Political Representation in Karam, Azza (ed.), *Women in Parliament: Beyond Numbers, Stockholm,* The International Institute for Democracy and Electoral Assistance. 1998.

Dalits in Modern India: Vision and Values. New Delhi: Vistaar Publications.

Damle, Y.B. and Jacob Aikara, *Caste, Religion and Politics in India.* New Delhi: Oxford & IBH Publishing Co.

Das, Bhagwan and James Massey, *Dalit Solidarity*, Delhi: The Indian Society for Promoting Christian Knowldege (ISPCK).

Dayananda, Swami, *The Light of Truth,* Allahabad (Translated and introduced by Ganga Prasad Upadhyaya).

Deshpande, V.G. *Why Hindu Rashtra?* New Delhi: All India Hindu Mahasabha.

Devanandan, P.D., *The Dravida Kazagham: A Revolt against Brahmanism.* Bangalore: Christian Institute for the Study of Religion and Society.

Devi, Indira V. *Secularisation of Indian Mind – A Study of Political Ideas in India from 1885 to 1914,* Jaipur: Rawat Publications, 2002.

Donald, E. Smith, *India as a Secular State,* Princeton University Press, Princeton, 1966.

Dwaipayan, Bhattacharyya, Niraja Gopal Jayal, Bishnu N.Mohapatra and Sudhapai (eds.) *Interrogating Social Capital: The Indian Experience,* New Delhi: Sage Publications, 2004.

Editorial, *EPW*, April 10, 2010, Vol. XLV.

Engineer, Asghar Ali, *Islam and Secularism.*

Engineer, Asghar Ali. *Secularism, Democracy and Muslim Experience in India – Understanding Communalism and Terrorism,* Haryana: Hope India Publications.

Esteves, Sarto, *Nationalism, Secularism and Communalism*. Delhi: South Asia Publications. 1996.

Formations of the Secular: Christianity, Islam, Modernity, Stanford: Stanford University Press, 2003.

Fred, Dallmayr, *Small Wonder: Global Power and Its Discontents,* 2005.

Gandhi, G.K., *Communal Unity,* Ahmedabad: Navjivan.

Gargarella, R. Full representation, deliberation and Impartiality in J. Elster (ed.), *Deliberative Democracy,* Cambridge, Cambridge University Press. 1998.

Geetha V., *Theorising Feminism-Patriarchy.*

Gellner, E. *Encounters with Nationalism*, Oxford: Blackwell.

Ghose, Sri Aurobindo, *Sri Aurobindo on Nationalism*, Pondicherry: Sri Aurobindo Ashram.

Ghurye, G.S., *Social Tensions in India.* Bombay: Popular Prakashan, 1968.

Glazer, Nathan. Minorities and India's Democracy. K. Shankar Bajpai (ed.), *Democracy and Diversity – India and the American Experience,* OUP, 2007.

Golwalkar, M.S, *We Or Our Nationhood Defined* (4th ed.), Nagpur: Bharat Prakashan.

Gore, M.S, *The Social Context of an Ideology. Ambedkar's Political and Social Thought,* New Delhi: Sage Publications.

Government of India, Ministry of Panchayati Raj. *Study on Elected Women Representatives in Panchayati Raj Institutions,* New Delhi, 2008.

Griffiths, Percival, *The British Impact on India,* London: McDonald & Company.

Guha, Ramachandra, Ambedkar's Desiderata in, *Outlook*, 1 February, 2010.

Gupta, Dipankar, Limits of Tolerance: Prospects of Secularism in India after Gujarat, *EPW*, 2002.

Habib, Irfan, *et al. After Ayodhya – Reclaiming the Secular.* New Delhi: SAHMAT, 2009.

Haq, Jalaul, *Nation and Nation-Worship in India*, New Delhi: Genuine Publication.

Hardgrave, Jr. Robert L, *The Dravidian Movement*, Bombay: Popular Prakashan.

Harrison, Selig, *India: The Most Dangerous Decades*, Princeton: Princeton University Press.

Hasan, Mushirul. Legacy of a Divided Nation – India's Muslims since Independence in *India's Muslims – An Omnibus*, OUP, 2007

Hastings, A. *The Construction of Nationhood. Ethnicity, Religion and Nationhood,* Cambridge: Cambridge University Press.

HDRC, *Decentralization in India: Challenges and Opportunities,* New Delhi, , HDRGC, UNDP. 2001.

Heehs, P. *Nationalism, Terrorism, Communalism. Essays in Modern Indian History*, New Delhi: Oxford University Press.

Heimsath, Charles H. *Indian Nationalism and Hindu Social Reform*. Princeton: Princeton University Press.

Historical Interpretations and the Secularising of Indian Society. Bangalore: Vistaar, 1999.

Iyer, Krishna, V.R. Some Tasks before the Indian Nation, *The Hindu*, 19 March, Chennai Edition, 2010.

Jacobsohn, Gary Jeffrey, *The Wheel of Law: India's Secularism in Comparative Constitutional Context,* Princeton: Princeton University Press, 2003.

Jaffrelot, C. *Hindu Nationalist Movement in India,* New York: Columbia University Press.

Jakobsen, J. R. and A. Pellegrini, World Secularism at the Millennium, *Social Text,* 2000.

Jalal, Ayesha, Secularists, Subalterns and the Stigma of Communalism: Partition Historiography Revisited, *IESHR,* 1996.

Jayal, Niraja Gopal, *Democracy and the State – Welfare, Secularism and Development on Contemporary India*, OUP. 1999.

Jordens, J.T.F., *Dayananda Saraswati: His Life and Ideas*, Delhi: Oxford University Press.

Jose, Casanova, *Public Religion in the Modern World*, Chicago: The University of Chicago Press, 1994.

Joseph H Carens and Melissa S Williams, "Muslim Minorities in Liberal Democracies: The Politics of Misrecognition", in Rajeev Bhargava (edited), *Secularism and its Critics*, Oxford University Press, 1998.

Juergensmeyer, M., *Religious Nationalism Confronts Secular State.* New Delhi: Oxford University.

Justice Jahagirdar, *Secularism in India: The Inconclusive Debate,* International Humanist and Ethical Union.

Keer, Dhananjay, *Mahatma Jotirao Phuley. Father of Indian Social Revolution*, Bombay: Popular Prakashan.

Kenneth, W. Jones, *Socio-Religious Reform Movements in British India.* Cambridge: Cambridge University Press, 1994.

Klostermaier, K.K., *A Survey of Hinduism*, New York: State University of New York Press.

Koenraad, Elst, *Decolonizing the Hindu Mind: Ideological Development of Hindu Revivalism*, New Delhi: Rupa & Co.

Kohn, H. *Nationalism, International Encyclopedia of Social Sciences,* The Macmillan & Co. The Free Press, Vol.II.

Kothari, Rajni The Problem, *Special Issue on the General Elections Seminar,* February, 1985.

Kothari, Rajni, Integration and Exclusion in Indian Politics, *Economic and Political Weekly*, October 22, 1988.

Kothari, Rajni, Towards a Politics of Intervention, in his *Politics and the People: In search of a Humane India,* Ajanta, Delhi, 1990.

Kymlica, Will, *Multicultural Citizenship – A Liberal Theory of Minority Rights*, Oxford: Clarendon Press, 1995.

Lambert, Richard D., Hindu Communal Groups in Indian Politics, in Richard L. Park and Irene Tinker, (eds.) *Leadership and Political Institutions in India*, Princeton: Princeton University Press.

Larson, Gerald James (ed.), *Religion and Personal Law in Secular India: A Call to Judgement*, Delhi: Social Secular Press, 2001.

Lata Mani, *Sacred Secular: Contemplative Cultural Critique*, 2009.

Lavkare, Arvind, quoting Dr. Subhash Kashyap, in *Them Counterfeits and Their Contentious Issues,* May 11, 1999.

Luthera, Ved Prakash, *The Concept of the Secular State and India. London:* Oxford University Press, 1964..

Madan, T.N. *Modern Myths, Locked Minds: Secularism and Fundamentalism in India.* Delhi: OUP, 1997.

Majumdar, R.C., *The History and Culture of the Indian People: British Paramountcy and Indian Renaissance II,* Bombay: Bharatiya Vidya Bhavan.

Malik, K.Y. and V.B. Singh, *Hindu Nationalists in India.* The Rise of the Bharatiya Janta Party. New Delhi: Vistaar Publications.

Martin, David, *On Secularization: Towards a Revised General Theory,* Aldershot: Ashgate, 2005.

Mauffe, Chantel, Religion, Liberal Democracy and Citizenship. Vries, Hent de and Lawrence E. Sullivan (eds.). *Political Theologies – Public Religions in a Post-secular World,* New Delhi: Social Science Press and Orient Longman. 2007.

Mazzoleni, Gianpietro., Julianne Stewart, Bruce Horsfield (eds.) *The Media and Neo-populism: A Contemporary Comparative Analysis,* Praeger, Westport, Connecticut, London 2003.

Menon, Dilip, *Blindness of Insight – Why Communalism in India is about Caste?,* Navayana, 2004.

Mernissi's, *The Veil and the Male Elite: A Feminist Interpretation of Women's Rights in Islam,* Addison-Wesley Publishing Company, The University of Michigan, for further elaboration, 1991.

Michael, S.M., Politicization of Ganapati Festival, in *Social Compass.* XXXIII.

Mihir Desai, *Combat Law,* Volume 3, Issue 4, November-December 2004.

Milbank, John, *Theology and Social Theory – Beyond Secular Reason,* Blackwell Publishers, 1990.

Mill, J.S. *Considerations on Representative Government*, London: Frontana, 1976.

Moore, R. J. (ed). *Critical Secularism* NC: Duke University Press, 2004.

Naicker, Ramaswamy E. V. *The Ramayana: A True Reading.* Madras: Rationalist Publications.

Nanda, Meera, "Secularism without Secularisation-Reflections on God and Politics in US and India", *EPW*, Vol. XLII, No. 1, January 6-12, 2007.

Nandy, Ashis, the Twilight of Certitudes – Secularism, Hindu Nationalism and Other Masks of Deculturation, in Ashis Nandy, *Bonfire of Creeds – The Essential Ashis Nandy.* OUP. 2004.

Needham, Anuradha Dingwaney and Rajeswari Sunder Rajan (eds.). *The Crisis of Secularism in India.* Ranikhet: Permanent Black, 2007.

Needham, Anuradha Dingwaney and Rajeswari Sunder Rajan (eds.). *The Crisis of Secularism in India,* Ranikhet: Permanent Black, 2007.

Nigam, Aditya. "Secularism, Modernity, Nation: Epistemology of the Dalit Critique", *EPW*, 2000.

Norma Claire Moruzzi's, *A Problem with Headscarves: Contemporary Complication of Political and Social Identity,* Political Theory, Volume 22, November 1994.

Norris, Pippa and Inglehart, *Ronald. Sacred and Secular – Religion and Politics Worldwide,* Cambridge: Cambridge University Press, 2004.

Norris, Pippa and Joni Lovenduski. *Blair's Babes: Critical Mass Theory, Gender, and Legislative Life,* John F. Kennedy School of Government, Harvard University, Faculty Research Working Paper Series , 2001.

Omvedt, Gail, *Dalit and Democratic Revolution,* New Delhi: Sage Publications.

Oommen T.K., Pluralism, Democracy, and Conflict: Situating the Indian Republic in M.N. Karna (ed.) *Democracy, Pluralism and Conflict,* New Delhi: Rawat Publications, 2006.

Oommen, T.K., *Understanding Indian Society: The Relevance of Perspective from Below.* Occasional Paper Series: Pune: Department of Sociology.

Palanithruai, G.; M.A.Thirunavukkarasu and G. Uma *Change Makers at Grassroots,* New Delhi: Concept Publishing Company, 2008.

Palanithurai, G. *Process and Performance of Gram Panchayat Women and Dalit Presidents,* New Delhi (2005), Concept Publishing Company.

Palanithurai, G. *Leadership Matters in Grassroots Governance,* (Path Finder Series-2), Gandhigram: Rajiv Gandhi Chair for Panchayati Raj Studies, 2005.

Palanithurai, G. *Leadership Matters in Grassroots Governance,* (Path Finder Series-3), Gandhigram: Rajiv Gandhi Chair for Panchayati Raj Studies, 2005.

Palanithurai, G. *Leadership Matters in Grassroots Governance,* (Path Finder Series-22), Gandhigram: Rajiv Gandhi Chair for Panchayati Raj Studies, 2006.

Palanithurai, G. *Management of Ethnic Conflict in India and Canada: A Comparative Analysis,* New Delhi: Kaniska Publishers and Distributors, 1993.

Palanithurai, G., Democracy, Development and Conflict at Grassroots, *Local Government Quarterly,* (July – September 2009), Vol. LXXIX.

Palanithurai, G., G. Uma and J. Vanishree, *Networking of Elected Women Representatives at Grassroots,* New Delhi: Concept Publishing Company, 2008.

Panikkar, K.N. (ed.)., *Communal Threat, Secular Challenge,* Madras: Earthworm Books, 1997

Panikkar, K.N., *Culture, Ideology and Hegemony, Intellectuals and Social Consciousness in Colonial India,* New Delhi: Tulika.

Panikkar, K.N., *The Ideas of Sovereignty and State in Indian Political Thought,* Bombay: Bharatiya Vidya Bhavan, 1963.

Parvate, T.V., *Gopal Krishna Gokhale,* Ahmedabad: Navjivan Publishing House.

Puri, Harish, The Akali Agitation: An Analysis of Socio-Economic Basis of Protest, *Economic and Political Weekly,* Vol. XVIII, January, 1983.

Rabbani, Attar, Secular India and its Communal Challenge, *Indian Journal of Secularism,* Vol. 11, No.3, Oct.-Dec., 2007.

Ragupathy, V., *Report on Empowerment of Women, Process and Status in Tamil Nadu,* Rajiv Gandhi Chair for Panchayati Raj Studies, Gandhigram Rural University, Gandhigram, 2007.

Rajan, Nalini, *Secularism, Democracy, Justice – Implications of Rawlsian Principles in India,* SAGE, 1998.

Rajan, Sunder (ed.), *The Crisis of Secularism in India,* Durhams NC : Duke University Press, 1983.

Rajasekhariah, A.M.; *B. R. Ambedkar: The Politics of Emancipation.* Bombay: Sindhu Publications.

Rajendra Prasad, Secularism, the Indian Concept, All India Radio Broadcast [as found in Christophe Jaffrelot (ed.), *Hindu Nationalism – A Reader,* New Delhi: Permanent Black, 1992.

Ram, P.R. (ed.). NA. *Secular Challenge to Communal Politics – A Reader,* Mumbai: Vikas Adhyayan Kendra.

Richard Bastien, *Are Secularism and Islam Cousins?,* Bastien is a freelance journalist based in Ottawa, 26th March, 2008.

Ritzer, G., *Contemporary, Sociological Theory and its Classical Roots:* The Basics. Boston McGraw Hill, 2007.

Robinson, Rowena. Democracy, secularism and minority rights in a globalizing India, *Indian Journal of Secularism,* Vol. 11, No. 4, Jan.-March, 2008.

Roy, Himanshu, Western Secularism and Colonial Legacy in India, *Economic and Political Weekly,* Vol. XLI, No. 2, January 14, 2006.

Rudolph, Lloyd and Susanne Rudolph, Confessional Politics, Secularism and Centrism in India, in J.W. Bjorkman (ed.), *Fundamentalism, Revivalists and Violence in South Asia,* Manohar, New Delhi, 1988.

Sarda, Harbilas, *Hindu Superiority – An Attempt to determine the Position of the Hindu Race in the Scale of Nations,* New Delhi.

Secularism, the Indian Concept, *Rajendra Prusad Lecture,* All India Radio Broad Cast (as found in Chrictophe Jaffrelot (Ed.), *Hindu Nationalism — A Reader, New Delhi: Permanent Black, 1992.*

Secularism and History, in Romila Thapar, *Cultural Pasts – Essays in Early Indian History.* OUP, 2004.

Secularism and Its Critics, Oxford University Press, for an elaboration of this theme, 1998.

Sen, Amartya *The Idea of Justice,* New York: Allen Lane an imprint of Penguin Books, 2009.

Sen, Amartya, Secularism and its Discontents, in K. Basu and S. Subrahmanyam (eds.), *Unravelling the Nation: Sectarian Conflicts in India.* New Delhi: Penguin. 1996.

Sen, Ronojoy, *Articles of Faith – Religion, Secularism, and the Indian Supreme Court.* OUP, 2010.

Seunarine, J.F., *Reconversion to Hinduism through Shuddhi.* Madras: Christian Literature Society.

Sharma, Arvind (ed.), *Hinduism and Secularism after Ayodhya,* New York: Palgrave, 2001.

Sharma, Jyoti, *Secularism and Ayodhya Politics in India.* New Delhi: Deep & Deep Publications Pvt. Ltd, 2007.

Shefali, Jha, *Secularism in the Constituent Assembly Debates,* 1946-1950. *EPW,* 2002.

Singh, M.P. Whither Indian Pluralism, in Urmila Phadnis (ed.), *Domestic Conflicts in South Asia,* Political Dimensions, South Asia Publishers, New Delhi, Vol. I, 1986.

Singh, Yogendra, *Social Processess and Dimensions of Indian Nationalism* in Social Transformation in India, (ed. By) Ghanshyam Shah, Jaipur: Rawat Publications.

Sivakumar, S. *Empowerment of Women Village Panchayat Presidents in Rural Local Governance* in Theni District, Tamil Nadu, Gandhigram: Unpublished Ph.D. Thesis, 2008, Gandhigram Rural University.

Smith, D. E., *India as a Secular State,* Princeton: Princeton University Press, 1963.

Smith, Donald Eugene, *India as a Secular State,* London: Princeton University Press.

Smith, W.C., *Modern Islam in India,* London: Princeton University Press.

Smith, William Roy, *Nationalism and Reform in India.* London: Yale University Press.

Sommerville, John C. *The Secularization of Early Modern England: From Religious Culture to Religious Faith.* New York: Oxford University Press, 1992.

Srinivas, M.N. *Village, Caste, Gender and Method,* New Delhi: Oxford University Press, 1996.

Srinivasan, T.N. (ed.), *The Future of Secularism,* OUP, 2007.

Stephen, Fuchs, *Rebellious Prophets – A Study of Messianic Movements in Indian Religions,* Bombay: Asia Publishing House, 1965.

Sumit Sarkar, *Writing Social History,* New Delhi: OUP, 1997.

Tagore, Rabindranath, *Nationalism.* Calcutta: Rupa & Co. 1992

Talreja, Kajnayalal M, *Pseudo-secularism in India,* Mumbai: Rashtriya Chetna Prakashan, 1996.

Talyabji, Badruddin, *The Self in Secularism,* New Delhi: Orient Longman, 1971.

Taylor, Charles, *A Secular Age,* Cambridge: Belknap Press of Harvard University, 2007.

Tejani, Shabhum. *Indian Secularism – A Social and Intellectual History 1890-1950,* Permanent Black, 2007.

Tejani, Shabhum. *Reflections on the Category of Secularism in India – Gandhi, Ambedkar, and the Ethics of Communal Representations,* 2007.

Thapar, Romila. *Is Secularism Alien to Indian Civilization*? In Srinivasan, T.N. (ed.). *The Future of Secularism*, OUP. 2007.

The Insurrection of Little Selves: The Crisis of Secular-Nationalism in India. New Delhi: OUP, 2006.

The Public Sphere, *British Journal of Political Science*, Volume 27, No. 3, 1997.

Thomas, K. Toms, *Auctioning the Left Out – Christians in Civil Society Building,* New Delhi: Indian Social Institute, 2005.

Upadhyay, Prakash Chandra, *The Politics of Indian Secularism*, New Delhi: Modern Asian Studies, 1992.

Vajpayee, Atal Behari, Secularism the Indian concept, Christopher Jaffralot (ed.), *Hindu Nationalism – A Reader,* New Delhi: Permanent Black.

Vajpayee, Atal Behari, The Bane of Secularism, in S. S. Bhandari (ed.), *Jan Sangh Souvenir,* Delhi: BJP, 1969.

Vanaik, Achin. *Communalism Contested: Religion, Modernity and Secularization,* New Delhi: Vistaar Publications, 1997.

Varma, V.P. *Modern Indian Political Thought,* Agra: Lakshmi Narain Agarwal.

Veer, Peter van der. *Imperial Encounters – Religion and Modernity in India and Britain,* New Delhi: Permanent Black. 2001.

Venkataraman, T.S. *A Treatise on Secular State,* Madras, 1950.

Verma, H.S. Secularism: Reflections on Meaning, Substance and Contemporary Practice, in B. Chakrabarty (ed.). *Secularism and Indian Polity,* New Delhi: Segment Books, 1990.

Viquaruddin, Mohammed, Secularism and Social Justice in India, *Indian Journal of Secularism,* Vol. 11, No. 4, Jan-March, 2008.

Vivekananda, Swami, *The Complete Works of Swami Vivekananda.* Calcutta: Advaita Ashrama.

Vries, Hent de and Lawrence E. Sullivan (eds.). *Political Theologies – Public Religions in a Post-secular World.* New Delhi: Social Science Press and Orient Longman, 2007.

Will Kymlica, *Multicultural Citizenship – A Liberal Theory of Minority Rights,* Oxford: Clarendon Press, 1995.

Wolpert, Stanley A. *Tilak and Gokhale,* Berkeley: Berkeley University Press.

Yechury, Sitaram, *Secularism* Versus *Communalism.* Hyderabad: Prajasakti Book House, 2008.

Zakaria, Rafiq, *Communal Rage in Secular India,* Mumbai: Popular Prakashan, 2002.

Zakaria, Rafiq. *Indian Muslims: Where have they gone wrong?* Bombay.

Index